DIVING THE WORLD

PHOTOGRAPHS BY NORBERT WU

Diving the World

PHOTOGRAPHS BY NORBERT WU

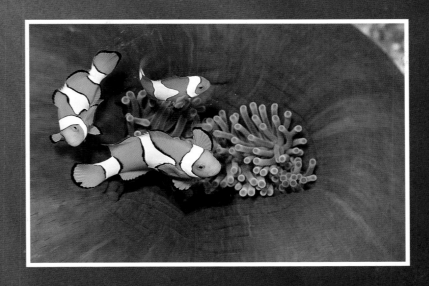

TEXT BY KEN McALPINE

HUGH LAUTER LEVIN ASSOCIATES, INC.

To my parents, James and Mei Ying Wu,
with great love and admiration.

Design: Lori S. Malkin
Editorial Production: Jeanne-Marie P. Hudson
ISBN: 0-88363-510-0
Printed in Hong Kong

Many of these photographs were made possible by a fellowship
from the Pew Fellows Program in Marine Conservation, an
initiative of The Pew Charitable Trusts in partnership with the
New England Aquarium.

Norbert Wu's work in Antarctica was supported by the Antarctic
Artists and Writers Program, National Science Foundation.

It would be impossible to list or photograph every deserving
diving site in the world. *Diving the World* highlights only some
of the most beautiful and diverse diving destinations around the
world. Travel and diving are not without risk. Never dive alone
or without proper training, and always check with the State
Department for travel advisories before visiting any international
dive destination.

*PAGE 1: Pugnacious and territorial, the male garibaldi cultivates a nest of
algae into which a female will lay eggs. It actively defends its nest against
all intruders, including other fish and algae-eating invertebrates, such as
this purple sea urchin. The garibaldi will take this urchin a few yards from
its nest and dump it. Channel Islands, California.*

*PAGES 2–3: Sunrays create dancing shafts of light underwater,
Revillagigedo Islands.*

*PAGE 3, INSET: Only in tropical Indo-Pacific waters, west of Hawaii to
the Red Sea, is a diver treated to the splendors of anemonefishes like these
Amphiprion percula and their hosts. Caribbean divers will have to settle
for books and aquarium displays because neither of these creatures nor their
ancestors existed when an open seaway connected the tropical Atlantic and
Pacific. Papua New Guinea.*

*RIGHT: The waters around Bonaire have been protected against fishing
and diving damage for many years. As a result, coral reefs here are among
the lushest in the Caribbean. Here, a diver swims past a stand of sponges.*

PAGES 6–7: World map by Howard S. Friedman, New York, NY.

*PAGE 8: A group of wild Atlantic spotted dolphins have interacted with
humans in their home range for over twenty years, after their initial discovery
by treasure hunters. They will often approach swimmers in the water, and
they seem to enjoy swimmers that try to match their speed and movements.*

*TABLE OF CONTENTS, TOP TO BOTTOM: Weddell seals under a breathing
hole, Antarctica; cowrie camouflaged in soft coral, Fiji; diver riding a manta,
Revillagigedo Islands; orange clump coral, Saba, Dutch Antilles; school of
masked butterflyfish and bannerfish, Red Sea.*

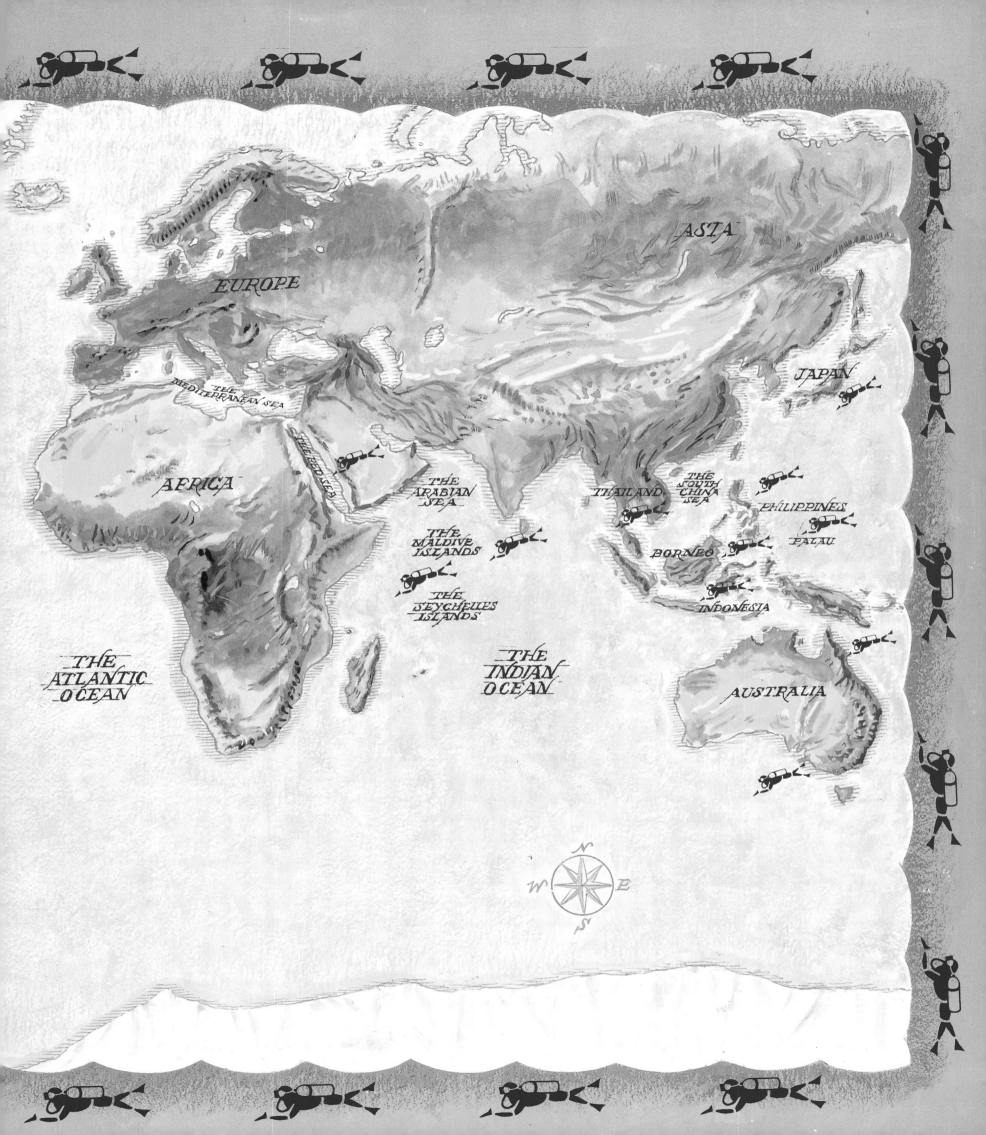

TABLE OF CONTENTS

INTRODUCTION

The first time I met Norb was at the Ventura, California, home of free diver Terry Maas. It was early in the morning, but not *that* early. Norb and Terry had flown in the night before from northern California. Terry greeted me bright eyed and alert. Terry looks like you would expect a man who spent a large part of his life around and under the ocean to look. He is lean and spare. On that particular day he was also slightly sun burnished from a recent dive.

ABOVE: A smooth trunkfish hunts invertebrates by blowing sand away from its prey. Bonaire.

RIGHT: Groups of strawberry anemones cover a rock wall. The individuals of each color are probably all clones from a common ancestor that has reproduced by splitting apart asexually, and they are more correctly termed corallimorpharians, not anemones. They possess very large nematocysts, or stinging cells, at the tips of the tentacles. Monterey, California.

Norb had come to Ventura to photograph Terry for an article we were doing together for American Airlines. I had spoken to Norb on the phone several times, and while he hadn't been unfriendly he hadn't been particularly effusive either. He was business-like, and to the point. Which was okay. He offered no personal information, other than the fact that he snored loudly and he got sick almost every time he went out on a boat—pertinent facts since we would be boating and sleeping together. He also took a moment to tell me he didn't look much like a diving photographer.

So I shouldn't have been surprised when Norb came out of the back room, but I was. He was short, rumpled, and bleary-eyed, with a physique leaning more toward Buddha than someone from Sea Hunt. He was bleary-eyed, but still observant. His handshake was brief and disinterested, but his eyes ran over me. I could feel it. Great photographers miss nothing, even if their subject is not all that interesting. Initially, I was equally unimpressed.

Since then I have worked with Norb in a variety of circumstances, circumstances that have taken us from a frigid winter in Yellowstone (yes, he can shoot dry land too), to the sparkling seas off Thailand. I am no longer unimpressed. Norb's professionalism, work ethic, and photography are second to none. Because of this he isn't always easy to be around. He expects the same high standards of everyone around him, and when you disappoint, he lets you know it. He is a straight shooter, sometimes with a short fuse. He has taken people by surprise by bluntly pointing out when they have dropped the ball; but I suspect their distaste for his style of people skills exists largely because Norb is often right.

The prize means a great deal to Norb, and his prize is a selfless one. Sure, it's fun to be recognized and, though it is hard to tell, I suspect Norb enjoys the notoriety he has gained. But he is in it for something bigger than self-promotion. Norb wishes to record the undersea world—its beauty, mystery, and fragility—so that people will better understand it, and, perhaps in understanding it, do their part to preserve it.

In pursuit of this aim, he is doggedly focused. I recall a time diving with Norb off Southern California's Channel Islands. I can't remember what island we were near—Anacapa, I think—but we had finished diving and we were heading back. It was a calm day, the seas were nearly flat, and, the day done, everyone's minds had drifted to wherever they go when their thoughts wander. On this particular day this was poor timing. We sensed it before we saw it, and I'm not sure who turned first, but whoever it was did so just in time, because out of nowhere an apartment-size wave bore down on the boat's starboard. The captain gunned the vessel and swung it up and over, the bow just barely clearing the hissing face. Had we been ten yards farther in, we all would have been in for a lot of swimming.

Norb turned to me and in a flat, even tone he said, "Shit. I thought I was going to lose my camera gear."

In pursuit of his life's work, Norb has earned plenty of honors. His photos have appeared in numerous magazines and on the cover of *Time*. He has a masters degree in engineering science from Stanford, and he studied ichthyology and marine biology at the prestigious Scripps Institution of Oceanography. He served a stint as chief still photographer aboard Jacques Cousteau's *Calypso*. He has been honored with the Antarctica Service Medal of the United States for work that eventually produced a first-of-its-kind high definition video of life beneath the most forbidding, and perhaps most beautiful, of the world's seas. He has also been awarded a prestigious Pew Marine Conservation Fellowship, which has allowed him to travel the globe in pursuit of many of the remarkable photos found in this book. But here's what impresses me most. I had to look all this up, because Norb never told me any of it.

His diving mirrors the same silent competence. In a world where many divers act like dogs

peeing on trees—name dropping locales, and otherwise staking their claim as the alpha diver in the vicinity—Norb dives quietly. He is humble and unobtrusive, and he stays down so long—typically everyone, including the dive masters, is back on the boat long before he is—I'm surprised he hasn't been left behind. He is not perfect, though. He does have a weak stomach and he has no problem sleeping through his own snoring. One night on a dive boat in Thailand, at the dive master's request, Norb gave a slide show. The dive master, also a photographer, followed Norb's slides with a presentation of his own. I was sitting next to Norb, and saw what was happening, but in the darkness the enthusiastic dive master didn't. At one juncture he had a question about a creature in one of his slides. "I'm not quite sure about this," he said. "What do you think Norb? Norb??"

Lest you think him uncaring, let me finish with my favorite Norb Wu story. We were in Yellowstone. It was cold. The two of us were out alone. I had gone with Norb because he wanted to photograph wolves. Wolves do not perform on cue. In fact, they often do not perform at all. My body and mind were numb when Norb stopped to fish around in a cooler. I waited for him to produce film or a different camera lens. Instead he produced lunch—a great stack of fried chicken, potato chips, and cookies he had packed for both of us—and gruffly waved off my gratitude.

If there is anything I have learned in my writing, and my life, it is to judge people not by how they appear to be, but by what they do. I am proud to be associated with Norb Wu, and to play a small part in this book. The photographs found within it show a remarkable world as seen by a remarkable man.

Gray whales undertake the longest migration of any mammal. Here, several show their characteristic heart-shaped spouts. Monterey, California.

13

THE ANTARCTIC OCEAN

ROSS ISLAND

It is the last real wilderness, and this is sorely understating things. It is a place so beautiful and pure that those who visit it are forever changed—and so harsh that plenty who visited never came back. It is the coldest, driest, windiest, darkest place on earth. To visit the bottom of the earth is to experience myriad emotions. Antarctica can thrill and infatuate, and, sometimes at the same moment, instill an equally overwhelming desire to get the hell out.

ABOVE: This icefall at Couloir Cliffs was colored by diatoms, minute, silica-encrusted plants that contain golden or brown pigments to absorb sunlight for photosynthesis. Most species of sea urchin scrape algae and other material from the substrate with an 'Aristotle's lantern'—five strong jaws, each with one tooth, which ring the mouth on the animal's lower surface and form an internal lantern-shaped structure.

PAGES 14–15: Sea ice stalactites are hollow, tapering structures up to several feet long. As ice forms from seawater, the salts are left as a brine solution. This dense, chilled brine drains down from the sea ice ceiling, entering the near-freezing seawater below. Ice forms around this draining, flowing brine, forming a hollow ice stalactite.

RIGHT: Jellyfish, or medusae, are among the most prominent midwater organisms seen under the ice at McMurdo. The giant Antarctic jellyfish has a bell that can reach more than three feet across and just a few, distinctive, cord-like tentacles. Larger jellies such as these are active swimmers.

A pod of orca, or killer whales, rests in pools of open water in an icebreaker channel. They are seeking the Antarctic cod, and are taking considerable risks to get at their food. The open water upon which they depend for breathing can close up within minutes, leaving them trapped without an air supply.

Icebergs may possess underwater spurs and ledges which extend a considerable distance from the visible topside portion of the iceberg. On these shelves, hundreds of fish (here, a "borch") sit within small holes in the ice. Most fish in Antarctic waters have glycoproteins in their bodies, a compound that serves as an antifreeze.

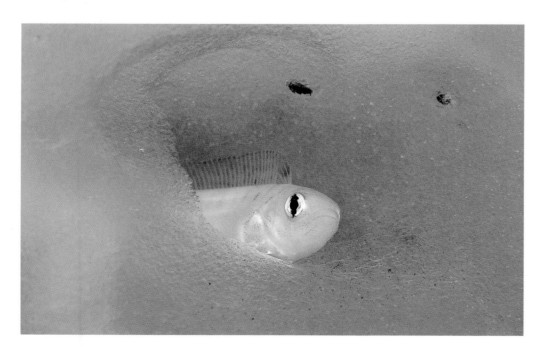

"In spite of this dusty workaday life I have ideals, and far away in my own White South I open my arms to the romance of it all and it abides with me now," gushed polar explorer Ernest Shackleton, who had more reason to hate the place than most.

Historian Stephen Pyne framed Antarctica in pithier terms. "Ice is the beginning and ice is the end of Antarctica," he wrote.

A simpler and truer statement has never been penned. At the height of winter—roughly July, though in a place so cold fixing winter's nadir is mostly quibbling—Antarctica's ice covers an area almost one and a half times the size of the United States, a slab that can be up to 15,600 feet thick. Starting in March (Antarctica's autumn) the ice grows at a rate of twenty-two square miles a minute, eventually covering 7 million square miles. Antarctica is barely fathomable in scope. In March 2000 an iceberg calved from the Ross Ice Shelf. Scientists dubbed it B-15, though they could have just as well called it Delaware, since the chunk of ice was larger than the state. Surface area, roughly 4,500 square miles. Water content? Enough fresh water to supply the United States for five years. Among those who understand it, Antarctica is simply, and rightly, known as The Ice.

By no means are all its marvels off-the-scale. The smallest, and yet grandest, adaptations are remarkable too. Living close to, and even within the ice (*Pagothenia borchgrevinki*, better known as "borchs" or icefish, inhabit the cracks and dimples of icebergs), is, as you might imagine, a physiological challenge. Many of Antarctica's fish have adapted via glycoprotein antifreeze compounds that lower the freezing point of their body fluids. Thus fish thrive as fish, and not as popsicles, wending their way through a world littered with sea stars, sponges, and soft corals.

Sea stars, sponges, and soft corals? Yes, life thrives beneath The Ice. Until the early twentieth century, scientists thought the waters of Antarctica, like the Arctic, were home to little life. Science has been required to execute an about face, as it is impossible to ignore a sponge the size of a bear. Proving that Nature has a sense of humor, Earth's harshest, emptiest land mass sits above a water wonderland.

Put aside all preconceptions and descend if you will into a world where the water can be so clear there is no sense of water at all; visibility is measured not in feet, but in football fields. Where jellies the size of barrels drift-cum-fly past. Where the electric-blue undersides of icebergs craft a ceiling akin to roiling thunderclouds and the sea floor is littered with sea stars, sea spiders, octopuses, nudibranchs, sea urchins, naked dragonfish, nemertean worms, and giant isopods performing a ballet in graceful, and sometimes horrid (anemones slowly devouring a jellyfish), slow motion. Where the water rings with the trills and chirrups of Weddell seals, and penguins swim like dark darts, trailing silver-bubble contrails. Alice in Wonderland, Timothy Leary, Ken Kesey, there is no stranger trip. A crazy, but very quiet dance hall—The Moulin Bleu.

Antarctica's climatic groundrules make for interesting divergences from diving's norms. The thick sea ice and its covering of snow keep light levels and water temperatures low, even in summer's twenty-four hours of light. Thus animals normally seen only in deep water (certain jellyfish, for example) rise up into diving depths. The water's shocking clarity—divers sometimes see other divers a thousand feet away—is clearest in winter and spring. After six months of darkness, the water is virtually empty of visibility-scuffing plankton. (In contrast, summer's post-plankton bloom viz can be as little as three feet.) Drifting icebergs grind across the sea floor, scouring away life. The tremendous cold, and relatively few predators, ensure many watery denizens a long life, not to mention bizarre gigantism. Sea stars

ABOVE: With little to fear from predators, this Weddell seal mother and her pup float in shallow water beneath their breathing hole. The survival of these mammals—the world's southernmost—depends on their ability to maintain year-round air holes in the ice. They have strong, forward-pointing teeth to do so, but when these wear out, the seals soon perish.

Adelie penguins jump out of the water in a group to confuse leopard seal predators. These penguins are returning to their colony after a foraging trip to replace mates left brooding eggs on their nests.

can live well over twenty years. In warm waters of the globe, sea spiders are typically smaller than a fingernail. Antarctic sea spiders grow to the size of a human hand. Rod Serling would have had a field day here.

And those are just the adaptations you see. The blood and muscle of Weddell seals have three to five times more oxygen-carrying capacity than humans do. Why? Human beings aren't limited to drawing their oxygen from a single ice hole that may be the only avenue to air for miles. While hunting for food a Weddell seal will typically hold its breath for twenty minutes and travel as far as two miles from its ice hole, sometimes as deep as two thousand feet. And, researchers have observed an eighty-two-minute dive. For these Houdini-like immersions, the seals actually alter their blood circulation to send oxygen where it is needed most, to the heart and the brain. Researchers have made another interesting discovery. Louder than Roseanne Barr on land, beneath the water Weddells are the consummate stealth hunter, coming within inches of their prey before the fish even notice. Stealth won't insure their continued existence on every front, though. Ice holes can freeze over quickly and over time an adult Weddell's sharp teeth dull. It's true the Weddells' uniquely angled teeth are perfectly suited to gnawing ice holes, allowing them to winter farther south than any other mammal on the planet. But eventually the seal may meet the ice ceiling it can't gnaw through, in turn providing sustenance, and life, for the creatures of the sea floor.

Life in Antarctica is harsh. Writers and poets have waxed on about Antarctica's profound silence, sighing ice floes, and lavish evening suns, huge and vermillion, framed by sun dogs, colored rainbows that appear when ice crystals are thick in the sunlit air. They can afford to focus on Antarctica's beauties because they are, at least in modern times, a short hop from shelter and safety. Antarctica's denizens aren't afforded such luxuries. Penguins and even Weddell seals are torn to bits by leopard seals lurking at the ice edge. Leaving the open seas, orcas follow leads (cracks) far into the ice in pursuit of their prey, the giant Antarctic cod. Many people suspect that orcas prey on unsuspecting seals and penguins who take a swim at the wrong time, but no one has actually witnessed this. Orcas that follow these inland leads have found themselves trapped if the ice closes behind them.

For the diver, conditions are equally unforgiving. With its freezing point lowered by salt, the water gets as cold as it can get on this planet—28.8 degrees F. in the Ross Sea of Antarctica, an appreciable degree warmer off the Antarctic Peninsula to the north. To prevent fogging during a dive, you spit into your mask; the spit freezes within a few seconds and you must clear the mask with seawater once you are in the water. Regulators can freeze up if you breathe too fast or work too hard. Currents can sweep you under the ice. Dry suits stave off the wet, but not the cold; hands and feet can still throb painfully. Some research divers who have made extensive dives find it takes several months for the feeling to completely return in their face, fingers, and toes.

There is no danger of Club Med gaining a foothold here. But man has discovered Antarctica and, in recent years, as much as is humanly possible, made it his home.

Until recently most visitors were researchers, many of them ensconced at McMurdo Station—

PAGES 22–23: At Little Razorback Island, our dive team explored passageways of ice that had been formed by pressure ridges. Seals used the passageways to move from breathing hole to breathing hole. These "living rooms" became spaces filled with invertebrate life below. Huge numbers of sea stars and a notothenioid fish have gathered beneath a breathing hole to feed on seal feces.

OPPOSITE: Crinoids, or feather stars, are primitive relatives of sea stars that are highly mobile. They are usually found perched on objects on a reef, using their many sticky, velcro-like arms to pick out food particles from passing water currents. Their mouths are located within the center of the ring of arms.

BELOW: Most pycnogonids, or sea spiders, are only about the size of a fingernail, but in Antarctica they can grow larger than the size of a human hand. In the extreme cold, where metabolisms are slow and there are relatively few predators, many invertebrates grow larger and live years longer than similar species in warmer waters. Here a sea spider appears to be consuming an unidentified prey item as it picks its way across a blanket of anchor ice.

Like missiles leaving behind an exhaust trail, emperor penguins shoot through the clear water at the ice edge—they are champion diving birds. The emperor penguin's thick feathers insulate it by trapping a layer of air next to the skin, but some of that air streams out when the bird swims.

MacTown to its residents—on Ross Island in Antarctica's far south, where temperatures, not including wind chill, can drop to nearly 20 below zero. McMurdo is the local headquarters of the National Science Foundation, which operates the U.S. Antarctic Program, a multidisciplinary research effort covering everything from glaciology to astronomy. The largest settlement on the continent—summertime population is roughly 1,100; winter roughly 250—McMurdo is a surreal and beautiful place. Sprawled over a rocky promontory on Ross Island, MacTown has a busy airfield, ATMs, and speed limit signs, backdropped by the breathtaking white panorama of the Royal Society Range. Most tourists visit Antarctica's northern peninsula, venturing south from the tip of Argentina. McMurdo lies worlds away in Antarctica's southernmost reaches; McMurdo Sound is as far south as you can travel and still find ocean. The Ross Sea, as you

might imagine, is a very remote and inhospitable place. For humankind, McMurdo and the far south remain the province of science and unspoiled natural beauty.

Smaller research stations are scattered about the continent, and more are being built. Antarctica has proven to be the ideal research laboratory in a wide variety of fields, from biology to astronomy, providing scientists with a forum for looking both up and down. The thin, dry atmosphere of the South Pole makes it the Earth's clearest window into space. Scientists drilling deep into Antarctica's ice have, by examining gas bubbles trapped in the ice, discovered that there are more greenhouse gases in the atmosphere today than there have been at any time in the past 420,000 years (the gas bubbles act as atmospheric time capsules).

No single country lays claim to Antarctica. Since the signing of the 1959 Antarctic Treaty, Earth's fifth largest continent has been set aside as a nature reserve devoted to science; in 1982, similar protection was extended to the surrounding ocean. The scientists have been working hard, and in their pursuit of heavenly and earthly mysteries they have made some enlightening and unnerving discoveries.

A close look at the ice has revealed the secret to Antarctica's surprisingly profuse sea life, and a critical keystone for life throughout the southern oceans. In winter, algae living on the ice provide food for krill, the tiny shrimplike creatures that, in their turn, serve as a staple food for just about everything—whales, seals, penguins, fish, and birds, on down to tiny zooplankton. Melt the right chunk of sea ice, and a healthy yellowish sludge will settle out—a collection of algae as rich as any that you'll find in any estuary.

Scientists may also be unearthing a related, and unsettling, trend. It is possible that the gradual warming of the earth has seen to it that not nearly as much ice forms, especially at Antarctica's northern reaches, just below South America. Where once the Antarctic was ensured a thick winter's ice, this is no longer the case. Some winters see a full ice pack, but they are followed by several warm, ice-scarce winters. Far less ice, far less algae, far less food for the krill. For the past fifty years, the Antarctic Peninsula, stabbing up toward Cape Horn, has registered temperatures a whopping ten degrees higher than normal. Scientists believe that, especially in Antarctica's northern reaches, krill populations are in danger of crashing. Should that happen, seal, whale, and penguin populations could follow.

Frigid water from Antarctica now travels north, where it affects the circulation of major ocean currents. Another concern: if the warming trend continues, eventually oceanic currents might shift, perhaps causing drastic changes in climate. Like all areas of science, even the concept of global warming is subject to debate; some studies have actually suggested some Antarctic areas might be cooling.

Man's hand has stamped Antarctica on other fronts. By 1912, seal hunters had killed nearly 3 million Antarctic seals, and nearly driven fur and elephant seals to extinction. They have now rebounded thanks to laws protecting them. Beginning in earnest in the early 1900s, whaling nearly drove several of the Antarctic's baleen whales to extinction. Whaling is outlawed in Antarctic waters, though Japan still kills roughly four hundred minke whales a year, ostensibly for research, though the meat is sold. The giant, and unfortunately tasty, Antarctic cod, some as large as two hundred pounds, are now being heavily fished. And geologists have discovered gold, platinum, and copper around the continent, though there will be no immediate harvest, due to an international agreement banning commercial extraction until at least 2048.

Recently, a different breed of animal has come to Antarctica. In 1967 Lars-Eric Lindblad built the first Antarctic cruise ship, claiming "you can't protect what you don't know." Self-serving logic certainly, but it would be unfair to close Antarctica off, and impossible now anyhow. Tourism is booming. Roughly fifteen thousand tourists a year visit The Ice, most of them puking their way across the tumultuous Drake Passage on cruise ships from South America. Few tourists stray south of the Antarctic Peninsula, but the fact you can buy an official Antarctic tartan tie at the gift shop in Port Lockroy signals an altered place. Many dive operators offer diving in the Antarctic Peninsula and some subantarctic islands. Tourism's impact to date has been small, but Antarctica is far more accessible than it was in the days when hardy explorers were forced to take long walks after their boats were crushed by pack ice.

Scientists are sorely concerned about global warming and other man-induced Antarctic impacts. But where other parts of the globe have weathered man's hand for centuries, put off by distance and horrid conditions man came to Antarctica late.

Nature also neatly illustrates man's Big Picture significance. Geologists have found remnants of deciduous trees 180 miles south of McMurdo, trees that were also found in Africa, Australia, South America, and India. Their conclusion is that 270 million years ago Antarctica was a lush wilderness of forest, marsh, and tundra, joined to all the other continents in a time when man's effects were nil.

An Antarctic minke whale takes a breath in a small pool, the only opening for miles around in the sea ice. Minke whales, the smallest and most common of the baleen whales, feed by gulping huge quantities of water and straining the microscopic plants and animals of the plankton with their specialized baleen plates. Minke whales are still hunted in Antarctic waters by the Japanese.

A nudibranch climbs up the stalk of a fan worm. Nudibranchs (meaning "naked gills") are among the most colorful inhabitants of the marine world, found in every sea and every environment, from the polar regions, to coral reefs, to kelp forests, and even the open ocean.

OPPOSITE: Every summer a U.S. Coast Guard icebreaker travels through ice floes, which have broken off the sea ice edge, to cut a passage for a freighter to bring in supplies to McMurdo Station. In the strips of open water behind the icebreaker, orcas and minke whales often appear. Both of these whales seize the opportunity offered by the ship channel to go as far into the ice as possible.

ABOVE: The helmet jelly is the most widely distributed and abundant jelly in deep water, and it is found worldwide. In most parts of the world it is found near the surface only at night, but diving in Antarctica is like diving at night. This jelly has been captured by an anemone and is in the throes of being consumed.

RIGHT: Ice caves below Weddell seal breathing holes are filled with life. Hundreds of red and orange sea stars, looking like roses, have gathered on the gritty black bottom to feed on seal feces. In the barren shallows where ice crystals form on anything that doesn't move, animals can't afford to be picky.

PAGES 28–29: A cluster of polychaete sponges grows in front of a grounded iceberg. This iceberg, calved from the front of a glacier the previous summer, drifted into the coast near Cape Evans, and became locked in by sea ice.

THE SOUTH PACIFIC

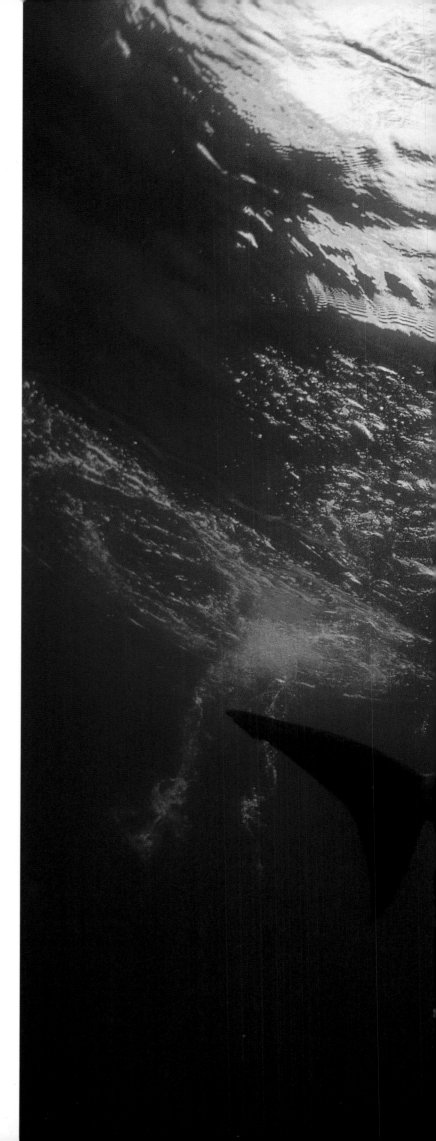

SOUTH AUSTRALIA

Seeing doesn't always afford comprehension, which is part of the attraction. To peer into the distance at a familiar shadowy shape, to watch it enlarge with alarming rapidity to impossible dimension, thick and broad, the shape almost like an oil drum, yet seductively streamlined too. To sense your own presence absorbed by black eyes, to watch the puggish snout lift and crinkle, to trust-cum-pray in the strength of the cage as the mouth yaws wide, a glory of pink ringed with serrated edges.

PAGES 30–31: A diver encounters a wealth of marine life surrounding Sipadan Island, Borneo.

ABOVE: The great white shark is the most famous of all sharks. It maintains a body temperature several degrees above that of seawater by utilizing a network of blood vessels working as a heat exchanger. A magnificent predator, it is now protected in many areas, including California and South Australia.

RIGHT: Being able to see a great white shark swimming freely in its natural habitat is something few divers have been able to experience. Great white shark attacks on man are usually a case of mistaken identity, where a shark mistakes a human for its usual prey, such as a seal.

To see the great white shark in its element is to be transformed forever. An adrenal jolt of primordial fear and fascination. "We're not just afraid of predators," wrote Harvard sociobiologist E.O. Wilson, "we're transfixed by them . . . In a deeply tribal sense, we love our monsters."

Though profoundly accurate, it's likely Wilson penned his assessment from the confines of Cambridge, not the innards of a shark cage dangling in the water off South Australia's Neptune Island. Had he been lucky enough to see the white shark in the open ocean, he likely would have developed an even profounder appreciation for predators, and the largest predatory fish in the world. Latin is a dry language, but in rare instances even Latin prickles the neck—*Carcharodon carcharias*: "Ragged-toothed" one.

The opportunity to see "whitey" in the waters off South Australia has made the place famous. To many divers South Australia *is* white shark diving, the great

sharks drawn here by a plethora of fat-rich sea lions. Even if you've never been within three times zones of South Oz, if you're a diver you've heard of Adelaide and Port Lincoln (a thirty-minute flight from Adelaide), the launching ports for white shark trips, and Dangerous Reef and the Neptune, Little English, and Sibsey Islands—the waters where the luckiest of divers experience one of Nature's rarest encounters.

What you may not realize is how rare these encounters can be. Though no one has matched the success of South Australia's commercial outfitters in bringing forth white sharks (prime whitey season runs from roughly December into May, Australia's summer), finding them is far from easy. Since 1976, when Rodney Fox took the first group of sport divers on a hunt for white sharks, it has been a merry game of cat and mouse. "Waiting for whitey" can consume a large part, and sometimes all, of a trip. It's not unheard of for divers to pay several thousand dollars

OPPOSITE: A New Zealand fur seal bellows. The areas around Kangaroo Island and the Neptune Islands are the most prolific breeding site for these once heavily hunted mammals. New Zealand fur seals are now protected in both New Zealand and Australia.

Australian blonde sea lions are a favored prey of great white sharks. They are found only in Australia and are becoming endangered, with a population of only 10,000 to 12,000.

for the opportunity to spend ten days scanning an empty horizon and inhaling the scent of chum. No one knows how many white sharks there are in South Australia's waters, or anywhere else for that matter. Additional simplicities—how big they can get, how long they can live, how many young they can carry—remain a mystery. Even the best commercial outfitters make no promises. Sometimes the sharks show, sometimes they don't. Sometimes they show in big fashion. Slack-jawed divers have watched sixteen feet of white shark leap from the water in pursuit of a doomed fur seal. Even when they do show, you're not

Shark diving is South Australia's marquee event, but it would be foolish to ignore its other dive, and dry land, offerings. The down under portion of Down Under often takes a backseat to the Great Barrier Reef, possibly because it doesn't offer the sunny ease of Barrier Reef diving. The southern coast of Australia is a land of rugged coastline, often edged by thick kelp, cool water (low to mid-60s and cooler), and strong currents. If it sounds wild, it is. Precisely why it is a magical place to dive.

It's also a vast stretch of coast, torn loose from Antarctica roughly 50 million years ago, so best first to pull out a map so you can follow along.

Starting to the east, the coastline of Victoria features Australia's southernmost point and one of its most popular national parks, Wilson's Promontory, where solid granite outcroppings drop below the sea to form a magnificent world of immense caves and strange animals like the exotically beautiful weedy sea dragon (more in a minute). Offshore from "The Prom," several islands also offer excellent diving—Norman Island, Cleft Island, and Great Glennie Island are each home to prolific sea life, drifting around and through granite outcroppings.

Move west, toward Melbourne, and you pick up some nice shore diving (diving at The Prom is best accessed by boat) on the seaward side of the Mornington Peninsula—spots like London Bridge and Diamond Bay—where rock caverns, hollowed out by big surf, serve as home to sponges, gorgonian fans, and fish, such as banded, bullseye, and magpie morwongs. It's worth noting that waves that can carve caverns, can make swimming and diving along these beaches precarious. In 1967 Australia lost a prime minister when Harold Holt went diving off Cheviot Beach. Best to dive these areas with someone who knows them. In fact, scan any dive guide for the Victoria and South Australia coasts and, under the heading "currents" you'll generally see the word "strong" or "unpredictable," oftentimes both.

For related reasons, parts of the coast, especially along Victoria's shores, are a wreck diver's dream. Lonsdale Reef, near Port Phillip Bay, is home to more

always apt to see them. The great white shark is one of the stealthiest creatures in the sea. One of Fox's earliest encounters occurred when a white shark he didn't see discovered him. Repairs from the 1963 attack left 462 stitches and no bitterness. "He was only doing what sharks do," Fox later told a reporter.

LEFT: A bronze whaler sweeps through a school of mackerel. Most shark species are not as dangerous as people think—they are shy and rarely attack humans.

PAGES 38–39: Three separate species of octopus display blue warning marks, the smallest being this South Australian species. It is difficult to see due to its small size (no larger than five inches across the outstretched arms) and because of its cryptic coloration. When it is cornered or harassed, brilliant rings and bands of electric blue appear on the surface of its normally drab flesh. Although the octopus will flee rather than fight, when agitated it will bite to defend itself. Its venom can paralyze a human's respiratory system in eight minutes.

than fifty wrecks. Further to the west, along the eighty-mile stretch of coast from Cape Otway to the town of Warnambool, over two hundred ships sank between 1850 and 1900, many of them ending the dreams of gold rush immigrants headed for Sydney. Probably the most popular wreck in the area is the *Loch Ard* off Mutton Island, a 1,623-ton sailing ship that went down in 1878, depositing bodies along miles of coast.

Crossing the border into South Australia, the first dive spot of note isn't on the coast at all. The Mount Gambier district has some of the finest sink-hole and cave diving in the world. The local topography is a Swiss cheese layout of over 140 sinkholes, containing crystal clear water, freshwater eels, and several species of saltwater fish that negotiate a long, arduous subterranean swim to rid themselves of para-sites that can't survive in freshwater.

But it's still in the saline waters where the best diving occurs, and that diving is often found along dozens of unspoiled islands. Consulting your map, the largest and most obvious of these is Kangaroo Island, a vast tract ninety miles long and roughly three hundred miles wide, that is home to more than a dozen conser-vation parks, and only a short, fifteen-minute plane flight from Adelaide. Ogling koala, emu, and kanga-roo, not to mention the aptly named Remarkable Rocks (monolithic blocks of granite that look like they were sculpted by Ken Kesey), occupies the eyes of the backpackers and tourists. But the diver knows too that Kangaroo Island's waters also offer wonders accessed by shore or boat. Descend off Kangaroo Head, and the explosion of sponges, coral, and ascidians offer silent, colorful testimony. Drifting through the water column, playful New Zealand fur seals eyeball divers, and huge four-foot wrasses, known locally as blue gropers, eat right out of your hand.

Kangaroo Island deserves special mention for another reason. White sharks hog much of South Australia's ink, but it is an arguable fact that the most amazing sea creature in South Australia's waters is the leafy sea dragon, and there are few better places to see them than Kangaroo Island. Actually, two types of sea

dragons (a kind of seahorse) reside in South Oz, and Kangaroo Island's, waters. The weedy sea dragon is smaller and slightly less ornate with bright blue bands along its upper body, though given the beauty and del-icacy of both species this is really only quibbling. To see either dragon is to understand that Nature's artistry knows no bounds. To see them period also takes some knowledge and effort, especially with the leafy sea dragon, which is so well camouflaged that it can disap-pear right before your eyes. (According to local dive operator Jim Thiselton, a good trick for spotting leafy sea dragons is to look for small clouds of mysid shrimp in protected water near rocky crags with lots of sea-weed—here too you might find their predator.)

Australians have always shown a blunt artistry with language and here again they don't disappoint. In local parlance the leafy sea dragon is known as LSD, and no amount of the hallucinogenic could concoct a stranger and more inspirational sight.

In fact, if you love wildlife in general, South Australia offers one of the world's tidiest assemblages of the stuff, sea life abutting impressive terrestrial variety. From Port Lincoln, a working fishing port with good tourist facilities, you can boat out to Spilsby, Thistle, and the Gambier Islands. After div-ing off Spilsby, twenty-eight miles from Port Lincoln,

OPPOSITE: The foot-long leafy sea dragon is a spectacular example of camouflage. Found only in South Australia, it blends in almost perfectly in its habitat of kelp and algae. It uses its camouflage for both protection and ambush feeding.

Remarkable Rocks on Kangaroo Island, granite boulders carved by wind and water and sitting on a promontory overlooking a spectacular coast, are truly remarkable.

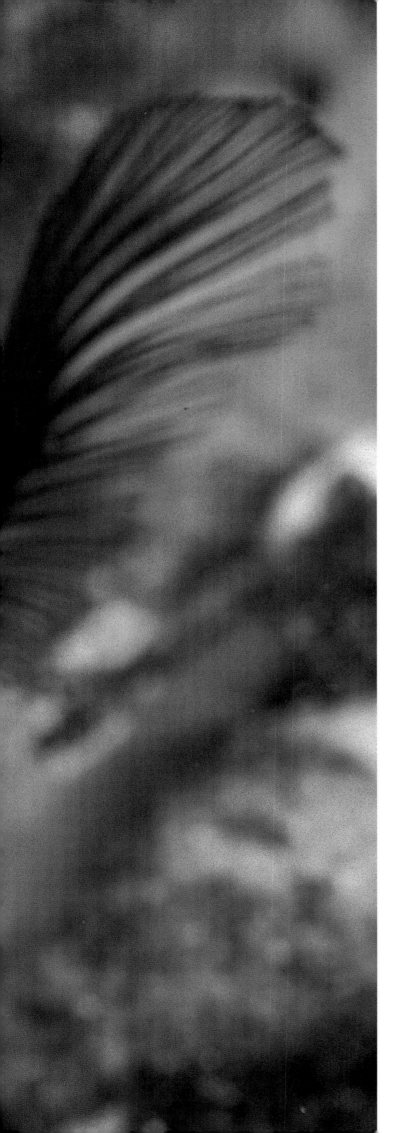

you can enjoy secluded beaches and rocky bays where great flocks of Cape Barren geese mass. Gaze skyward and see rare sea eagles and parrots wheeling overhead. Walk inland and emus, wallabies, and wombats commingle.

It's important to note that diving in South Australia isn't solely about islands. The once booming grain fields of the Yorke and Eyre Peninsulas saw to the construction of huge wooden jetties, where ships docked to load and transport the grain overseas. Most of the jetties are now out of commission, but not for divers, who can enjoy the vast array of sea life that jetties attract. The most famous of the jetties is at Port Noarlunga, just to the south of Adelaide. Pronging out to a reef four hundred yards offshore, the jetty at Port Noarlunga may make for the world's most convenient shore dive. Divers can nearly walk to a reef, protected as a marine reserve since 1971, fat with life—blue devilfish, boarfish, green groper, brilliant sponges, and colorful hydroids, some two hundred species of marine plants and animals in all. Convenience and location mean something unusual in South Australia—crowds. Noarlunga offers another rarity. It's a great place for beginners, complete with an easy-to-follow Aquatic Trail.

LEFT: The blue devil is common in the waters of South Australia. It is a favorite among divers because it is inquisitive and will approach humans.

This large wrasse, called a blue groper, was once hunted almost to extinction. Now a protected species, individuals will follow divers around for handouts.

OPPOSITE: The bluefin tuna is the most expensive animal in the world. A 444-pound bluefin sold at a Japanese auction for $175,000. These southern bluefin tuna caught in the open ocean are swimming in a pen where they are raised and then sent to Japan.

Move farther to the west and things quickly get remote. Australia's vast size (slightly smaller than North America), coupled with its small population ensures plenty of nothingness, assuming you measure presence by the presence of man. Around the bend from Port Lincoln, but still off the Eyre Peninsula, lie the Investigator Group of islands—two of the islands, Pearson and Topgallant, offer especially good dives, with little chance of crowds. Some of the best island diving may be farther north still, in the remote Nuyts Archipelago off the town of Ceduna. The odds of finding a glitzy dive resort on these farther reaches of the Eyre Peninsula are equally remote; in some instances it might be hard to find any place to stay, but it's exploratory diving at its best.

Also worth noting, the waters of the Great Australian Bight are one of the few places you can see rare Southern right whales (world population estimates for these whales range from 1,500 to 3,000), particularly at the Head of the Bight, where they come in close to shore to calve and mate, close enough that they can be seen from shore. It's a spectacular sight, and the only way to see it is from dry land, as the area around the Head of the Bight is a protected marine park. The whales typically congregate between May and November (Australia's winter), and the place to see them is Collosity Point. South Australia has been one of Australia's most progressive states when it comes to founding marine reserves, and its remoteness also serves to protect it well. But roughly 85 percent of Australians live in the continent's coastal zone, and Victoria and South Australia are no exception. In Victoria, humanity cloves particularly close to the coast—most Victorians live within fifteen miles of the water, and the state has the highest population density per kilometer of coast of any state in Australia. This has its impacts, from agricultural and sewage runoff to development of wetlands.

But the main problems are still confined to the bays and estuaries, particularly around the larger cities, because much of the southern reaches of Australia remain, in large part, a wild place (though, for the same reason, much remains unstudied, and so unassessed). Population numbers are low, and the vast acreage of ocean is high.

But big numbers don't tell the whole story, because man can have an impact when he simply numbers one. Several years back, in Adelaide Australia, twelve thousand people stood in line to see and touch an awesome spectacle, an eighteen-foot three thousand-pound female white shark, the greatest predator in the sea, a corpse, accidentally hooked, but effectively drowned, on a fisherman's longline.

Scientists guess that female white sharks start to breed at twelve to fourteen years of age. They also guess, because guessing is all they can do, that the number of white sharks in South Australian waters are falling off. Hooked on a line meant for snapper, the mature Adelaide female wrapped herself taut and died.

With apologies to E. O. Wilson, the white shark is not a monster at all, but a creature as fragile as it is remarkable.

A school of old wife fishes, found only in Australia, swims in the cold waters off Kangaroo Island. Its somewhat derogatory common name is based on the grinding sound of its teeth when it is captured.

THE GREAT
BARRIER REEF

You may be familiar with some of the statistics pertaining to the Great Barrier Reef and its nearly incomprehensible vastness. The reef stretches more than 1,250 miles, a numbing collection of limestone and polyp spanning fourteen degrees of latitude and ten of longitude off Australia's northeast coast. The GBR (even the name is large) actually comprises some 2,800-plus different reefs, as well as 940 islands, innumerable small islets, and immense tracts of water. It spreads across 135,000 square miles, an expanse—pick one—greater than Poland, equal to Arizona, or half the size of Texas. It is one of the most biodiverse regions of the world. It supports 37 species of mangroves (over half the world's total), 350 species of coral (over two-thirds of the world's total), and over 2,000 species of fish, with new species uncovered on a regular basis. It is the world's largest living organism, the only life form that can be seen from the moon. It is nearly bigger than hyperbole itself.

A "bommie" is a popular name for a coral formation that rises abruptly from the depths to near the surface. Like seamounts, these coral bommies serve as gathering places for marine life, such as these vast schools of sergeant majors and fairy basslets.

On Lizard Island, in the tropical northern Great Barrier Reef, a few mangrove trees have taken root. Mangrove forests trap sediment, thus creating more land where there once was none.

The statistics are certainly impressive, but you need to look at a smaller picture to really appreciate what's going on. Tallying creatures on the reefs around Heron Island, near the GBR's southern end, researchers took a count on a single volleyball-size coral chunk. They found 1,441 worms from 103 species. Now go back to the big picture, with volleyballs scattered everywhere.

The sheer volume of life enfolded by the GBR is numbing, and that's just the stuff that is visible. Walk a section of Heron Island's beaches at low tide and you'll unknowingly tread on millions of microscopic algae and photosynthetic bacteria swarming among the sand grains—a square mile of beach breathes out as much oxygen as an equal area of rainforest canopy. Life pulses, and succeeds, even where you don't see it.

Of course most people—divers included—are interested in what they can see, and, no surprise, the range of what you can see on the GBR is nigh on endless. The broad, shallow continental shelf of tropical northeastern Australia, overlain by an abundance of blistering sunshine, provides the perfect foundation for coral growth, and the corals have responded. There are patch reefs, fringing reefs, platform reefs, barrier reefs, and atolls whose inner lagoons are pocked with hundreds of coral bommies. In, under, and around this, almost everything swims and squats. Sharks, mantas, invisible stonefish, gargantuan potato cod, dwarf minke whales, and swirling masses of chromis, surgeonfish, and triggerfish in heart-stopping floods. Really, it's silly to go on. Equally important are the small numbers. The GBR is home to the threatened giant clam and dugong, and six of the globe's seven species of sea turtles, several of those species also threatened or endangered.

But as anyone who has ever been to Australia knows, any assessment of this great continent would be woefully incomplete without mention of its grandest life form. While it is unfair to define an entire populace by a single tale, it isn't far from the truth either. In a grassy meadow in Queensland's Eungala Rainforest, Norbert Wu was engrossed with photographing a

OPPOSITE, RIGHT: Coral reefs are built up by tiny, extremely delicate animals. The touch of a finger can damage and kill them. Here, a trained guide is leading a group of tourists safely over a dead section of reef on Heron Island, at the southern part of the Great Barrier Reef.

Symbiotic algae within the mantles of giant clams form wondrous displays of swirling colors. The clams use food and waste gases produced by the algae in their tissues.

PAGES 50–51: Like a string of jewels, the far-flung atolls and reefs that form the Great Barrier Reef are shown in this aerial photograph.

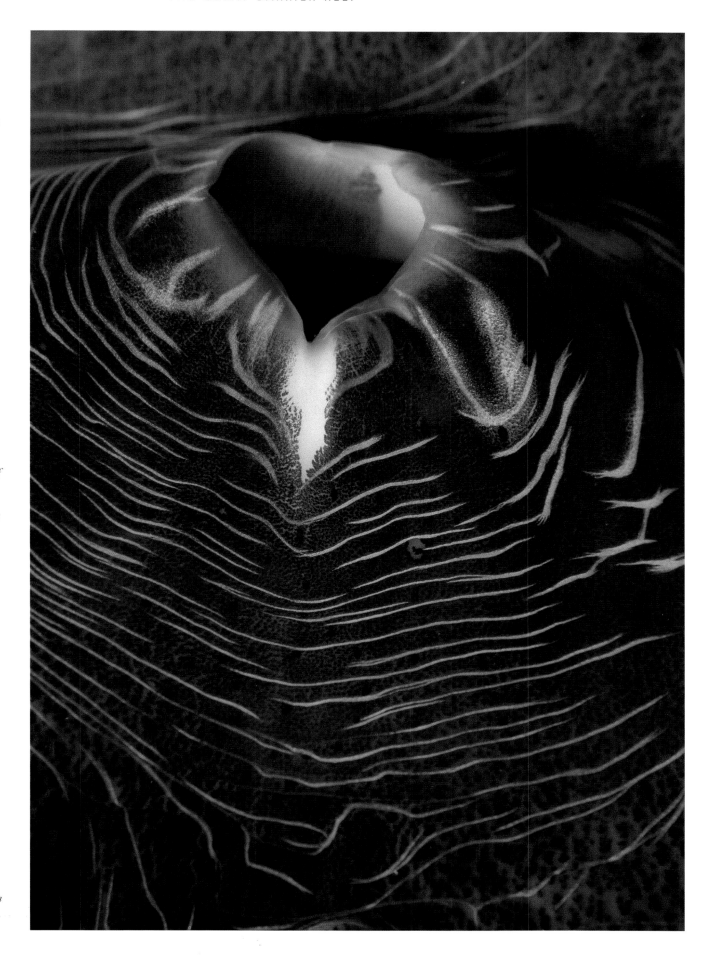

OPPOSITE: *This grouper is being cleaned by a cleaner wrasse. A fish being cleaned by a wrasse has a peculiar understanding. It allows the cleaner to go all over its body, even within its mouth and gills.*

Sea stars are echinoderms, a class of animals that features radial symmetry and includes sea cucumbers and sea urchins. They have great powers of regeneration; if an arm is cut off from the body of the star, the arm (called a "comet") can grow back the remaining body parts to form a completely new individual.

ten-foot python, his concentration necessitated by the highly aggressive snake that struck out whenever Wu got too close. At one point, a pair of black leather shoes appeared in Wu's viewfinder. The shoes were attached to a dapper, eighty-something matron, who deftly sidestepped the python's next strike, snatched it behind the head, and, crooning soothing endearment to the creature now coiled around her arm, trotted off to show her prize to her friends. She returned after a time, laying the snake down in the spot from whence she had snatched it. Standing erect, she calmly regarded her arm. "Oh dear," she said. "He shit all over me."

Australians are unique. Any diver's trip to the GBR (or anywhere else in Australia) is sure to be enhanced and enlivened by the locals.

When diving the GBR, what you see—and the effort involved in seeing it—will vary depending on where you go. As a general rule, the diversity and volume of life increase as you move north. Not that the south suffers a paucity of life. Roughly 350 species of coral dwell in the north (versus 450 in the Indo-Philippine region, the epicenter of global coral diversity), but there are still 240-plus species in the south. On the reefs around Heron Island, in the GBR's southernmost region, researchers discovered 250 types of shrimp. Finning over Heron Island's reefs, divers who don't thrill to shrimp will still see everything from wobbegong sharks and astoundingly colorful harlequin

tuskfish to turtles and manta rays—often in a single dive. On the Great Barrier Reef, numbers are relative.

The majority of the Barrier Reef islands lie north of the Tropic of Capricorn and have a monsoon climate. The seasons are reversed Down Under, and summer brings tropical downpours to the Great Barrier Reef. It gets hotter as you head north, and those in the northern reaches often prefer the tolerable temperatures and balmy nights of the Australian winter. Still it is true that the farther north you go, the more life you'll find, and the farther offshore you go, the better the diving conditions will be, as reefs closer to shore can be affected by runoff and diver traffic. Travel by liveaboard to the Eastern Fields, an atoll two hundred miles east of the tip of Australia's Cape York Peninsula, and you will descend into a gin-clear (viz 150–200 feet), china-blue world where pelagics (southern bluefin tuna, marlin, whales and sharks, sharks, sharks) reign. Distant reefs like Bligh, Mantis, Star, Holmes, Boomerang, and Bougainville produce magic. Rock gently on the surface beneath naught but a flood of stars—yours the only boat for hundreds of miles—then descend to Osprey Reef, the stars above mirrored by the dozens of pockets of light drifting over the reef—flashlight fish, finding their way and observing zooplankton via their enormous headlight-like luminous organs under their eyes.

This sort of thing sounds poetic and enticing, but it is rendered less so if you spent the previous twenty hours vomiting. There is a reason for the scarcity of *Homo sapiens* at the dive sites in the Far North and beyond. Getting there can be time consuming (twenty-plus hours) and rough.

Explaining the popularity of Cairns. Large portions of the GBR rest far offshore, but not far from Cairns. Once a sleepy town drowsing in tropical torpor, today Cairns hosts roughly eight hundred thousand tourists a year. They don't come for the kangaroo steak or the emu pate—though both are available. They come because Cairns offers easy access to the Reef, which wends in as close as twenty-five miles from shore.

Diving in Cairns—and also in Port Douglas to the north and Townsville to the south—is a refined

business. This has its benefits and drawbacks. You can't turn around in Cairns without falling over a dive shop willing to take you where you want to go. It's also possible you'll be falling over nearly three hundred other people who want to sign on for the same day trip to Agincourt Reefs aboard a high-speed catamaran with rubber-gloved crew members at the ready (seasickness can strike during an hour-long trip too). Arriving at the reef you step on to the massive Agincourt Reef Platform, where hundreds of other people mill about trying to decide whether to see the reefs via snorkel, by diving, by helicopter, or glass-sided semi-submersible. At first glance this might seem less like a nature experience and more like a cattle drive, but the happy fact is it introduces thousands to the wonders of the GBR, and it's a great offering if you're traveling with someone who doesn't dive.

If the clamoring intimacy of a day-trip scares you, fine. Fierce competition between dive operators assures myriad offerings. There are two- to four-day trips, allowing a longer reach to less impacted reefs, and time ashore for Queensland's stunning terrestrial wonders like Daintree National Park and the Atherton Tablelands. These shorter trips often include diving off the Ribbon Reefs north of Cairns, ten of them,

OPPOSITE: An enormous potato cod, actually a type of grouper, approaches divers for handouts at Cod Hole on the northern Great Barrier Reef. The yellow pilotfish beneath it make their living by feeding on scraps left behind by this five-foot, 150-pound fish.

A large male parrotfish sleeps at night in a coral reef within a cocoon of mucus that it has created. Parrotfish are so named for their beaklike mouths, which consist of hard, fused teeth and strong jaws used for crunching coral. The mucous net serves to mask the fish's scent from nighttime predators like moray eels.

Like birds that flock together, schooling reef fishes such as these Hussar take advantage of additional sets of eyes to avoid a lurking predator or to discover passing prey.

a seamount, its surface festooned with waving soft corals, the waters around it clouded with life flicking through gauzy beams of sunlight, big-eye trevally, Maori wrasse, kingfish, batfish, turtles, and banded and olive sea snakes. Much ado is made of the Yongala, with good reason.

Also worth any serious diver's attention is Lizard Island. Officially one of the GBR's northern islands, Lizard Island sits 170 miles north of Cairns, a sparkling piece of tropical beauty replete with first-class resorts, a breathtaking lagoon, and excellent fringing reefs. Added plus, staying on Lizard Island puts you a short boat ride away from the spectacular Ribbon Reefs and the aforementioned Cod Hole. In 1770, during a voyage to find the rumored conti-nent of Terra Australis, a beaten and battered Captain James Cook of England clambered to Lizard Island's 1,178-foot summit for a beseeching look around, in the hope of finding a way out of what he viewed as an endless barricade of reefs. From his vantage point (now known as Cook's Look), the good captain learned there was lots more reef. Today our knowl-edge of the GBR continues to grow at the highly respected Lizard Island Research Station.

And there is the Coral Sea. Here is the very best diving, out beyond the Great Barrier Reef, at the atolls and reefs—Osprey, Holmes, Bougainville, and Flinders—peppered with hard and soft corals of sometimes gargantuan proportion and swept by visible currents of schooling fish. Diving here takes time and devotion, but the reward is memorable. Close your eyes. Imagine waters swept with armies of pelagics, including sharks, lots of them—grey reef, zebra, silvertip, whitetip, tiger, and bronze whaler. Above the ocean's skein, a sun-blasted realm of wild emptiness, filled only with blue and seabirds. Would that there was time to explore over a million square miles of water.

Thankfully, sheer expanse helps, in large part, to buffer the Great Barrier Reef from man's impact. Since 1975 the Reef has also been protected, to a degree, by the Great Barrier Reef Marine Park, the largest marine sanctuary in the world. The Australians take their environment seriously, and the GBR has been well

imaginatively numbered one to ten, perched at the edge of the continental slope where it begins its long slide down to the Papua Abyssal Plain. Also on the hit list for the shorter (and longer) liveaboard trips are the famous Cod Hole (home to thuggish, enormous—some 150-pounds plus—potato cod) and, about sixty miles south of Townsville, the wreck of the *Yongala*, whose misfortune it was to miss a cyclone warning and carry no telegraph equipment. On March 24, 1911, the vessel came to rest on a wide sandy bottom in ninety-six feet of water, providing the only hard substrate for miles. The sea is an opportunistic arena. Today the *Yongala* is less a wreck and more

The Napoleon, or humphead, wrasse once reached lengths of seven and a half feet. Large humpheads are becoming rare due to extensive fishing pressure.

ABOVE: The Great Barrier Reef, the world's largest living organism, is not one reef but thousands of small reefs extending across a vast expanse off the east coast of Australia. This small coral cay on the Great Barrier Reef shows a typical atoll formation—a coral reef forming a protective lagoon, in the center of which has grown an island.

PAGES 58–59: Predators on coral reefs will eat many of the eggs being released by corals. By spawning en masse, the corals ensure that at least some eggs of every species will be fertilized, and drift away to colonize new reefs.

PAGE 59, RIGHT: As sport divers and researchers have spent more time underwater at day and night, previously unknown behaviors have revealed themselves. The spawning of corals and other marine animals is rarely seen and occurs only at certain times of the year and lunar cycle.

managed within human constraints. A happy statistic, roughly 95 percent of tourists visit just 5 percent of the park, thanks in large part to management efforts funneling them there. Oil drilling and mining on the GBR are outlawed, and commercial fishing, sportfishing, and collecting are regulated as best as can be expected when policing a territory so vast.

But the GBR is not without problems. While the outer reefs and remote areas beyond are still in good shape, the inner reefs feel Man's hand. Much of Queensland's seaside wetlands—Nature's natural filtration system—have been replaced by cane fields, croplands, and development. Runoff—and its sediments and reef-wrecking nutrients—from towns, farms, and industries now pour onto the inner reefs in greater concentrations than ever before. Some reefs have stopped growing, a halt tied directly to higher nitrogen levels from Queensland's rivers. (Anything beyond moderate levels of nitrogen harms growth and reproduction in corals, at the same time fertilizing algae that can smother the coral.) Overfishing on

The epaulette shark is a small, nocturnal shark that feeds on small fishes and invertebrates which it finds in coral, rock, and sand.

the GBR isn't the problem it is in many areas of the world, but there are exceptions, the most notable being prawn trawling. Because the large majority of the reef is relatively shallow—and inhabited by prawns—prawn trawling, done by dragging nets across the sandy bottom, is lucrative. Studies have also shown it to be ruthlessly destructive. A single trawl sweep removes around 10 percent of the biomass attached to the sea bed. Twelve more passes, and up to 90 percent of the biomass is removed. The GBR is impossible to police, and illegal trawling is rampant. Politics raises an added problem. Commercial fisheries aren't controlled by managers of the Marine Park, they're controlled by the State of Queensland, and fishermen are a powerful lobby.

Though important, these are transient quibbles. Another problem on the Great Barrier Reef and anywhere else in the oceans—Nature is not designed for

management. Nutrient runoff arrives on the GBR from areas outside the Marine Park's jurisdiction. Endangered green turtles may be protected within Australia's waters but they have to get there first, and they are slaughtered by Asian fishermen to the north. Nature aids in destruction too. In 1998, the El Niño-mediated coral bleaching event afflicted 87 percent of the inner reefs and 28 percent of the outer reefs, and repeated outbreaks of crown-of-thorns starfish accomplish ongoing damage.

But oversize issues in an oversize place tend to obscure a reassuring fact. As you read this, beneath a tropical sun polyps die and accrete, their limestone skeletons joining generations before, Nature working patiently to restore, operating on a timetable so leisurely it is often overlooked.

It's a vision worthy of a master, and certainly worthy of a look.

Two bobtail squid mate at night. These tiny squid are bottom-living, burying in sand during the day and emerging at night to forage. These squid use glowing bacteria to hide their presence at night; they produce just enough light from their underside to hide their silhouettes.

This large hermit crab feeds on mollusks, breaking open shells with its large claws.

Fiji

Conditions were less than idyllic when Captain Bligh and a lip-cracked, sun-stroked contingent of his men passed, via longboat, between Viti Levu and Vanua Levu in the middle of the South Pacific. Bligh, after all, had been cast adrift by Fletcher Christian after the mutiny on the *Bounty*, and was in the midst of his four thousand-mile, forty-eight-day epic of open-boat survival from Tonga to, eventually, Timor.

LEFT: Palm trees sway behind the pink coral sand of an idyllic tropical beach.

RIGHT: A crinoid, or feather star, catches food particles in the current at the edge of a lettuce coral. Crinoids catch food particles in their bristly arms. Coral colonies like these provide shelter for thousands of species of animals.

OPPOSITE: *This close-up photograph of a soft coral tree shows stinging polyps and silicon spicules embedded in the calcareous skeleton. Soft corals are among the most brightly colored invertebrates on the reef, coming in all colors of the rainbow. Were it not for a camera's underwater flash, this rosy soft coral would appear mono-chromatic due to the absorption of red light from the visible spectrum within the first few meters.*

An allied cowrie closely resembles the soft coral upon which it feeds.

Yet even Bligh appreciated the otherworldly beauty of Fiji, noting, in his log, the "marvelous cockscomb mountains" that rose, high and green, into tufts of clouds. Happily Bligh and his journal narrowly escaped a closer look at the islands, outpaddling several canoes crewed by fierce Fijians who, Bligh believed, not unjustly, were hoping to make a meal of him.

Today the passage between Viti Levu and Vanua Levu is named Bligh Water. Had the good captain the leisure to look below the surface of that water, he would have noted the astonishing beauty there too.

The Fiji islands are part of one of the largest reef systems in the world, a vast tract of fringing, barrier, platform, and patch reef enveloping the roughly 844 high islands, cays, and islets that make up the Fiji chain. In terrestrial terms, most of these islands are little more than insignificant splotches. Viti Levu and Vanua Levu together account for almost 87 percent of the total land area, and the rest is largely dispensed with courtesy of Fiji's other larger islands: Kadavu, Taveuni, Gau, and Ovalau.

But it's what hugs, rings, and wanders through this island chain that's of real interest. Roughly one thousand reefs in all, ranging from small—less than fifty yards long—to impressively expansive—over two hundred miles long. The archipelago and its singsong islands also house one of the largest mangrove systems in the South Pacific. The astute diver will recognize this combination for what it is—nursery and home for life.

Fiji has been tagged the soft coral capital of the world. It's true the soft corals around Taveuni Island and along Great Astrolabe Reef are a dreamland splotch of red, vermilion, yellow, blue, and twenty shades of each. This is quite nice, but there are hard corals too. Along the Lau group of islands, hard corals crowd up against each other for miles. Fish life is impressive, too—over one thousand species, perused in visibility that, on the right tide, can reach two hundred-plus feet. Visibility is at its peak from June through October, when the islands are drier, cooler, and far less humid.

Fiji offers convenience too, and for this it has been both lauded and maligned. Calm emerald lagoons sit directly off powdered sugar beaches, their waters housing delicate lettuce coral gardens larger than a football field. Great Astrolabe Lagoon and stunning Rainbow Reef off the south coast of Vanua Levu are easily accessible from shore. Beqa Lagoon, a huge platform off the south coast of Viti Levu between Beqa and Yanutha islands, is famous not only for its fifty-plus coral pinnacles, but for its proximity to Fiji's capital city of Suva. There is even ease within this ease. Some of Beqa's pinnacles rise to within ten feet of the surface.

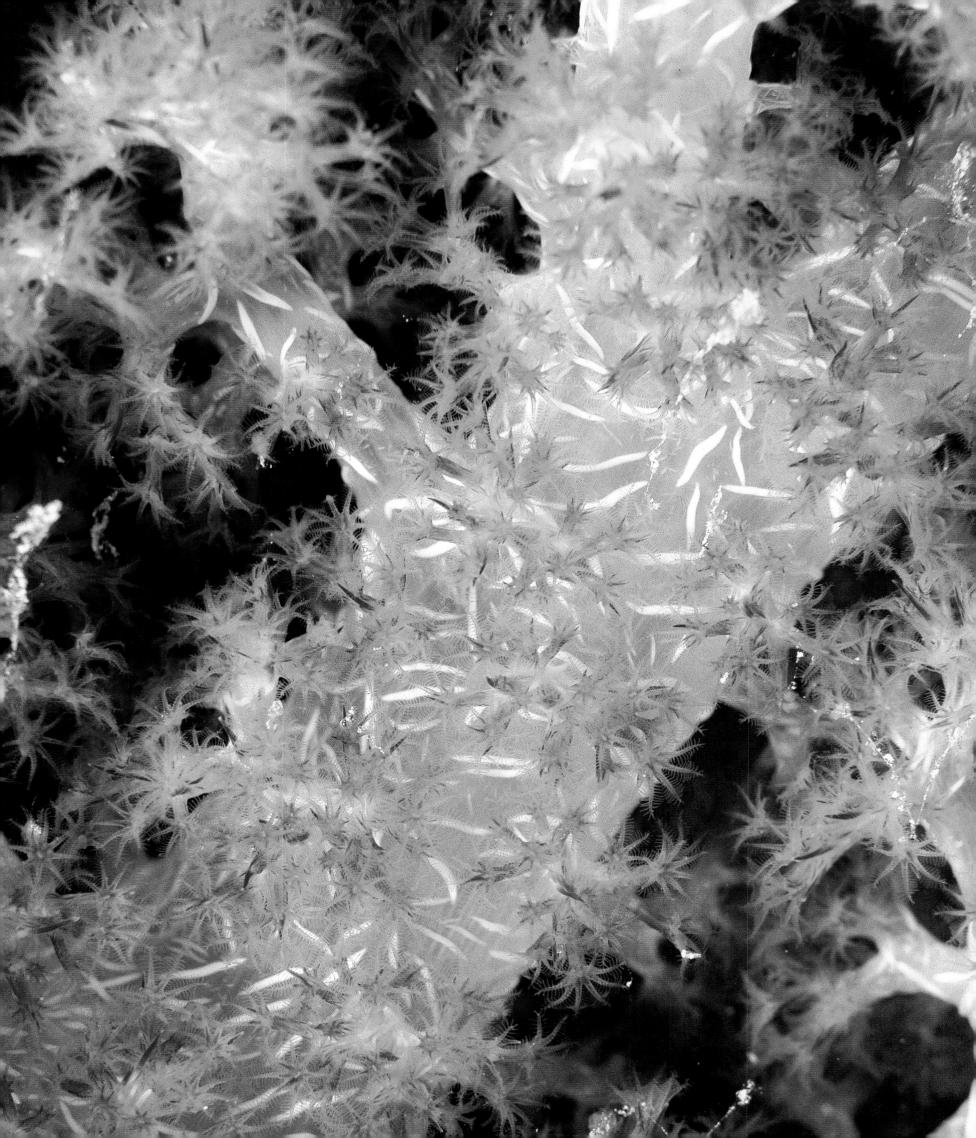

A staghorn coral colony provides shelter for hundreds of damselfish, which feed on plankton being brought past the coral by currents. Damselfishes are among the most conspicuous fish on the reef, forming large plankton-feeding schools above the reef.

RIGHT: The thick matt of floral-like tentacles of the organ-pipe coral obscures the underlying mass of slender scarlet tubes of this octocoral.

Certain divers view this ease with haughty disdain, an outlook both myopic and petty, and certainly of no concern to any diver drifting above the fantastic coral gardens of Rainbow Reef. Besides, if ease of access irks you (and even if it doesn't), your best bet is to hop a liveaboard accessing Fiji's lesser-known islands like Namena, Wakaya, Gau, and the Lau group. It's also worth noting that roughly 90 percent of Fiji's population lives on Viti Levu and Vanua Levu, with roughly three-quarters of that mass dwelling on Viti Levu. Head out into the archipelago, and more than just ease of access drops away.

In transit from the close-at-hand to the farther-flung you'll happen across some stellar dives too. There's E-6, an extraordinary seamount named after the film-processing designate because of all the film divers burn there; home also to a sky-lit cavern lined with stunning gorgonian fans and soft corals. And Koro, a labyrinth of coral bommies adjacent to a barrier reef, home to myriad pelagics. And nearby

Namena, a tiny cay good for several days of diving, its coral pinnacles topped with a blinding sway of colors.

And then there's Fiji's famous Great White Wall, one of those rare places whose pre-visit hype won't distract from its actuality one whit. The White Wall is one of the spots that first drew slavering divers to Fiji, and it remains a unique dive that will touch you both during and after. Located along a stretch of

outer fringing reef on the southern side of Vanua Levu, the wall drops off into the deep Somosomo Strait. From roughly 90 to 240 feet the near-vertical wall is smothered solely by ice-blue soft coral, a sheer snowy face that, were it not for drifting schools of fish, might be the world's ultimate black diamond run. Christmas comes eternally to tropical waters. A good dive operator will time your dive to catch the sun on the wall's face, and time the tide so that the corals are inflated in all their splendor.

In Fiji's farther-flung places quality is, if possible, even further enhanced. Fiji is known for terrific pass diving, and Gau Island's Nigali Pass may be one of the best. Dropped outside the reef, divers are immediately privy to giant schools of jack and barracuda, and possibly mantas and hammerheads, often milling about in two-hundred-foot-plus visibility. Divers position themselves where the channel narrows—a spot dubbed "the bleachers'"—and when the tide begins to run, the show stoppers appear with it, fat two-hundred-pound

A school of barracuda swims together. Fierce predators, barracuda have streamlined bodies and large mouths with saber-like teeth. Fortunately, barracudas in schools like this have never attacked divers, or shown the slightest interest in divers as prey.

PAGES 68–69: Longnose filefish are found in the same habitats as staghorn corals. They swim in small groups between or over the tips of the coals, feeding primarily on the polyps.

OPPOSITE: A crinoid, or feather star, has numerous arms which pick plankton out of the water. A system of arms and hairs transport food particles down to the mouth, at the center of the feather star's arms.

BELOW: This squat lobster steals food from the arms of the crinoid, or feather star, on which it makes its home.

groupers, writhing sea snakes, and opportunistic sharks that may cruise inches past your face.

Off Kadavu Island lies the spread of Astrolabe Reef, pocked with great dives, among them Purple Wall, Evil Trench, Mellow Reef, and Naingoro Pass, probably Fiji's most reliable spot for seeing big fish—tuna, billfish, tiger sharks, and hammerheads among them.

Sharks—*qio* (pronounced "ghio") in Fijian—illustrate an interesting point. The tiger sharks of Kadavu Island may raise a hair or two on the necks of visiting divers, but they raise nary a heartbeat among Kadavu islanders. Suva may be one of the largest cities in the South Pacific, English may be the archipelago's official language (until 1987 Fiji was a British Crown Colony), your hotel room may be equipped with e-mail and fax access to Peoria, but Kadavu Islanders believe they are protected from sharks for timeless reasons. Long, long ago Dakuwaqa, the arrogant shark god, wandered the islands challenging various reef guardians and summarily thumping them. Dakuwaqa got wind of a giant octopus occupying the reefs off Kadavu and so, like most thuggish bullies, set off to vanquish that which was getting

OPPOSITE: *An anemonefish rushes out to assert her territory. An anemone usually contains a single pair of mature anemonefish and a few immature juveniles. The female is the largest and most dominant. If she is removed, the largest male will change sex to take her place.*

more ink than he. Dakuwaqa charged the octopus, but the creature enveloped the shark's body, wrapping his jaws shut. Dakuwaqa begged for mercy and the giant octopus acquiesced, but in return he required his subjects, the people of Kadavu, forever be protected from shark attack. Today's islanders show no fear of sharks, and, in a nice twist, the sharks have little to fear from them. Most Fijians won't eat shark or octopus out of respect for their gods.

Tradition still holds sway on other fronts too. Fiji is governed by a central government, but on many of the islands this doesn't matter much to the local chiefs—the *ratus*—who hold firm sway over their respective village. For a time, all diving off Kadavu Island was summarily shut down by local chiefs who believed the bubbles were scaring fish away.

Fijian tribal roots and traditions still run deep. Much ado has been made about Fiji's ceremonial kava drink, which, depending on who is doing the talking, has no effect, produces numbness in the lips and legs, elicits mild euphoria, leads to stupor, or renders one senseless as a tree stump. No matter. If you travel to Fiji you'll probably get to try it yourself, as the drinking of kava is part of ceremony and day-to-day life. The roots of the yaqona tree—the pepper plant *Piper methysticum*—are ground up in a bowl,

The lionfish, also known as turkeyfish or devilfish, possesses poisonous spines, and its stripes can serve both to camouflage it and warn of its presence. They feed primarily on other fishes and are often seen herding smaller fish.

eventually producing a liquid that looks like dishwater and tastes like a mixture of mouthwash and mud. Perhaps with an eye to the side effects, the ceremony is simple. A bowl is passed to the drinker, who claps, downs the contents, hands the empty shell back, and claps again. Probably not a ceremony to engage in before diving, but an important part of Fijian culture, and no harm to try.

Fiji is often portrayed as paradise, and when you're drifting lazily above delicate lettuce coral gardens swept by bright fish and brighter sunshine, this seems rightly so. But the waters are by no means untouched. Sugarcane farming, a critical export, sends masses of sediment and chemicals into rivers, and both are swept out on to reefs, especially around Viti Levu and Vanua Levu. The interior of these bigger islands is rugged and virtually uninhabitable, so most people live on the coast. Sewage systems, where they exist, aren't up to snuff. Fiji's population is growing, and development sees mangrove areas filled in and coral sands gobbled up for cement construction. Tourism, of course, plays a role here too.

Burgeoning population has also seen to the tailspin of sea life. The waters around the larger islands are sorely overfished. Two species of giant clams in Fiji's waters—harvested for their meat and shells—recently became extinct. Hawksbill and green turtles are seriously endangered. The world's largest parrotfish, the humphead parrotfish, is in danger of being fished to extinction in Fijian waters. Attempts on the part of the Fiji government to establish marine protected areas have run into a traditional glitch. Local villagers, who hold centuries-old customary fishing rights over their local reefs, often won't acquiesce. An attempt to establish Fiji's first National Marine Park off Makogai Island—and protect a clam hatchery in the process—failed when local villagers balked at giving up their fishing rights for the equivalent of $250 a year. Over the years, scientists have recommended marine protected status for diving grails like Beqa lagoon, Great Astrolabe Reef, and Taveuni Island's Rainbow Reef, with no luck.

But there is hope. As far back as the 1970s, resorts and privately owned islands have established private sanctuaries by leasing local waters from villagers, and this practice continues. Awareness is growing, villagers and the central government recognizing the value of eco-tourist dollars. And the waters and life of the outer islands remain largely pristine.

In Fiji, the *tabua* is a ceremonial whale tooth that, among other roles, marks the forging of a lifelong commitment in marriage. In a culture tied to the sea, a similar commitment to a different cause may be possible.

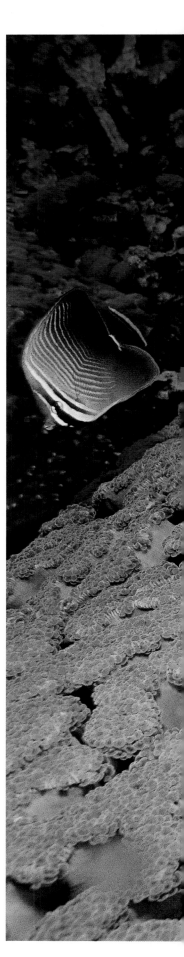

RIGHT: An endangered hawksbill turtle has the flesh around its face stung from eating organ pipe coral. Hawksbill turtles are coveted for their beautiful shells.

The most commonly seen ray on Indo-Pacific coral reefs, the blue-spotted stingray is usually seen under corals or in ledges. Its mouth and platelike teeth, on the underside of its body, crushes the invertebrates that it finds in the sand. Like all stingrays, it has a barb on its tail which it can use for defense.

The whitemargin unicornfish, found here sleeping at night, is a member of the surgeonfish family. The function of its prominent long horn is unknown. Schools of unicornfish are often seen in the waters off coral dropoffs, swimming about feeding on plankton.

PAGES 76–77: A golden damselfish keeps close to the shelter of a soft coral tree, feeding on plankton passing in the current. It is commonly seen on the edges of steep coral walls.

The blue-ribbon eel's flaring nostrils aid in its sense of smell. This eel is sometimes seen stretching out from its burrow, trying to grab a small fish for dinner.

Two red fire gobies hover above their burrows in coral rubble. These fish, usually found in pairs, feed on zooplankton, using burrows for refuge. The burrows are often made by other fishes.

BELOW: This species of commensal shrimp lives only on the surface of sea stars. This one is on the dotted, colorful surface of a Linckia *star.*

FRENCH POLYNESIA

Moorea, Tahiti, Bora Bora—these are the islands of romance, and romance, of course, takes many forms. In the eighteenth century, it was practical. When a foreigner arrived on the remote Austral Islands, far to the southwest of Tahiti, he was often offered a woman, in hopes of adding new blood to the community, and preventing inbreeding. On the larger, more populated islands, romance took a more mercenary tack. Romantic favors were traded for goods, a ploy so successful that at least one captain had to keep a close eye on his crew to ensure that they didn't dismantle their ship beneath their feet, nails being popular among the islanders.

RIGHT: Children enjoy a boat ride in Moorea's lagoon.

OPPOSITE: Clear, shallow water covers the sand in the middle of the lagoon off Moorea.

OPPOSITE: *A regular feeding by a dive operator in Moorea attracts hundreds of fish, including snappers, groupers, and sharks. The positive and negative aspects of fish and shark feeding have been subject to debate in the past few years. Yet, it cannot be denied that seeing sharks in their natural habitat is a powerful incentive to saving sharks.*

In 1768 French explorer Louis Antoine de Bougainville, who must have possessed more focus than most men, could only throw up an unanswerable question in lament when his vessel was surrounded by pirogues, filled with beautiful, and quite naked, women. "I ask you, given such a spectacle, how could one keep at work four hundred Frenchmen?"

Certainly there is no answer to this question, just as there is no real hope of describing the exquisite beauty of this sprinkling of 118 atolls and islands in a vast, vast sea. All sorts of famous sorts have tried to put a finger to French Polynesia. The wiser ones gave up, asking questions—"These trivial islands have imposed on history the most lasting vision of the earthly paradise. Why?" (James Michener); or making simple, unassailable statements—"I knew right away," wrote Somerset Maugham, "that there was the place I had been looking for all my life."

Physically, French Polynesia is all about water— happy news for the diver, or, for that matter, anyone who enjoys a flaring sunset reflected on a mirror-still lagoon. The French territory comprises five sets of islands, plunked in the South Pacific roughly 2,700 miles south of Honolulu. To the west are the Society Islands, including Tahiti, Moorea, and Bora Bora. In the center rests the islands of the Tuamotu Archipelago,

The generally shy sicklefin lemon shark seems to keep to a relatively small home range.

Rangiroa, with its famed reef passes, among them. The Gambiers sit to the southeast, the Australs to the southwest, and far to the north, the Marquesas. The weather is subtropical in the southern archipelagos and steamy and equatorial to the north.

Unless you're a mapmaker, you don't need to concern yourself with the layout. But you will better grasp French Polynesia if you understand this. The total land mass of all the islands is 1,359 square miles. French Polynesia's watery territory enfolds over one million square miles, a chunk roughly the size of Western Europe. Land at Bora Bora airport—on a small island on the outer edge of the atoll—and, until the resort catamaran comes to pick you up, you can pass the time peering down at pufferfish staring directly back at you.

The dry land that does poke itself above the waterline is astonishingly beautiful. Jagged mossy peaks snare high clouds, frame rainbows, or both. Ice-still lagoons throw off myriad shades of blue and green. Bright-white beaches serve as bleachers for implausible sunsets and fat tropical moons.

Ironically, islands famous among moony couples for terrestrial tranquility are, in dive circles, revered for their adrenal rush. If you want to lollygag above lush coral gardens, French Polynesia is not for you. Compared to Australia or Indonesia, for example, there aren't that many corals. Plus, lollygagging will see you miss the sharky, electric, reef pass dives for which French Polynesia is famous. French Polynesia has been dubbed "the shark diving capital of the world." Understand that writers are forever trying to pigeonhole, and there are plenty of other dive opportunities in these islands (more on this in a minute). But know too that the reef pass diving and the sharks and shark feedings will give you a buzz you'll carry with you for a long, long time.

Probably the best known of the reef passes, and deservedly so, are those that join Rangiroa Atoll and its massive lagoon to the ocean. Located in the northern Tuamotus, Rangiroa is a ring of 240 motus with only two breaks leading from the lagoon to the open ocean. Rangiroa's lagoon is massive. Forty-eight miles

In a pass at Rangiroa, gray reef sharks congregate by the hundreds. Gray reef sharks have a reputation for aggressive, territorial behavior and have attacked many divers. However, in areas that are frequented by divers, gray reef sharks may have grown accustomed to intrusions by humans, and will keep a distance.

long by fifteen miles wide, the whole of Tahiti could be plopped in it. When the tides move in and out of the lagoon, they do so with e-ticket suction.

These passes-cum-Hoover vacuums are where the sharks mass—blacktip, silvertip, whitetip, grey reef, and lemon sharks flicking about in the blue. Under ideal conditions, here is how a dive at Tiputa or Avatoru Pass might go. Plunge into the open ocean a few hundred yards outside the pass. Descend quickly into the gloom, catching glimpses of massive curtains of jacks and barracudas; see the reef plunging from the surface to the bluish sandy bottom. Feel suddenly— and unexpectedly, even though you were told to expect it—the inexorable suction, which, in a blink, clicks to tremendous speed. Understand in the same click that you are powerless. Soar over the bottom, backward, forward, upside down. Once you damp down the brief anxiety, speed becomes a carnival ride.

See them hanging outside the reef pass, hazy shadows at first, then, fifty yards gone in a wink, discernible forms, and, depending on your experience your heart does a brief jig or a powerful slam dance. A hundred sharks, maybe more, and, blink again, you are among them, and if you are attentive you notice that they loll easily as if there is no current, an impassive, patient cloud of cold-eyed forms regarding you with little interest. Wink again, and they have dissolved back into the haze, and you are being swept into the lagoon, the current slowing, the water a bit murkier, and what you want more than anything is to pass through that no longer menacing cloud again.

Shark rush hour can be experienced at other passes on other atolls (Manihi and Fakarave are two) and the bee-swarm shark feedings off Moorea's Tiki Point are deservedly eye-popping. But Rangiroa is something special.

ABOVE: This aerial view of Rangiroa atoll, one of the largest atolls in the world, shows the classic atoll structure of an outer barrier reef surrounding an inner lagoon. Small islands (motus) have formed on the outer edge of the atoll.

Napoleon wrasse are prized for their flesh, and are uncommon except in areas that are protected from fishing. In areas where they are protected, they are a welcome presence on reefs, where they will often approach divers.

It is a mistake, however, to equate French Polynesia, or for that matter Rangiroa (a one-hour flight from Tahiti), strictly with sharks and adrenaline. Rangiroa's vast lagoon is its own world with its own unique ecosystem, and the diving on its outer reef walls, depending on the season, can showcase mantas, dolphins, hammerhead sharks, tuna, jacks, and barracuda. And, if big fish are what you pine for, there is great opportunity elsewhere in the island chain. The chance to snorkel with humpback whales off Rurutu in the Australs, or dive with huge schools of melonhead whales off the Marquesas. Drift about

PAGES 86–87: At the lagoon pass of Rangiroa, a school of mullet pass under a wave as it crests.

Bottlenose dolphins frequent the pass at Rangiroa. Dolphins can work together to round up schools of fish, then take turns feeding on the school.

Ironically the one place you probably won't dive is Tahiti, the biggest island of the lot, home to the capital Papeete and the international airport, and point of departure for the best diving, which is on the other islands. Manihi offers another rare experience, the chance to visit a black pearl farm and so better understand why you might pay a thousand dollars for what amounts to an undersize marble. More than 98 percent of the world's black pearls are cultured in French Polynesia, and the island chain's pearl farms—roughly five hundred of them, some tiny one-man operations, some huge operations—are fascinating places. Black pearls are manufactured—and this is precisely the right word, because today nearly every single pearl on the market is cultured by man—using *Pinctada margaritifera*, the black-lipped pearl oyster. The process is actually fairly simple. First little oysters are lovingly raised from their beginnings as pinhead-size larvae, hanging suspended in a warm lagoon for the better part of two years in baskets. At this point the oysters are removed and wedged open, one by one, by nimble-fingered grafting operators who make a slit with a scalpel near the oyster's gonad and insert a bit of mantle tissue and then a small bead. Returned to the lagoon, the oyster slowly, doggedly, covers the inserted bead with the pearlescent substance that will turn the bead from its former self—a piece of shell from an American freshwater mussel—into the pricey item that will win a lover's heart and dent a suitor's billfold. After about three years the pearls—which aren't really black at all, but maybe grey, purple, green, or champagne yellow—are ready to harvest.

Black pearls aren't the only pricey items in French Polynesia; fact is, they only occupy one spot in line. Almost everything must be imported, so almost everything is expensive. The famed over-the-water bungalows go for seven hundred dollars a night and up, and, in the wrong place, a Coke can cost six dollars. But don't be scared off because the locals can't pay those kinds of prices, and you don't have to either. Move off the water and on to the beach, and a "pension" will provide you a room or a bungalow, complete with breakfast, for as little as

in Bora Bora's magnificent lagoon or head to Manihi Atoll—330 miles northeast of Tahiti and one of the prettiest atolls in French Polynesia—and wile away time exploring the aptly named Drop Off, a wall that plunges over four thousand feet. Liveaboards can take you to these places and, in many instances, shore-based diving centers can too—zipping you out to your dive of choice in fifteen minutes or less. (The vast expanses of Rangiroa and Bora Bora are two exceptions to this brief commute.)

sixty dollars a night. And if the French, who have ruled Polynesia in one form or another since 1842, impact anything it's cuisine. The exterior of a restaurant may resemble your twelve-year-old's tree fort, but inside they are serving delectable escargot with garlic butter or carpaccio of tuna with ginger.

It is, of course, hard to keep Paradise a secret. France took Tahiti and its islands from the English in 1842. Even by the turn of the century, when French artist Paul Gaugin came to Papeete to flee civilization, he took one look around, and fled further (to the Marquesas). French Polynesia discovered the modern traveler in 1961 with the opening of the international airport, and discovered modern technology in 1967 when the French began detonating nuclear bombs on Mururoa and Fangataufa atolls (an experiment that continued until 1991). Papeete today is citified and faces problems familiar to any city that is growing fast with nowhere to go. Ninety-one percent of French Polynesia's population already lives in the capital and its nearby environs, and, given Tahiti's rugged interior, virtually everyone lives on the coast.

No coincidence that 20 percent of the fringing reefs around Papeete have been destroyed. What has transpired off Papeete is a perfect example of Nature's web gone awry. Man—through sediment and sewage runoff—has seen to an increased nutrient presence in the waters off Papeete. Algae have capitalized on this, covering parts of the reef. Urchins, which feed on algae, have capitalized on this. The fish that would normally keep the urchins in check have been largely fished out. End result, the reef is being grazed away faster than it can regenerate. Reef quality has declined in Bora Bora and Moorea too. Because French Polynesia's islands (and reefs) are so far flung it is harder for them to regenerate because they can't expect much larval contribution from other reef systems.

Nature, however, can be hardy, sometimes rebounding back from the harshest of adversity. Many of French Polynesia's reefs are so far flung they haven't been studied. But ironically two of the most isolated atolls have been extensively examined, and the news there is, if not wildly optimistic, at least

hopeful. Many coral reef species on Mururoa and Fangataufa atolls, pounded by nuclear armament for nearly twenty-five years, were able to recolonize the reefs quickly once the bombing stopped.

And, like many South Pacific archipelagos, once you move away from the overrun center, man's fingerprints disappear proportionally. Of the 118 islands in the five groups, roughly one-third are still uninhabited, and it is a fine thing, post dive, to stroll your own private *motu* beneath an arc of eggshell blue, the sun on your back and a lick of tradewind in your face.

When Captain James Cook pulled anchor during one of several departures from the lovely islands, his lieutenant came as close as anyone to capturing Polynesia's magnetic spell. "They are," wrote Charles Clerke, "as pleasant and happy a spot as the world contains."

Pacific double-saddle butterflyfish swarm a snorkeler in Bora Bora.

Papua New Guinea and the Solomon Islands

The term Heaven on Earth is greatly bandied about, but Papua New Guinea may just be that place. As recently as 1995, in the rugged central Highlands of Papua New Guinea, anthropologists came upon tribes who had never been in contact with Westerners, certainly a blessing for the anthropologists and quite possibly a blessing for the Guinean tribes too.

LEFT: An islander steers a canoe in Kimbe Bay.

RIGHT: A false-eye puffer keeps close to a sea fan for protection.

PNG, as it is informally known, is a place of impressive numbers. Over fourteen hundred islands to the north of Australia are spread over hundreds of miles of open waters, comprising the Coral, Bismarck, and Solomon seas. Roughly one-third of the world's languages are spoken here, a reflection of the far-flung islands and the rugged topography—mountains as high as 15,400 feet—some islands possess. On certain islands the terrain is so rugged that neighboring tribes dwelled only a mile apart, unaware that the other existed. This same isolation has helped buffer PNG from the modern world. Port Moresby, the ramshackle capital, is no stranger to the outside world, but beyond its dusty sprawl lie little-touched natural havens.

Happily for divers, the boons of isolation are best reflected beneath the sea. Much of PNG's coast-line is uninhabited; habitation, where it does appear, consists of small coastal villages whose residents exist by farming and fishing. Roughly fifteen hundred square miles of reef support almost no large commercial fisheries; experts guess that the subsistence catch is four times the total commercial catch. PNG is one of the few places left where Nature is the dominant force affecting the reefs—weather, outbreaks of coral-eating sea stars, heavy seas. What you have, in short, is a vast arena that Man has yet to unreservedly finger.

And what an arena it is. Currents from the Great Barrier Reef, the South Pacific, the Indian Ocean, and Japan sweep into PNG's waters, carrying a potpourri of everything from larvae to very large life. Infant fish are nourished by some of the world's largest and most pristine mangrove systems. Pounding rains during the

A diver approaches a huge sea fan. Sea whips and sea fans are colonies of stinging invertebrates, with polyps that catch plankton in currents.

PAGES 94–95: A school of black-tipped fusiliers swim past an elephant ear sponge at twilight. Dusk is a great time for activity on the coral reef. The reduced light reduces the risk of day-time predators seeing them, so many fish species spawn at dusk.

monsoon months (January through March) fill rivers, which spew a cargo of silt and nutrients into the sea, a soup for life. Life reflects its appreciation. An estimated nine hundred species of fish and four hundred species of coral dwell in the Bismarck, Coral, and Solomon seas. Most alluring, these estimates are likely quite low. The area is little studied. Local divers who have descended into PNG's waters hundreds of times see new creatures almost every dive.

But it would be a mistake to equate diving in PNG strictly with numbers, because the real joy is in form. PNG's waters—calm, sunny, and ideal for diving April through June and September through November— are home to sea shapes so bizarre that Abstract Expressionism suddenly looks clear. Dive Restorf Island, accessed by boat from Kimbe Bay on

the north coast of West New Britain, and a post-dive name-dropping might proceed like this.

"Happen to see that harlequin ghost pipefish? I nearly swam into it, I was so mesmerized by the blue ribbon eels."

"Ghost pipefish? Certainly. Though I have to say the crocodilefish, devil scorpionfish, and the three species of seahorses were annoyingly distracting."

Nicely illustrating how well balanced PNG diving can be, along with the requisite floods of jacks and barracudas and splendid coral-covered walls, the calm waters of Kimbe Bay might also house orcas, pilot, sperm, minke, humpback or melonhead whales, or pygmy seahorses. In recent years pygmy seahorse sightings have been cropping up at dive spots around the globe, largely because divers now know to look for

BELOW: Shrimpfish, or razorfish, use their long bodies to hide within stalks of sea whips. The entire school of fish turn and swim as one, all head-down.

BELOW, RIGHT: Only the head of the blue-ribbon eel shows, with its very long body hidden in its burrow. This eel is a hermaphrodite and can change sex and coloration quickly. Males and juveniles are black; females are blue with yellow fins, or all yellow.

Corallimorpharians are considered to be intermediate between corals and sea anemones. Some species in some areas are reputed to have a very painful sting.

A freckle-faced blenny peers out from a crevice. Blennies are generally small fishes that hide in cracks and holes, coming out only to search for food. They defend their tiny territories vigorously.

OPPOSITE: The tiny pygmy seahorse is smaller than a fingernail, and it is well-camouflaged in its sea-fan home. The seahorse's colors match the color of its host; even the warts on its body match the polyps of the sea fan. In recent years pygmy seahorse sightings have been cropping up at dive spots around the globe, largely because divers now know to look for them.

them. Kimbe Bay has its share of seahorses, from the large (six inches plus) to the impossibly small, explaining why you often see divers scouring the bottom, bubbling Sherlock Holmeses peering intently at red gorgonians with magnifying glasses. Magnification isn't always required. On one occasion in Kimbe Bay, stunned divers watched a mother orca and her calf hunt a twelve-foot hammerhead.

For the open-minded diver, things can get weirder still. Muck diving off Loloata (Lion) Island—diving shallow sand and seagrass—may not sound appealing until you discover the wonderfully strange creatures that call muck home—seahorses, warty frog-fish, banded snake eels, juvenile batfish, and juvenile striped catfish massed in tight balls. A wet page out of Weird Science.

Need more? There's stunning drift diving off Rabaul in St. George's Channel and off Kavieng on the northern tip of New Ireland, where hopefully you won't be forced to choose between Silvertip, a shallow pinnacle crowded with sharks, and Planet Channel, with its whopping sea fans, sponges, and soft corals. Valerie's Reef may very well be the pelagic capital of PNG. Dive World War II wrecks off Madang, and experience some of the best sheltered wreck dives

anywhere at Bootless Inlet just off Port Moresby. Travel by liveaboard to Eastern Fields, an atoll in the Coral Sea eighty-six miles southwest of Port Moresby, and explore a remote barrier reef fat with life—tuna, sharks, turtles, giant groupers, and gorgonian sea fans ten feet high.

You may be hard pressed figuring out when to rest, because night dives in PNG delight too. Pin a fire urchin in your light's beam and watch in rapt silence as the day-glo ball prowls the blackness, molten orange at its center and thick with a tuft of spines glimmering yellow-gold and bright blue. Watch opportunistic lion-fish make the most of your beam, following you in the darkness until you illuminate the right size fish, then gobbling the floodlit repast.

Unicorn surgeonfish are found in schools here. Giant green and hawksbill turtles drift through the blue, as do brown-spotted cod the size of a refrigerator and ten-foot dugong seacows with calves on their backs.

Though it might seem obvious, it's important to realize that life above water will be equally foreign. PNG is not yet tuned to cell phones, drive-thru eateries, and smartly dressed, multilingual ticketing agents. The pace of life in PNG reflects this. Arrive in Port Moresby, and your connecting flight to the outer

ABOVE: A divemaster blows a series of perfect rings of bubbles while waiting for his group of divers to perform a safety stop after a dive. Diving, far from being a strenuous sport, is a relaxing and peaceful activity.

RIGHT: *A diver examines the lush marine life that has grown around the wreck of the* Kinugawa Maru, *a Japanese vessel from World War II. The waters around Guadalcanal in the Solomon Islands are filled with such wrecks.*

OPPOSITE, TOP LEFT: *A pair of clown anemonefish, immune to the stinging tentacles of their host, guard a nest of eggs they have laid at the base of the anemone.*

OPPOSITE, BOTTOM: *A whitetip reef shark swims among a school of pyramid butterflyfish. Out of 375 species of sharks, less than a dozen have been implicated in unprovoked attacks on humans. The whitetip reef shark will only bite if handled.*

island of your choice may be on time or it may be *Balus I bagarap* (buggered up) and out of fuel. You will wait, possibly in a very warm equatorial sun, possibly for quite some time. In times like these it is best to see such delays in an optimistic light. What inconveniences you is what makes PNG special.

It will also help to bone up on your Pidgin (Pidgin pocket guides are available, and they're worth the investment). Though plenty of islanders speak English, plenty more speak Tok Pisin, and they greatly appreciate it when you try too. It can come in handy, as in these two random examples: *Planti tumas sharks* (Plenty of Sharks); *No Ken Bagarupim Haus Pek Pek* (Do Not Misuse the Toilet).

"Planti tumas" variety in the wondrous Solomon Islands too, the vast chain of nine hundred-plus islands and atolls that string their way across roughly one thousand miles of Pacific to the east of PNG. Like the coral and life-rich reefs of Indonesia and the Philippines, the reefs and overlaying life in PNG and the Solomon Islands are as diverse as any place on the globe. But, unlike Indonesia and the Philippines, which have been impacted by trades like cyanide and blast fishing, the majority of the reefs in PNG and the Solomons are still in excellent condition.

Appropriately, the Solomons were named by a dreamy Spanish captain, Alvaro de Mendana, who sailed from Peru inspired by Inca stories of immense stocks of gold six hundred leagues to the west. It is quite possible the Incas were simply ridding themselves of another conquistador, but when de Mendana sailed into the vast, but goldless archipelago, he tagged them in honor of King Solomon.

There is gold in the Solomons, though gold of a different sort. A single day's diving among the Solomons might proceed like this. Morning dive on a World War II plane, perfectly preserved in turquoise lagoon waters. Rest and decompress in the sun. Explore a cave system that meanders through the middle of a coral island. Rest, decompress, sun, barter with local islanders who have paddled out in canoes to offer up fresh fruit, nautilus shells, and wood carvings. Glide through sun-spackled eighty-degree water, float-

ing above coral gardens as diverse as any place in the world. Sea life? Massive schools of barracuda, seven species of anemonefish, grey reef sharks patrolling in the blue haze, maybe even an orca or a saltwater crocodile. Your biggest concern? *Watkaen dei blong wik hem I nao tude*? What day of the week is it? Just another evening under pink and purple sky, the sea the color of rose water.

Six major islands serve as centerpiece in the Solomons—Guadalcanal, Malaita, New Georgia, Santa Isabel, Makira, and Choiseul. Because of their equatorial location, the islands enjoy a year-round tropical climate. (The southern winter—May through December—is slightly cooler and drier than the

OPPOSITE: A diver investigates a crack in a coral island. In rare places, a split in a coral reef may leave huge fissures.

A World War II Corsair lies in shallow water near Munda. Corsairs were also flown against jets in Korea and were used in Vietnam by the French, giving them the longest combat life of any aircraft of the time.

ABOVE: *Double rainbows appear above the tropical rainforest of the Solomon Islands.*

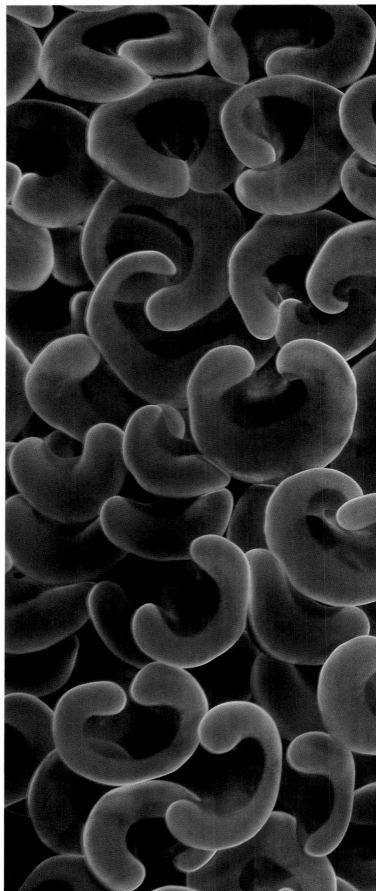

summer months.) Guadalcanal is home to the Solomon's capital city, Honiara, and the largest collection of Solomon Islanders, roughly one hundred thousand at last count. Honiara, and Gizo on New Georgia Island, serve as the centers for diving in the islands, with day-trip operators offering nearby dives and liveaboards sailing from there to explore what amounts to a large step back in time. Imagine empty emerald isles slipping silently past; canoes filled with jostling, goggle-eyed children peering down into the water to watch your every move; distinguished, straight-backed elders who, in less serene times, reported the movements of Japanese ships and aircraft to American forces; villagers who worship the shark and eagle. A place where *kastom* (tradition) still reigns.

Proving that no place is removed when global powers decide to have a go at each other, the Solomons, of course, played a pivotal role in the outcome of World War II. The six-month ordeal of Guadalcanal, which ended in American victory in February 1943, at the great cost of thirty thousand lives, was perhaps the turning point of the war. Today, in the waters and the jungles, Nature has enveloped history, vine-tangles embracing downed warplanes, soft corals festooning the hulls of now-silent destroyers.

Poignant yes, but also opportunity for terrific wreck diving. Iron Bottom Sound, just off Honiara

The Euphyllia coral is a type of stony coral with distinctive polyps. These coral colonies look like a spilled tray of typesetters' parentheses.

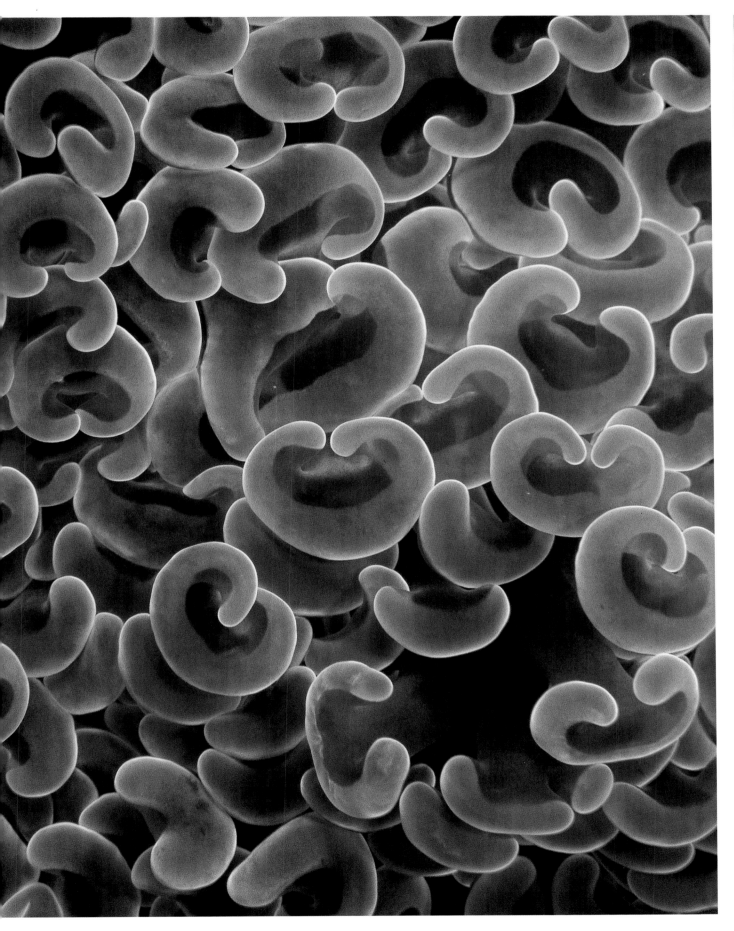

This mantis shrimp strikes with its stiletto-shaped claws, one of the fastest movements in the animal kingdom. Other species use blunt claws to smash the shell of mollusks upon which they feed.

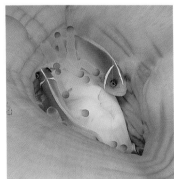

Many anemones on a coral reef have a small community of fish and shrimp that live within their tentacles. Here, a pair of anemonefish is settling in for the night. Juvenile anemonefish typically hatch from a nest under the anemone's body, drift in the ocean current for about two weeks, and then seek a new host anemone.

Harbor, is so named for the sixty-odd wrecks littering the bottom. There are wrecks off the Russell and Florida islands (some of the best diving in the Solomons, reached only by liveaboard vessel). Off Munda, on New Georgia Island, a bomber lies in thirty-five feet of water, its last flight, on July 23, 1943, abruptly ended by antiaircraft fire. It is important to note that the current liveaboards don't usually spend much time on the Guadalcanal wrecks, but there are day-boat operators who do. If wreck diving's your joy, best to allow a few days in Honiara before or after your liveaboard adventure, easily done since almost all flights come through Honiara.

The intricate and bizarre players of PNG are here too—harlequin ghost pipefish, scorpionfish, leaf scorpionfish, frogfish, and Caledonian stingers dragging themselves across sandy bottoms on chicken-claw feet. There are dives that rival, and surpass, the best on the globe. Grand Central Station, a beach dive on New Georgia Island, moves from idyllic, palm-cusped South Pacific beach directly to shallow lush coral reef and then, on a slow current, out to deeper water where vast silver-blue curtains of fish waver and dart about like indecisive commuters at, you guessed it. Custom Cave in the Russell Islands may be the underwater world's Sistine Chapel. Sunlight pours through a surface opening (you swim through a gaping entrance fifty feet below the surface), spotlighting divers in the cavern below with arrow-beams of light that pierce a stage of saw-blade blue. Palau's Blue Holes, Sipadan's Turtle Tomb—merely pretenders.

Striking out from centers in Honiara and Gizo, liveaboards open up the Solomons' vast and stunning world: Korumolun Island, walls fat with coral and fish life; Mane Island's Mirror Pond, famous for a sometime-resident saltwater croc; Mary Island's underwater point flooded with massive schools of barracuda and jacks.

Added plus, you'll share the diving with a select few. Very few tourists visit the Solomons, explaining why the international airport is, more accurately, a narrow strip of asphalt and the terminal is presided over by a few locals who have been known to take a

Divers off Gizo admire a large cuttlefish. Of all the cephalopods, the cuttlefish have the greatest ability to alter their color.

PAGES 106–107: A nudibranch crawls over a tunicate. Most nudibranchs feed on stinging or chemically noxious animals such as hydroids and sponges, and store the stinging cells or the noxious compounds within their own bodies. Scientists theorize that the bright colors advertise the fact that nudibranchs are poisonous, or terribly untasty.

ride through the X-ray machines so as to admire each others' bones.

The Solomons and Papua New Guinea represent something not yet lost. Vast swaths of healthy mangrove and seagrass nurture life as it begins. Expansive tracts of reef shimmer with color and healthy adult life. But the standard of living is low, and the temptation is high. In the Solomon Islands hunting for crocodile skins and turtle shells quickly drove estuarine crocodiles to near extinction and put a severe dent in hawksbill turtle populations. Local regulations have slowed the hunting of both animals, and crocodile farming has also helped ease the strain, but in a remote and unpoliceable place it's impossible to put complete brakes on poaching. Asian-market

The masterful camouflage of the weedy scorpionfish mimics the sea fans and crinoids of its coral reef habitat.

desire for sea cucumbers has seen them sorely depleted. The use of cyanide for the lucrative live reef-fish trade is on the rise. Grouper, wrasse, stonefish and spiny lobster that arrive alive in Hong Kong, China, and Taiwan bring high prices at the restaurant table and a tidy profit for the fisherman. In a small village without electricity or running water, where life depends on what you grow and catch, the environment is not the first concern.

Excepting a knowledgeable few, the Solomon Islands and Papua New Guinea are neither tourist mecca nor a place of environmental concern. This will change. And the next moves will decide whether these glorious outposts become something less, or remain *nambbawan*—the best.

A master of camouflage, the flattened crocodilefish can hardly be distinguished from its habitat. Its shape and mottled coloring make it an effective ambush predator.

BELOW, LEFT: This reef stonefish lying in sand resembles a rock. The stonefish is the most venomous fish in the world. A sting from its dorsal spines has caused human fatalities. First aid treatment for all scorpionfish stings is heat applied to the wound with hot water, and, absent that, hot air from a hair dryer.

BELOW: The Caledonian stinger is venomous. It usually hides in sand by day, emerging at night. It uses its lower fins to "walk" across sandy bottoms.

Palau

They sweep through the water with careless and uncaring grace, the fine edges of their wings furling like lace curtains in a delicate wind. Their smooth broad backs, eight feet from wingtip to wingtip, sweep past, then their pearly white undersides. The mantas, five of them, turn languid somersaults here in German Channel, mouths agape. Intent on feeding, they pirouette less than an arm's length from your mask, inhaling plankton with regal aplomb. Yet another impossibly beautiful brushstroke in Palau's collective palette.

ABOVE: The Seventy Islands of Palau are limestone islands which have been cut into strange mushroom-shaped formations by ocean action. They are the oldest national wildlife preserve in Palau and Micronesia.

RIGHT: The steep walls of Palau offer a rare opportunity to see the chambered nautilus, a fascinating and primitive cephalopod. During the day, nautiluses rest in water as deep as several hundred feet and rise at night to feed in shallower depths. Their shells are separated into a series of chambers that fill with gas or water to regulate the animal's buoyancy.

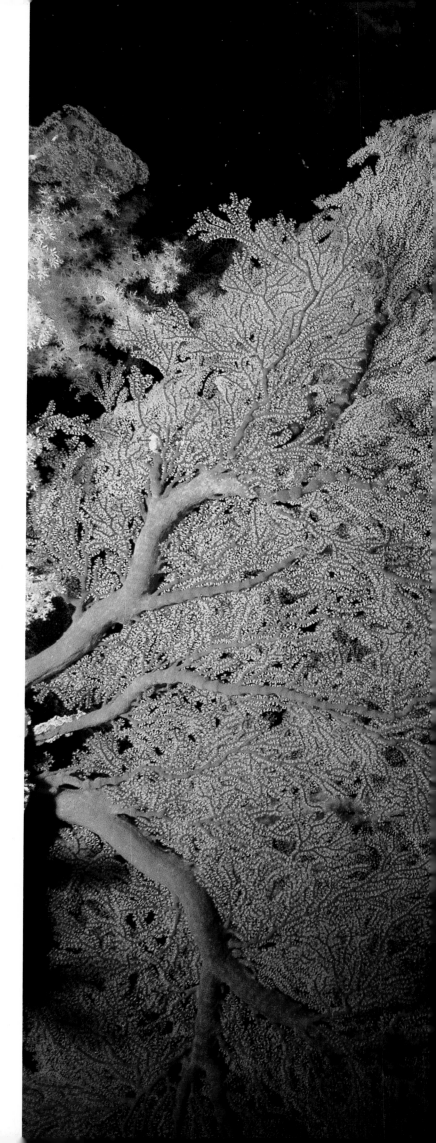

The famous Blue Hole dive site boasts two large tunnels at the top of a coral reef that lead into the open ocean.

ABOVE: Batfish are relatively large fish that often follow divers or hang motionless in the waters above coral reefs. The juveniles have very tall fins compared to those of adults.

The large eyespot on this eclipse butterflyfish may serve to confuse or scare predators. A black line covers the butterflyfish's real eyes, and the false eyespot may confuse predators into thinking it is the eye of a much larger fish.

The pajama cardinalfish is found in lagoons among branching corals. Like most, if not all, cardinalfish, the male of the species incubates eggs in its mouth for about a week after spawning occurs.

PAGES 114–115: *This commensal shrimp lives only on the surfaces of sea stars. This one is on the dotted, colorful surface of a cushion star, avoiding predators by keeping to the underside of its host.*

Much ado has been made of Palau (*Belau* to the locals). With good reason. You can go to the Galapagos and see more sharks, to Sipadan to see more turtles, even to neighboring Yap for more mantas and Truk for more wrecks. But Palau's stunning diversity includes all of these, and then some. "It is," states a local diver, "a biological phenomenon not repeated elsewhere."

It is also plain and simply beautiful, a natural beauty that defies words, because your stammerings and mine would be different, though equally inadequate. To behold a manta ballet, to watch huge schools of fish feed in rocketing currents, to drift quietly on blue waters among the mushroomed Rock Islands beneath an equally blue, cloud-fleeced sky is to be assured that Nature's creations are unsurpassed.

Cartographically, the facts are thus. The island nation of Palau, a tropical archipelago of several hundred Micronesian islands, is scattered across roughly 750 square miles of Western Pacific Ocean, part of a vast mountain range rising up some twenty-seven thousand feet from the ocean floor. North of New Guinea, east of the Philippines, and southwest of Guam, of Palau's 586 islands only a handful are inhabited. Of critical importance to the diver (and the local sea life), the islands are located at the confluence of several major currents, delivering nutrients and species from the biologically rich waters of the Philippine Sea and New Guinea right to Palau's reefs. Some fourteen hundred species of reef and pelagic fish call Palau home, along with roughly seven hundred kinds of hard and soft coral and sea anemones. There's Big Stuff (sharks, sea turtles, mantas, and the giant technicolor tridacna clams), Small Stuff (nudibranchs, black seahorses), Unique Stuff (*Nautilus belauensis*, the chambered nautilus) and a collective profusion of all that stuff.

Bluntly put, smack dab in the center of coral reef diversity Palau is among the best diving in the world. (Year-round temperatures average a moderate 82 degrees, but December through May boasts calmer seas and greater visibility.) Blue Corner, Siaes Tunnel, and Chandelier Cave (Palau's limestone reefs are pocked with caves and caverns), German Channel, New Drop Off, Ngemelis Wall, the Quadruple Blue Holes, and Jellyfish Lake have become the stuff of dive legend. As such, they are well visited. In 1980 Palau's visitor numbers—five thousand that year— were a mere trickle. By 1985, the number had gone to thirteen thousand. By 2000 it was seven times that. They are not, of course, all divers. But the numbers are representative. These days Palau's signature spot, Blue Corner, can see heavy dive crowds.

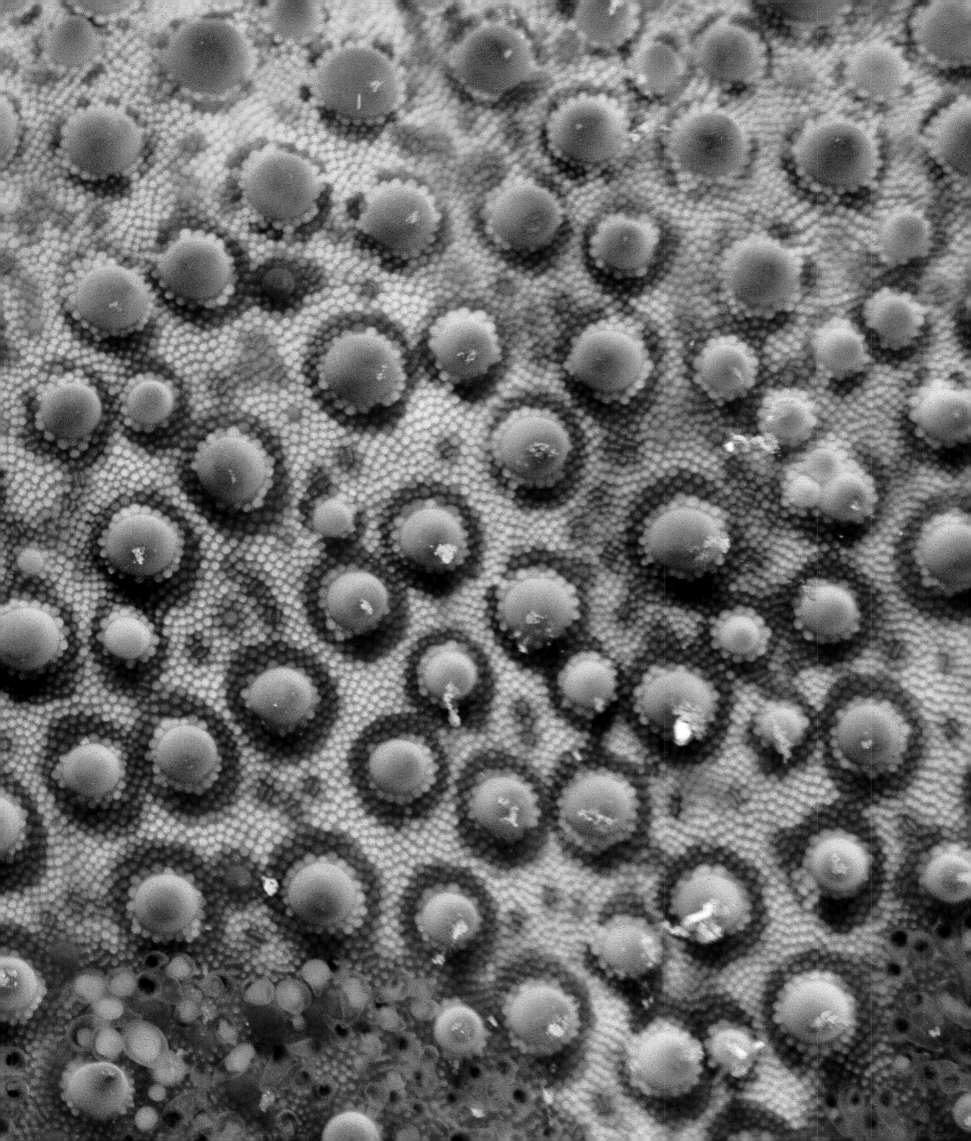

An elegant squat lobster hides among the base of a crinoid, or feather star. It almost perfectly matches the colors of its host's arms.

To drift dive Blue Corner (many of Palau's dives are drift dives, courtesy of the same strong currents that deliver microscopic nutrients and visible sea life) when conditions gel is to experience diving's best. Blue Corner is a section of reef that juts out into the Philippine Sea. Just past the Corner, the wall drops off to great depths. The time to dive Blue Corner is when the tidal currents are running. The currents have been the subject of much hyperbole—two of three divers are NOT swept off to the distant reaches of the Philippine Sea. But the currents do require attention and respect, precisely why divers are issued reef hooks—big fishing hooks with about three feet of line (the line attaches to the chest strap of your BC, the hook to a dead section of reef).

Diving Blue Corner actually means taking in two of the world's best dive sites as one. A dive at Blue Corner proceeds thus. First you drop into the famed Blue Hole cavern, descending through the cavern's ceiling and into the enormous cavern, where beams of surface sunlight flicker through the shroud of darkness. After enjoying cathedral serenity you fin through an enormous arched opening and out into the open sea, and just off a spectacular wall. Here the current does its trick, swooping you past a kaleidoscopic blur of lavender soft corals, swaying bushes of black coral, and undulating sea whips. Nearing Blue Corner you pass swirling balls of pyramid butterflyfish and red-tooth triggerfish. A glance at the distant, though rapidly onrushing blue, might reveal a seething cloud of silver. In a few rapid blinks you are at the Corner, applying your hook. The line tugs taut and there you fly, the current mashing your mask down while blizzards of fish swirl and flit past your face. Drawn by this conveyor belt of foodstuffs, Big Things arrive to dine. Grey reef sharks, whitetipped reef sharks, and the silver cloud that is hundreds of barracuda.

Blue Corner often dominates Palau's PR, and it is a world-class experience. But to focus on Blue Corner is as wrong-minded as ogling tour buses with your back to the Grand Canyon. The diversity of life in Palau's waters is rivaled by the diversity of dive

But fame has yet to ruin Blue Corner, or any of the rest of Palau's dives. Part of the reason, unless you live in Yap, Palau is one hell of a long way from home, fourteen hours flying time from Los Angeles, with layovers in Honolulu and Guam. The Palauans have also exhibited a commendable degree of preservation forethought (more on this later). But mostly spots like Blue Corner remain world-class dives because they are so shockingly beautiful they are difficult to spoil.

offerings—sheer walls, caves and caverns, wrecks, and shallow reefs. Palau is not known as a spot for beginners, and this is a sad misunderstanding. Many of the shallow reefs offer delicate pastel beauty, calm water, and prime snorkeling, happy news if a significant other doesn't dive.

And while neighboring Truk, also part of the Micronesian archipelago, grabs understandable glory regarding wrecks, Palau is unfairly overshadowed. First

the Japanese (by 1940 Koror, Palau's provincial capital, was home to roughly thirty-one thousand Japanese) and then World War II visited Palau in a big way. In March 1944 American air strike Operation Desecrate One sent more than fifty Japanese Imperial Navy vessels to the bottom, many of them in shallow, protected waters not far from Koror, which is still Palau's economic center. Drifting above the silent, shadowy bulk of a ship or a Japanese Zero is both serene and

At Blue Corner in Palau, current rising up from the wall can be so strong that it can rip a dive mask right off your face. All manner of fish patrol the wall, seemingly oblivious to the current. Here, a Napoleon, or humphead, wrasse swims in front of a massive school of jacks.

sobering. Six months after Operation Desecrate One, American forces invaded the Palauan islands of Anguar, Ngedebus, and Peleliu en masse. Eventually American troops walked into Koror, but not without a price. The Japanese lost twelve thousand men, the Americans more than sixteen hundred. A visit to Palau is incomplete without a stop at Peleliu, roughly an hour's boat ride through the mushroom maze of Rock Islands. Yes, the tiny five-mile-square island is home to some stellar diving (Peleliu Corner and Yellow Wall to name two). But it is also a place to think. On its beaches, in its cemeteries, in the front yards of its residents lie the rusted and etched reminders of war. "Lest We Forget Those Who Died" reads the stone monument on Bloody Nose Ridge.

Serenity without sadness can be had in, and on, Palau's seventy-plus marine lakes. Some are completely landlocked. Others touch the ocean. All are sparkling, pan-smooth bodies of water mirroring blue skies, lying serene in a wrap of silent mangrove, thick foliage, and crying birds (Palau is also a birder's paradise, home to more than fifty species of birds, from kingfishers and

RIGHT: Water quickly robs sunlight of warm colors. At a depth of 60 feet, reds are seen as brown. These corals were photographed at a depth of 80 feet, where nearly all subjects look blue on film. These corals are flourescing red light, which can be seen as dots encircling the coral polyps.

BELOW: Light from an underwater flash unit brings back the true colors of underwater subjects. These corals are brown when illuminated by the light of an underwater flash unit. The flourescence of the corals is negligible compared to the power of the artificial light source.

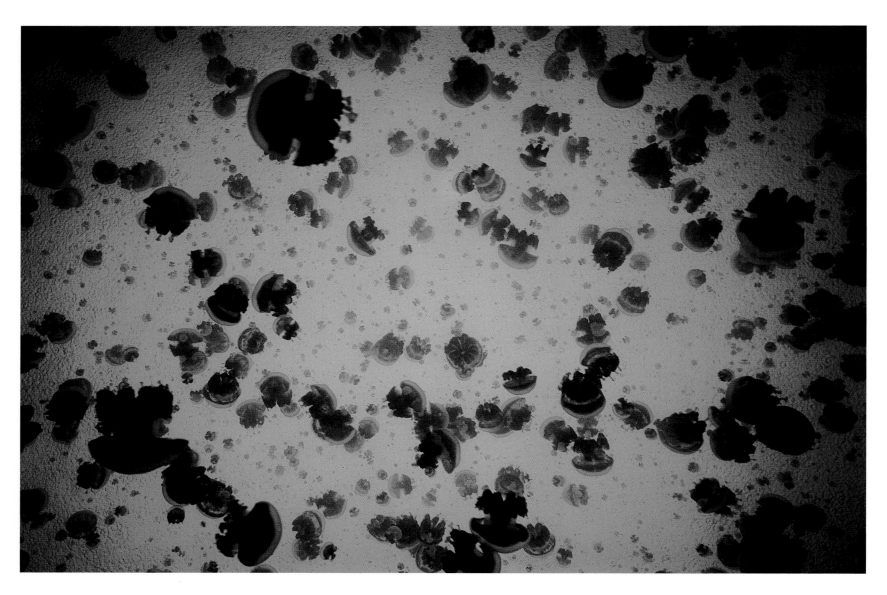

cockatoos to owls and the Palauan fruit dove). Again, there is a headliner—Jellyfish Lake on Eil Malk Island just south of Koror, the famed lake of millions of sting-less jellyfish into which snorkelers plunge in a sort of oozy orgy. (There is no deep diving in Jellyfish Lake, as below about fifty feet the water is dark due to the influx of nutrients from the surrounding islands, pro-ducing deoxygenated water with toxic concentrations of hydrogen sulfide.) Algae living on the jellies produce food for their hosts via photosynthesis, so the mass of jellies follow the sun across the lake each day like an obedient retriever. Jellyfish Lake is also home to a jelly-fish-feeding anemone resembling a beautiful white flower. It is a weird and wonderful place.

Jellyfish Lake is stunning, and a visit to Palau is incomplete without a slurpy swim. But as with Blue

OPPOSITE: *Jellyfish Lake in Palau is one of the diving world's preeminent attractions. This landlocked lake features enormous numbers of jellies that have lost their ability to sting through years of isolation. Algae living within the jellies produce food for their hosts via photosynthesis, but during the massive 1998 El Niño event the algae died and so did millions of jellyfish. Now that the waters have cooled, the jellyfish have returned.*

OPPOSITE, BOTTOM: *The mangrove jellyfish is commonly found in shallow bottoms of lagoons or bays. This species is very similar to the non-stinging species found in Jellyfish Lake. The difference is that this jelly can sting. Like most jellyfish, it has two life stages: the free-swimming medusa stage and the polyp form, which is attached to a substrate.*

The crown-of-thorns starfish feeds on the polyps of stony corals, leaving behind a bleached skeleton. For some reason, populations of these coral predators have exploded in some areas, devastating entire coral reefs. Whether these population explosions are caused by natural cycles or human activities is not known.

Corner, it is foolish to ignore its brethren. Though the lakes themselves show no end to the possibilities of imagining, man has approached them with the creativity of cement. So there is Flatworm Lake (filled with millions of marine flatworms) and Shrimp Lake (you guessed it). No matter. The lakes are fascinating. Mandarinfish Lake (actually a shallow bay nearly rimmed by Rock Islands) is filled with an incredible number of jaunty mandarinfish, particularly jaunty at dawn and dusk when they often engage in elaborate courting and mating rituals.

Comfort has come to these islands too. For years Palau's diving was done via day trips out of Koror, making for a long day of boating and a shorter day of diving. Now liveaboards have come to stay. Equally enticing, and still rarely visited even by the liveaboards, are Palau's remoter islands. To the north, Kayangel Island. Some two hundred miles south of Koror, the Southwest Islands. And some say the real magic is had right at home—diving, snorkeling, and kayaking among the Rock Islands just off Koror. To drift the placid expanse of Long Lake (a mangrove-

filled channel between two Rock Islands) is to experience tropical idyll at its finest. Frankly, your hardest decision is where to turn.

The island nation is not untouched. In 1980, tourists were mostly limited to nostalgic Japanese and a few very wise divers. That has changed, and now Palauans are working to balance their economy (tourism is their top revenue generator) with their environment. Palau gained its independence from the United States in 1994. As part of that break, and in exchange for access by the military (not exercised to date), the U.S. agreed to pay Palau roughly $450 million over fifteen years. That nest egg dries up in 2009, and then Palau must rely fully on tourism. When the money runs out, Palau's master plan projects a need for four hundred thousand tourists a year to make up the difference.

Already there are plenty of growing pains. Sewage is a problem, mangrove removal, overfishing, and chemical pollution too, though these ills are centered primarily around Koror, where most of the population lives. But that might change. To the north

of Koror is Babeldaob Island. Palau's largest island by far, Babeldaob will host the new Palauan capital, which is nearly complete. To that end, construction has invaded the once secluded volcanic island, bringing with it environmental problems including soil erosion, runoff, and the dredging of sand flats and seagrass beds for road fill.

But, though some are not above the avarice that development breeds, the Palauans revere the sea, and a dedicated core of preservationists are taking an active hand in trying to protect their islands. No take and no entry reserves are already in place. Projects

RIGHT: Roots of red mangrove trees extend into salt water, while young saplings rise up from the sediment. Mangrove trees are one of the few land plants that thrive in salt water. Mangrove forests serve to trap sediment before it reaches coral reefs, and they also serve as nursery grounds for hundreds of species of fish and invertebrates.

BELOW: Many of the limestone islands of Palau have been cut by wave action into strange mushroom-shaped formations.

are underway to protect mangroves and endangered dugongs (sea cows) and promote catch-and-release fishing and low-impact kayaking. Organizations and government agencies like the Environmental Quality and Protection Board and Palau Conservation Society monitor reefs and development, and work toward sustainable tourism.

Nothing stays the same. For a time, two dogs lived on one of the Rock Islands. Dive boats visited the informally dubbed Two Dog Island regularly, feeding the island's namesakes scraps. Sweet story has it that the dogs often returned the favor. Campers on the island would wake to find a fresh fish deposited outside their tent flap.

The dogs are gone now, but the idea remains. Man and dogs or entire ecosystems, happy coexistence is a matter of give and take, without an overabundance of either.

A green sea turtle swims off a coral wall. Most sea turtles are threatened and many are in danger of extinction. The green sea turtle is named for the color of its flesh rather than any outward features.

A school of jacks swims above a wall of sea fans at Blue Corner.

The male yellow-margin triggerfish creates large, three-foot-long nests made of coral rubble. It will guard these nests vigorously, attacking any animal venturing into the sand flats where the nest is located. Many divers have been bitten by these aggressive fish.

INDONESIA

Let's dispense with the numbers right away, because they are both illuminating and numbing. The Indonesian archipelago comprises roughly seventeen thousand islands, spanning a distance of roughly three thousand miles and 46 degrees of longitude, an area about the size of the United States. Roughly half of these islands have names; only about one thousand of them are inhabited. Around these islands lie 10 to 15 percent of the world's reefs. In Indonesian waters there swims (pick one) over 2,000 species of fish, over 2,500 species of fish, or over 3,000 species of fish. If there is anything constant here, it's the word "roughly." Point is, Indonesia is simply too vast to precisely know.

ABOVE: Kungkungan Bay Resort is situated right by a coral reef in the Lembeh Straits of North Sulawesi. It is famed for the diversity of life found in the area, as well as the ability of its guides to find elusive and bizarre creatures in what is called "muck diving."

RIGHT: The striped catfish, here seen feeding in a school, are the only species of eeltail catfish commonly observed on coral reefs. The fin spines are highly venomous; stings are extremely painful, and repeated stings can be fatal.

The geography is of interest because it reflects Indonesia's vast potential; there are still plenty of places where no diver has ever slipped beneath the water. But for the diver it is the biology that really grips the imagination. Within the, yes, rough triangle formed by Northern Sulawesi, Bali, and Irian Jaya live more marine species than at any other spot on the globe. In science-speak, this area (extending into the waters of the Philippines and Papua New Guinea) is a zone of megabiodiversity. In comparative-speak, the waters of the far Western Pacific are home to eight times the corals and four times the fish of the Caribbean. This is the Epicenter of Undersea Life, and, barring cataclysmic change, everything else will never catch up. One hundred and twenty-three species of damselfish are found in Indonesian waters, 118 species in the Philippines, 60 in Fiji, 12 in the Galapagos, and 16 in the entire Caribbean.

But numbers still fog the reality. To drift betwixt Indonesia's isles is, in many instances, to experience Nature at her peak. When a Dutch scientist named Umbgrove beheld the reefs of Jakarta Bay in 1928, he lost all head for science, penning instead an assessment as good as any: "The unrivaled splendor and wealth of forms and the delicate tint of the coral structures, the brilliant colours of the fishes, clams, sea anemones, worms, crabs, starfishes, and the whole rest of the reef animals are so attractive and interesting that it seems impossible to give an adequate description of such a profusion of serene and fascinating beauty."

Indonesia is both vast and varied. Warm waters, cold waters, still waters, raging currents, muck diving, fallaway visibility, coral cays, fringing reefs, sheltered bays, rocky coasts, long shallows, massive drop-offs, strung together by a common denominator. In few, if any, places will you see so many fish, so consistently in

A pair of robust ghost pipefish look like pieces of eelgrass or seaweed. Ghost pipefishes are only found in quiet environments, usually in bays or off coral walls. They usually hover head down.

OPPOSITE, BOTTOM: An octopus brooding eggs in an empty bottle sprays a cloud of ink as defense. Most cephalopods can produce ink. Its main function is to distract predators, but it is also used for other purposes ranging from egg coloring to aiding communication. The ink is composed of concentrated melanin, the same pigment responsible for dark hair and skin in humans.

so many different places. And, this is repeated here for your benefit, Indonesia's waters (and dry land) offer a potpourri of everything. From the Little Stuff (pygmy seahorses, crinoid shrimps, nudibranchs, soft coral crabs), to the Big Stuff (sharks, turtles, huge school of barracuda), to the Rare Stuff (ornate ghost pipefish, waspfishes, flying gurnards, frogfishes, comet fish). Komodo Island, near the middle of the Indonesian island chain, is famous as the home of the world's largest lizard, but only a diver would know that Komodo is also home to *Hippocampus bargibanti,* the world's smallest seahorse.

This commensal shrimp is found only within feather stars. It is colored like its host, and probably steals food from the crinoid's arms.

And, no surprise but happy surprises, there are surprises everywhere. Not long ago a liveaboard operator and his party was stuck on Alor Island at Kalabahi Harbor, occupied with a morning of bureaucratic paperwork. Alor Strait and its three beautiful tropical islands (Pura, Reta, and Buaya) are famous for teeming fish life, but the harbor is best known as a port for large oil ships. Anchored in Kalabahi, with few options, they opted to take a chance on a muck dive around a heretofore-unexplored pier. End result, a mimic octopus, eight harlequin shrimp, an *Inimicus* (devil fish), banded pipefish, stonefish, juvenile batfish, three species of seahorse, Pegasus sea moths, and an assortment of nudibranchs. Total dive area, one hundred square meters.

Its nutrient-rich seas and thousands of miles of mangrove-lined coastline (providing critical nurseries for many juvenile species) account for the shocking amount of life in Indonesia's waters. Why the shocking diversity? Indonesia's vast distances and huge numbers of islands have led individual species to fragment again and again as they adjust to new environments. Darwin would have been rendered stupid with glee.

When it comes to diving, plenty of areas deserve special mention, and frankly there's not room enough for all of them here. One glance at a map will convince you of the silliness of even trying to list a fraction of Indonesia's dive options, much less highlight all of them, though hauling out a good map will help you follow along.

Generalizations have their many exceptions, but it is probably safe to say that as you move eastward through the Indonesian archipelago the diving gets better. It is scientifically safe to say Eastern Indonesia has the greatest diversity of life, and, the two are related, the farther east you go, the more remote it gets. In the easternmost reaches of the chain, off Irian Jaya (also known as *Papau Barat* or West Papau), there are still plenty of places where a diver has never placed a mask in the water.

Bali, of course, is the best known of Indonesia's isles. For this reason it is far from undiscovered. Divers began diving the island just to the east of Java in earnest in the late 1960s, but Aussie surfies on the dole

(unemployed) and adventurers had already claimed it for their own. Back then, the island was still a place of sweet innocence. Today it is what you should expect of Indonesia's number one tourist destination. Denpasar, the capital, is a full-fledged city, with all a city's dirt and noise, and nearby Kuta Beach is as unapologetically honky-tonk-a-tourist-trap as you'll find. Most of Bali's development is along the south (Kuta) and east coasts, and, unfortunately, this is where a lot of the diving occurs too. But the best diving is, not coincidentally, as far away from the development as possible, on the far western edge of the north coast. Tiny Menjangan Island, for example, offers fine diving, at the price of a long, but worthwhile, haul from the tourist meccas. Bali's stunning natural scenery makes any drive worthwhile. Away from the tourist centers, Bali remains a place of cool lakes, dripping forests, small villages, lush green rice paddies, and cloud-shrouded volcanoes.

One interesting, and important, footnote is that Indonesia's vast geographic spread insures an equally vast cultural range. Ninety-five percent of Bali's population is Hindu. Just to the east, on Java, the populace of the world's most crowded island is overwhelmingly Muslim. Travel to Manado (on the northern tip of Sulawesi) and the people, mostly ethnic Minahasans (more closely tied to the southern Philippines than they are to Indonesia), are largely Christian. Take a leap (actually several leaps) farther to Irian Jaya, and its native people have nothing to do with Asia, belonging as they do to the Melanesian culture of the South Seas. Indonesia may have taken control of Irian Jaya in 1963 (and forty years later it is still working hard to make it its own), but as recently as the 1970s a highland tribe killed and ate a mission preacher and a dozen of his assistants, after deeming them guilty of stealing land and taking liberties with local women.

Indonesia has experienced more than its share of violent unrest. But to equate the problems, and potential hazards, of Muslim extremists with all of Indonesia is as right-minded as believing every American is a cowboy. Not that divers are immune to danger. While a few liveaboard operations in Indonesia are first-rate, many are not up to Western levels of comfort, nor are

their crews properly trained. Things are worse when it comes to many land-based dive operators. Plenty of day boats have never seen a first aid kit, and rental equipment, expensive to replace, can be used to within an inch of its life, explaining why at least one diving guide book includes the phrases "*Angin tidak bagus*" (The air is no good) and "*Di mana jukung*" (Where is the boat?). Best to thoroughly research your choice of dive operator before you arrive.

Being as far-flung as it is, the best way to explore Indonesia is by liveaboard. Ensconced on a boat, the true glories of Indo diving are available to you. Magical isles—Sangeang, Satonda, Alor, Padar, Tatawa, Komodo, Rinca, Bunaken, Lonta, Hatta, Ai; the deservedly famous, and eye-popping, life in Lembeh Strait; and, far to the east, in the waters off Irian Jaya, the spectacular islands, and diving, of the Rajah Empat group in the Seram Sea. The list goes on and on. Equally wonderful is the possibility that, excepting the teeming sea life, in many spots you will be the only one around.

Because it straddles the equator, Indonesia tends to have a fairly even climate year round, but storms during the rainy season (October through April) tend

PAGES 130–131: A pair of commensal harlequin crabs is found on the underside of a sea cucumber.

OPPOSITE: These juvenile black snappers are hiding among the stinging spines of a venomous fire urchin. As they grow larger, they will become drab in coloration and move off into the reef, no longer needing the protection of their host.

The squat lobster, or pink fairy lobster, is only found within the central cavity of barrel sponges.

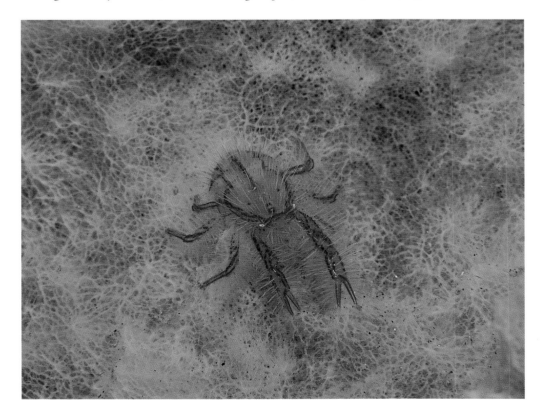

to reduce visibility. Much ado is made of Indonesia's powerful currents, and with good reason. In some areas—the islands of Komodo National Park, for one—currents can be tremendous. Strong currents, transporting nutrients, also mean lots of life. Komodo throws in the added challenge of surprisingly cold water. While diving in Indonesia is primarily mid-80s bathwater warm, along the southern perimeter of the National Park, deep water upwellings can turn the water far colder; divers at 120 feet have stuck their hands into thermoclines and found 62-degree water on the other side.

RIGHT: A group of brightly colored tunicates shimmers on a coral reef. All tunicates possess a notochord and a nerve cord, although they are invertebrates.

LEFT: The larvae of many reef fish are planktonic with unusual shapes. When they settle onto a reef, they mature into recognizable fish. Here, a tiny, juvenile spotted pufferfish has just settled on a coral reef.

BELOW: The bigfin reef squid is active at night, typically found on coral reefs and seagrass beds.

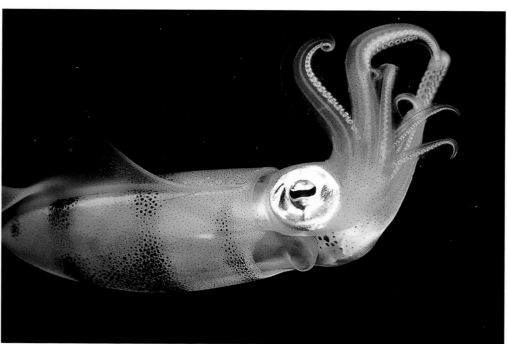

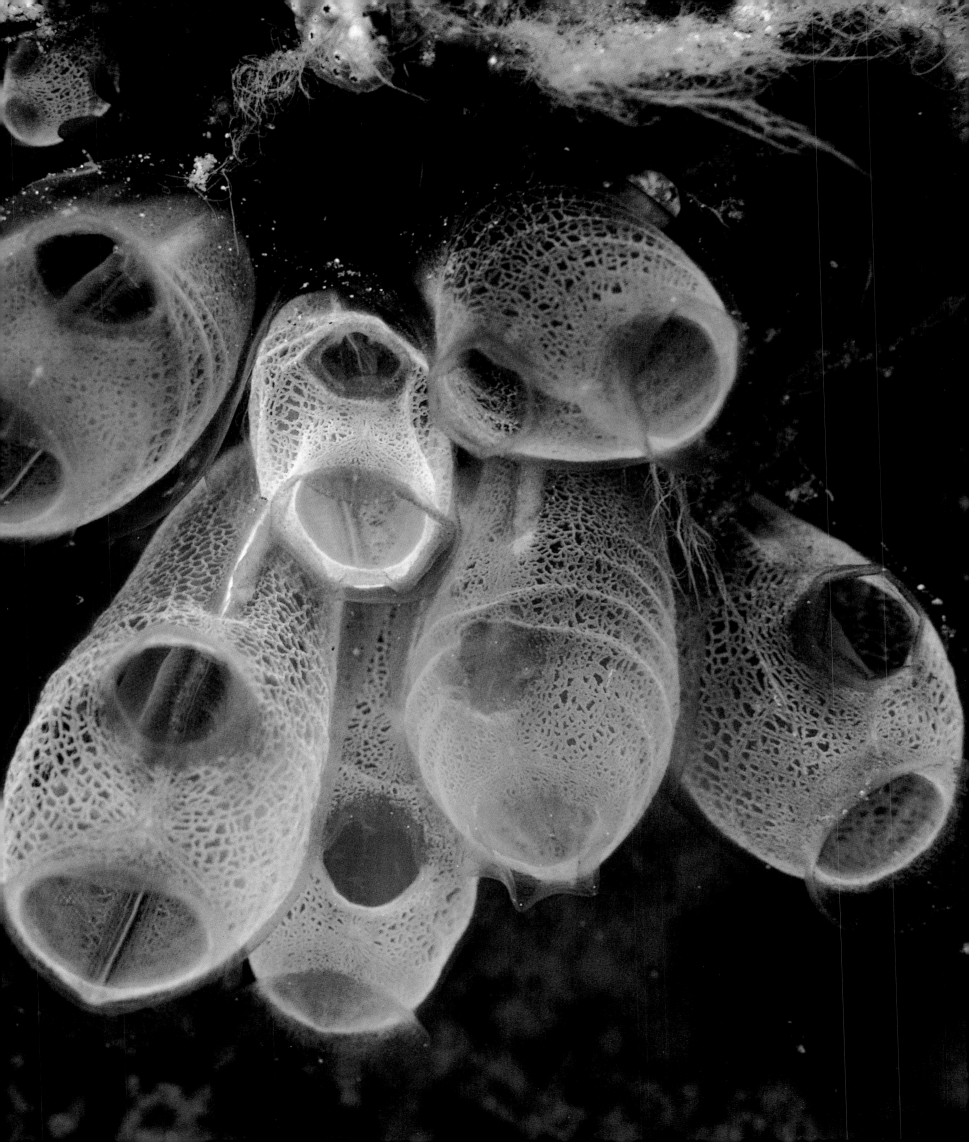

But Indonesia has plenty of beginner-friendly
spots too, from the popular wreck of the *Liberty* (a
WWII cargo ship), a popular beach dive on Bali's
north side, to the quiet waters of Bunaken island (off
Manado), and, farther east, the moderate-current-to-
still-waters off Ambon Island's Leitmur peninsula.
Sometimes even in the eye of the hurricane there is
calm. Currents can sometimes roar through Lembeh
Strait (thus its explosion of life), but along some
shores they also produce eddies of perfect stillness.

Amidst a wealth of diving such as this it may
be slightly misleading to single any place out, but in
recent years the waters off Irian Jaya ("Victorious hot
land" in Indonesian) have created serious excitement.
Again, a blow-by-blow of the known (important distinction here) dive spots and creatures in these waters
takes too much space. Just remember two simple, and
enticing, facts. As you move east, there is more sea life.
And in Irian Jaya, at this writing, there is almost no
dive life. A single resort hunkers on Kri Island (part
of the Rajah Empat group), and liveaboards are only
just beginning to make forays into the area. Dive
magazines are never short of hyperbole, but in this

*RIGHT: Golden sweepers are often
seen in dense schools, filling coral caves
during the day. Numerous predators,
such as frogfish, leaffish, lionfish, and
others, can often be seen occupying
positions within such caves, hoping
for a meal. These weakly bioluminescent fish disperse at night to feed on
plankton in open water.*

Hundreds of hinge-beak shrimp gather at a rock in the middle of a sandy area in Lembeh Straits, North Sulawesi.

BELOW: The small bubble coral shrimp is transparent, and is found only on bubble coral. These tiny shrimp dance and wave their tentacles about to attract the attention of a client fish. They will leave their host to clean their client of parasites.

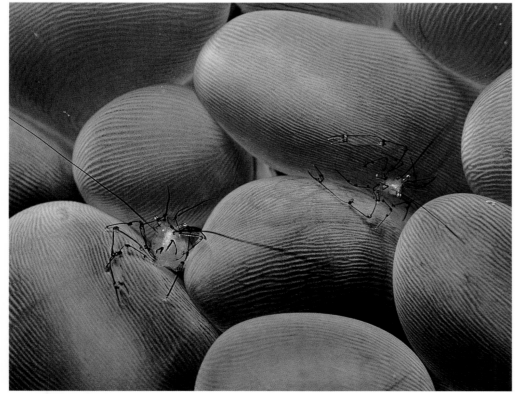

instance hyperbole equals truth. Irian Jaya's waters, wrote one dive scribe, "are destined to become the standard against which all diving is measured."

Hopefully they will stay that way, but if history is any indicator it will be a tough task. Though Indonesia can be spectacular and wild, few places are more beset by environmental ills, and, to date, little to nothing has been done to address them. There is a reason you find little or no mention of diving to the west of Bali. The seas off western Indonesia, particularly around Java and the capital city of Jakarta, are beset by everything from oil spills to staggering influxes of garbage. It's been estimated that eighty-six thousand tons of garbage is left uncollected each year in Jakarta, and plenty of it washes into the sea. Blast fishing, cyanide fishing, inshore trawling, and the sad, but effective, practice of muro-ami fishing have decimated many western reefs. (In muro-ami fishing children swim over reefs banging at the reef with rocks and

A frogfish, seen here sitting on a sponge, resembles its background in shape and color to an astonishing degree. Frogfish sometimes use a lure to attract prey. The lure is attached to a modified dorsal spine, located between its eyes, and acts much like a fishing pole.

BELOW: A banded sea snake goes about its rounds during the day, swimming into holes in a coral reef in search of its prey, small eels. Extremely venomous but not aggressive, these three-foot-long snakes should nevertheless be given a safe distance.

pipes to scare fish into waiting nets. The children are often forced to dive to dangerous depths. Many drown, sometimes trapped in the nets. The practice is illegal, but children have little say and in remote areas muro-ami continues.) Blast fishing, though illegal, is so pervasive in western Indonesian waters that it is considered a traditional means of fishing. Considering a successful blast fisherman can earn up to three times the salary of a government official, it is not hard to understand the attraction—or why officials hired to enforce the law are easily persuaded otherwise. And destructive fishing practices are spreading eastward as bombed, poisoned, and dragged reefs are reduced to lifeless rubble.

Efforts are being made to stem the tide, but in a poor country often besieged by political problems, environmentalism isn't a top priority. Small victories are being won in small, but important, areas. The Nature Conservancy has issued a twenty-five-year plan for the Komodo National Park that includes

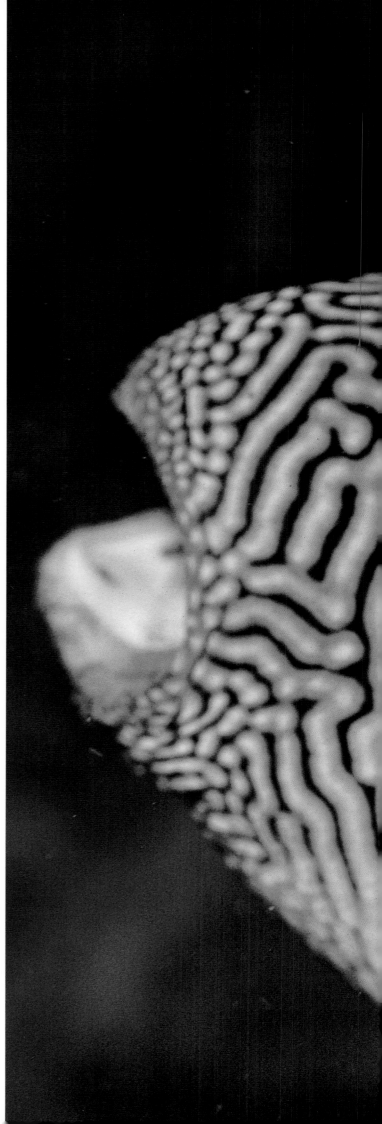

innovative ways to raise money and floating ranger stations to keep blast fishermen out of park waters. But it is too late for the Jakarta Bay reefs so glowingly described by the Dutch scientist Umbgrove in 1928. They are gone. In scientific parlance, they have become "functionally dead systems."

In a place as vast, poor, and complex as Indonesia, there are no simple answers. But it is equally simplistic, and fatalistic, to assume that the fate of Jakarta Bay awaits the rest of Indonesia's waters. If there is any good news in man's destruction of Nature, it's that it serves as a warning cry. As more and more undersea glories are discovered in the vast tracts of healthy sea that remain, hopefully such cries will serve a positive purpose.

A pair of mandarinfish are either mating or fighting. These colorful dragonets only come out at dusk. They can be very common on Indo-Pacific reefs, but are very difficult to find.

BORNEO

It's true, Sipadan Island, twenty miles off the coast of Borneo in the Celebes Sea, has been called the crown jewel in the world's richest sea, so we'll start there. But when it comes to Borneo and diving, the story ranges far wider than an island that can be circumnavigated in twenty minutes. Borneo is one of the most biologically rich regions on earth, a cornucopia of wild things that nearly defies imagination (gliding lizards, more than twelve hundred species of orchids), and the rich soup of the South China, Sulu, and Celebes seas takes no backseat to its dry land counterpart.

ABOVE: Because of its isolation, its abrupt 2,000-foot rise from the sea floor, and its position in the richest sea in the world, tiny Sipadan Island is a gathering point for marine life. It can be circumnavigated in twenty minutes.

RIGHT: A cleaner wrasse services a blue-faced, or yellow-masked, angelfish at a cleaning station, which operates much like a neighborhood barbershop. Larger fish come to a cleaning station to be cleaned of parasites and dead skin by brightly colored cleaning shrimp and wrasses. The cleaning wrasse or shrimp dances in a peculiar rhythm, designed to catch the attention of the larger fish which it cleans.

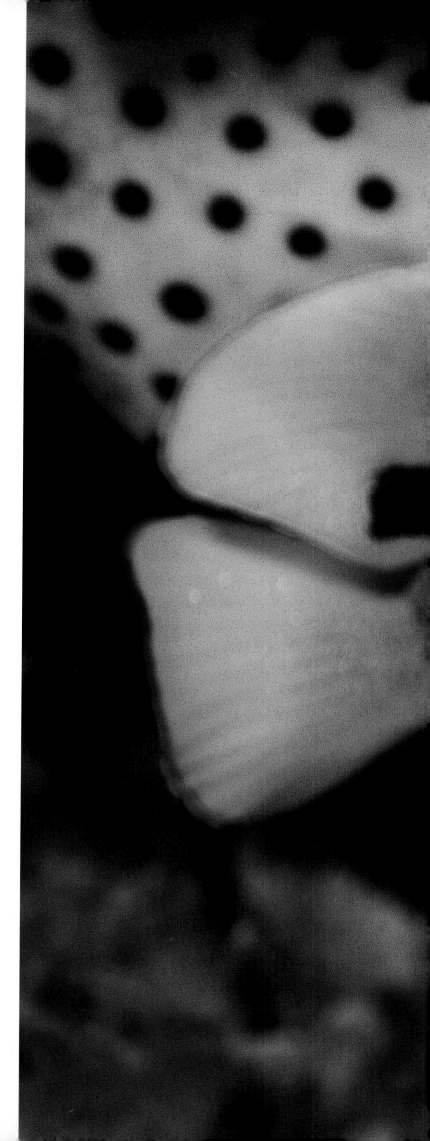

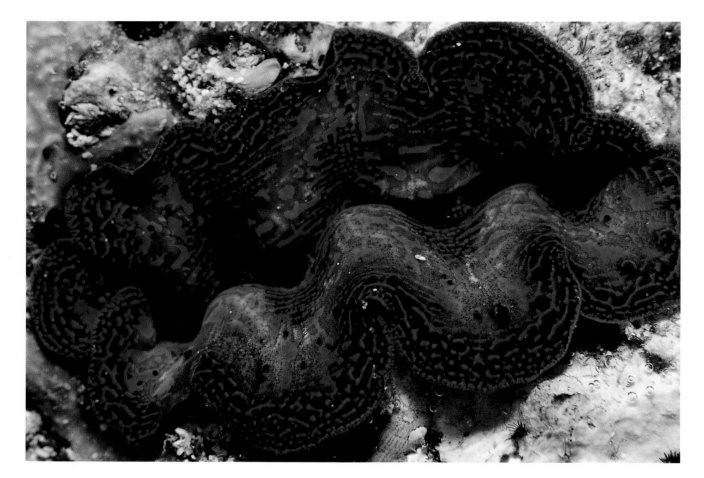

Giant clams are harvested by many cultures, to the point where they are now extinct on many Indo-Pacific coral reefs. Researchers have been successful in cultivating them and planting them back on coral reefs.

Perched just north of the equator, Borneo exhibits little seasonal variance—it's always hot and humid. It is dry from March through November, but you can expect frequent heavy rains between December and February. Back though to Sipadan, or more properly *Pulau Sipadan* ("Border Island" in Malay), because Sipadan does deserve its banner headlines. Picture strolling across a sugar-fine beach, adjusting your fins in water clear and warm as sky, then finning across thirty feet of sandy bottom to a drop off of nearly two thousand feet, and a wall festooned and frequented by a shocking explosion of color and life. From goby-and-blind-shrimp-shallows, to nudibranch, butterflyfish, giant clam, green turtle, and a spiraling mass of jacks in fallaway blue in but several handfuls of fin strokes. A beach dive? Correct. Disney couldn't have made things more convenient, or more phantasmagorical.

Here's why. Sipadan is perched on a volcanic sea mount rising from depths of almost two thousand feet. The island itself is the tip of this needle spire, a mushroom bulb atop a lance. This explains the Grand Canyon plunge. It also explains, in part, the remarkable collection of life, more than two hundred species of fish and over seventy genera of corals. Sipadan is life's only gathering spot for miles, in a sea that is the epicenter of marine biodiversity. Picture a hundred

This chromodorid nudibranch's bright colors advertise its bad taste. Many nudibranchs retain noxious compounds from their food and store these chemicals in their body. This nudibranch regularly flutters its mantle when crawling.

ABOVE: *Most shrimp on coral reefs hide in crevices during the day and come out at night to feed. Their enlarged eyes help them to see in the dark.*

This brilliantly colored nudibranch, or sea slug, breathes through the yellow gills on its back.

dollar bill giveaway in Central Park. When Jacques Cousteau first glimpsed Sipadan's waters in 1989, he uttered this bittersweet accolade: "I have seen other places like Sipadan, forty-five years ago, but now no more. Now we have found an untouched piece of art." Divers didn't even start coming to the island until the late 1970s, and only in 1988 did Borneo Divers receive permission to establish permanent accommodations on the island.

Sipadan has since received serious attention so that now its dive sites—Hanging Gardens, Barracuda Point, Turtle Tomb—chime like familiar bells. There are several resorts on the island, each ferrying divers about in boats that really do have less mileage than granny's Oldsmobile. It might be five minutes to a dive spot, possibly fifteen. Visitors to Sipadan do make one long boat ride, roughly twenty-eight miles from the docks in Semporna on Sabah's east coast (Borneo is currently divided into Brunei, East Malaysia, (Sabah and Sarawak), and Indonesia (Kalimantan), and out through the open waters of Mabul Passage. But after that you can forget about amassing frequent boater miles, unless you opt to dive the nearby islands of Mabul and Kapalai (more on them later), visible eight miles to the south across an expanse of *air biru* (blue water). Getting to Sipadan takes some doing, generally a bleary-eye, jet-lag whopping flight into Kota Kinabalu ("KK" to the insider), then a forty-five-minute flight to the small town of Tawau, then a ninety-minute bus ride to Semporna and the trip across the Mabul Channel. But once ensconced on Sipadan, travel to world-class diving can be negotiated by a preschooler with water wings. The diving itself isn't particularly easy —it's almost all drift diving, and the currents can be impressive—but not a spot on the globe offers better diving with more convenience.

Pulau Sipadan, as any diver knows, is famous for its turtles. Of the seven oceanic turtle species, six—the green, hawksbill, loggerhead, leatherback, Pacific olive ridley, and flatback—are found in Malay waters. Greens and hawksbills are most commonly seen off Sipadan, but whatever the species, the things are everywhere, gliding through the azure waters by

Green turtles come to Sipadan Island by the hundreds to mate and to lay eggs at night.

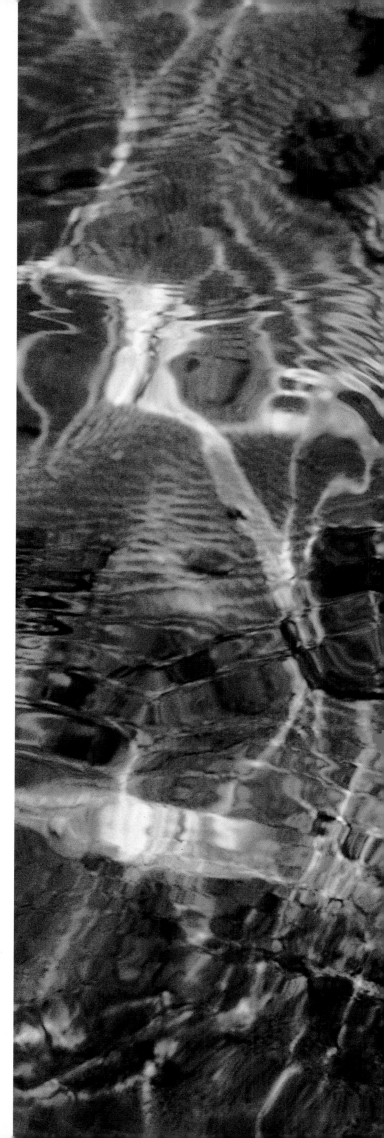

the dozens, and sometimes the hundreds, and humping up the beach to lay eggs almost nightly. In pursuit of propagation they are dogged. On Sangalakki Island, off the east coast of Indonesian Kalimantan, where there are even *more* turtles, resort proprietors have had to usher turtles out of the kitchen.

Their profusion makes it easy to take the sea turtles for granted, and many divers do. This is a shame, because their life is a remarkable one. The young hatchlings make their way off the beach, through the surf line, and out into the open sea. If they are lucky and strong, they eventually find their way to the equator, where they drift in the spaces between the major ocean currents for several years before making their way back to the island of their birth. It is a hard, and often very short, life. Of a hatch of one hundred, roughly one turtle survives to adulthood. To walk a morning beach and see the sweep

marks of a mad rush of tiny flippers end suddenly where the tracks of a monitor lizard begin is to understand bluntly that Nature offers few happy endings.

Malaysian Borneo possesses other diving gems. Visible from Sipadan lie the islands of Mabul and Kapalai. Mabul actually offers more species of nudibranchs and other macro creatures than Sipadan, but fewer big animals, and good visibility is chancier. But Mabul is special because it has been protected from blast fishing and cyanide fishing, rampant around other islands, for years, and its reefs have responded. Sipadan currently enjoys protection too, but as recently as the mid-1980s (shortly before Borneo Divers established residency on the island) blast fishing on its reefs was common place. Plenty of divers stay on Mabul, which has more luxurious accommodations, then make the thirty-minute boat ride to Sipadan to dive. And divers on Sipadan boat

Small anemone-like animals, a colony of zoanthids is connected by a membrane underneath the individual animals. Zoanthids are primarily tropical, and are found in shallow water and intertidal zones.

The blacksaddle mimic filefish is a remarkable mimic of the poisonous sharpnose puffer. It mimics the puffer's color and shape in great detail, and it shares the same habitat.

BELOW: The world's largest parrotfish, the four-foot-long humphead parrotfish, sleeps in a coral cave at night. These fish reputedly break coral apart with their foreheads. Most wrasses and parrotfishes undergo sequential hermaphroditism. Females can change into brilliantly colored males, known as terminal males.

to Kapalai and Mabul to dive their equally impressive reefs—a wild assortment of nudibranchs, blue ribbon eels, crocodile snake eels, frogfish, mandarinfish, ornate ghost pipefish, and exotic on and on. Mabul and Kapalai lie within a mile of each other. Kapalai itself barely qualifies as an island. More accurately it's a sandbar that is only exposed at low tide, though this hasn't prevented the opportunistic Malay government from allowing a resort, on stilts, to exist there.

Also worth noting is Layang Layang island. Mabul, Kapalai, and Sipadan lie off the east coast of Sabah. Part of the Spratly islands, Layang Layang sits off Sabah's west coast, about 185 miles west of Kota Kinabalu, in the South China Sea. A narrow island with a huge circular lagoon (guests of the island's resort are flown out from KK by private plane), Layang Layang has a singular advantage—it is far from civilization, and its burgeoning reefs reflect that fact. The island has its own collection of glories—masses of

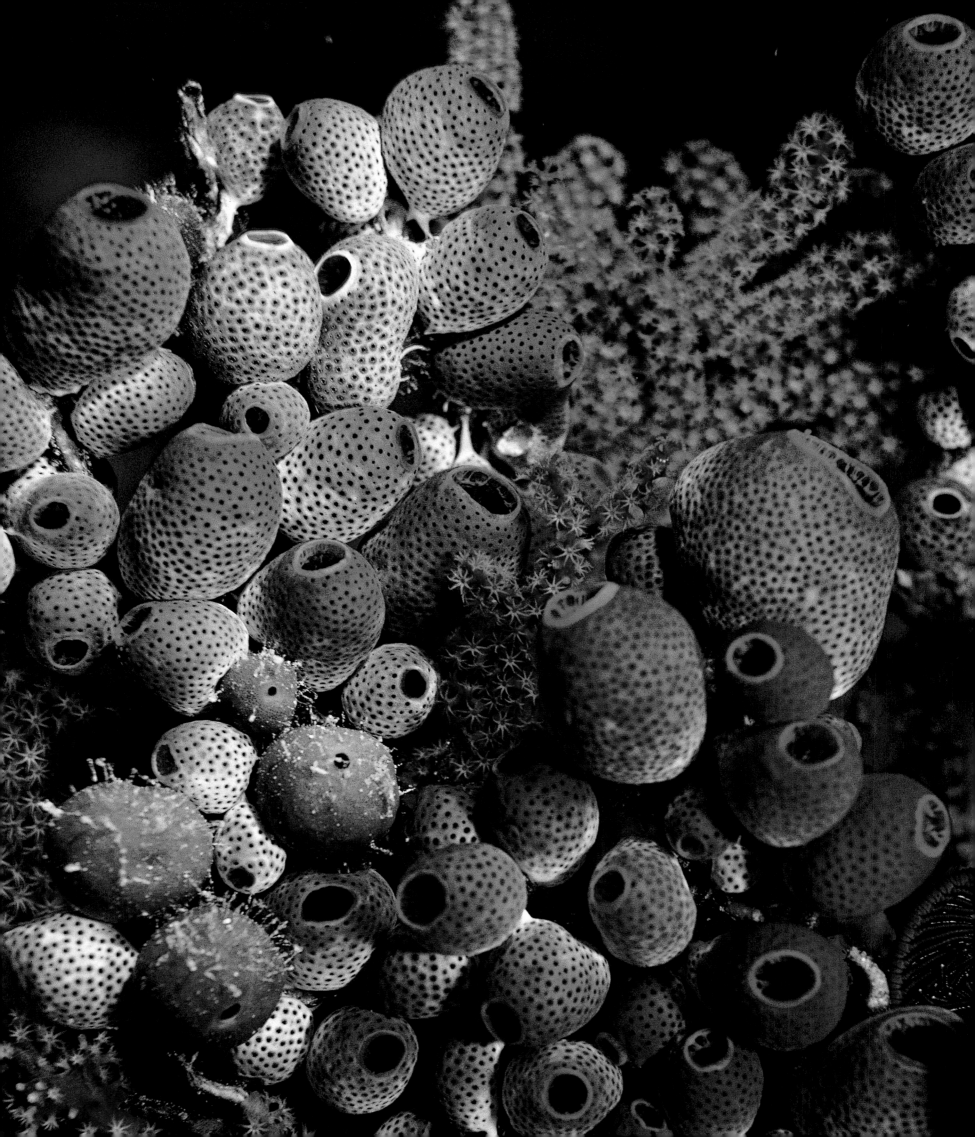

lionfish, sweetlips, triggerfish, and butterflyfish, wonderful small stuff (ornate ghost pipefish, mandarinfish), and, because it sits smack dab in deep ocean, big fish as well, including scalloped hammerheads and an occasional whale shark. There is other life too. *Layang Layang* means "swallows" in Malay. If you're a birder and diver you won't know whether to gaze dumbstruck up or down. From July to October more than ten thousand birds, a vast combination of residents and migrants, inhabit the island. In the water column, hammerheads, grey reef sharks, and giant trevally pick panicked schools of yellow parrotfish apart.

And off the east coast of Kalimantan lies beguiling Sangalakki Island. This one belongs to Indonesia and it is a gem. (The Borneo region is rife with territorial squabbling, both Indonesia and Malaysia claim Sipadan, and at least five Asian countries lay claim to the Spratly islands, hoping to capitalize on natural gas that may or may not be there.)

It is Man's wont to always be looking elsewhere. Once established on Sipadan, Borneo Divers made the logical leap, assuming similar islands must exist elsewhere. Eventually local fishermen told Borneo Divers' Ron Holland of another island 120 miles to the south. Holland investigated and found a near-Sipadan clone, roughly thirty acres of island, only with more turtles, as well as huge mantas reaching widths of twelve feet from tip to tip. An added plus, twenty-five minutes by boat puts divers on *Pulau Kakaban*, with its own walls descending to eight hundred feet and—surprise—a freshwater lake filled with non-stinging jellies (such lakes were once believed unique to the islands of Palau).

Sangalakki is a special place. It is home to one of the largest turtle nesting populations in the entire Malay-Indo archipelago, a place where giant multicolored Tridacna clams squat on equally bright reefs like psychedelic monoliths and golden eagles snatch turtle hatchlings from the lagoon. The lucky diver can drop into a vast forest of coral trees, and follow a gentle current toward the shallows where mantas swoop and feed.

With its jaw-dropping reefs and white sand beaches, Sangalakki represents all that is glorious, and

all that is threatened, in Borneo's wilds. No doubt Borneo is still a place of unspoiled beauty, with huge areas of undisturbed mangrove swamps, pristine reefs, river dolphins, and vast turtle nesting areas. But it is also heavily assaulted on many fronts. Mangroves are being destroyed at an alarming rate. It's been estimated that Borneo has lost up to 80 percent of its mangroves, though in a place so vast and empty, reliable measures are hard to come by. Though there is little industry, Borneo's population is growing and a lack of sewage treatment is a serious problem for nearshore waters. Overfishing is widespread. Blast fishing and cyanide fishing are rampant, and even the remotest, and

OPPOSITE: A colorful display of sponges and tunicates has grown on this dead piece of coral.

A diver swims over a giant barrel sponge near Sipadan Island. Sponges filter food particles from seawater using a network of canals within their body.

A decorator crab has covered itself with sponges and hydroids for camouflage.

BELOW: A huge school of barracuda surrounds divers. Swimming in the midst of it is exciting, and fortunately not at all dangerous.

ostensibly most protected, reefs are not immune. In the remote reefs of the Spratlys many of the large fish are gone, taken, via cyanide fishing, for the lucrative Asian live fish trade. In northern Sabah, it's possible to hear up to fifteen bomb blasts an hour, and many reefs are now little more than rubble and sand. In the unlikeliest of places, destruction continues. Sangalakki may be home to an eco-friendly dive resort and a national park, but that hasn't stopped villagers from collecting turtle eggs and practicing blast and cyanide fishing. Sipadan is protected, through efforts by the island dive operators and happy circumstance; because Indonesia claims the island too, the Malaysian Navy and Marine Police frequent Sipadan's waters more regularly.

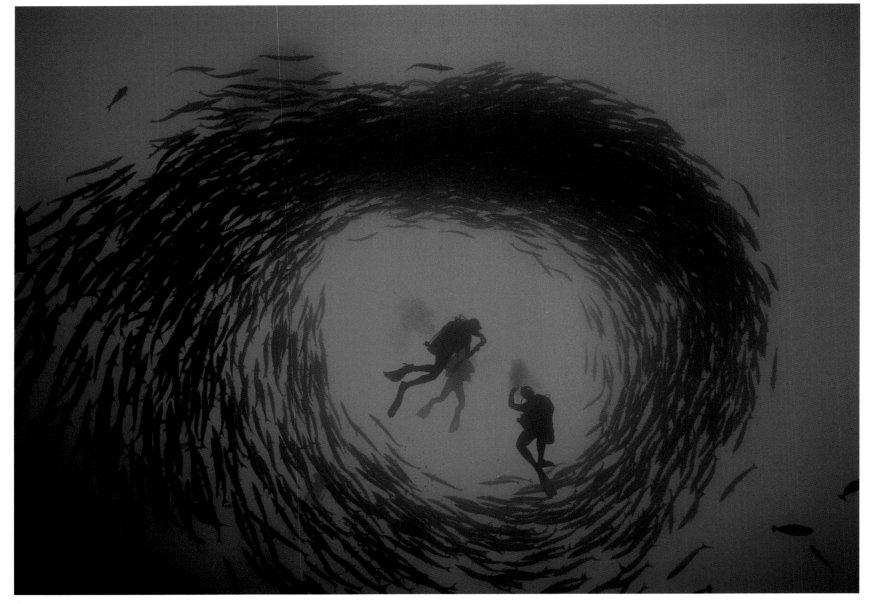

A tiny goby, so small that it is almost invisible, watches for passing food particles while resting on a colony of bubble coral. Not unlike anemone-fishes that reside among anemones, these gobies live only upon certain corals. Scientists have yet to explain the relationship.

PAGES 154–155: A tiny goby rests on a purple sponge. Gobies are among the tiniest of living vertebrates. Some species mature to be only about the length of a human fingernail.

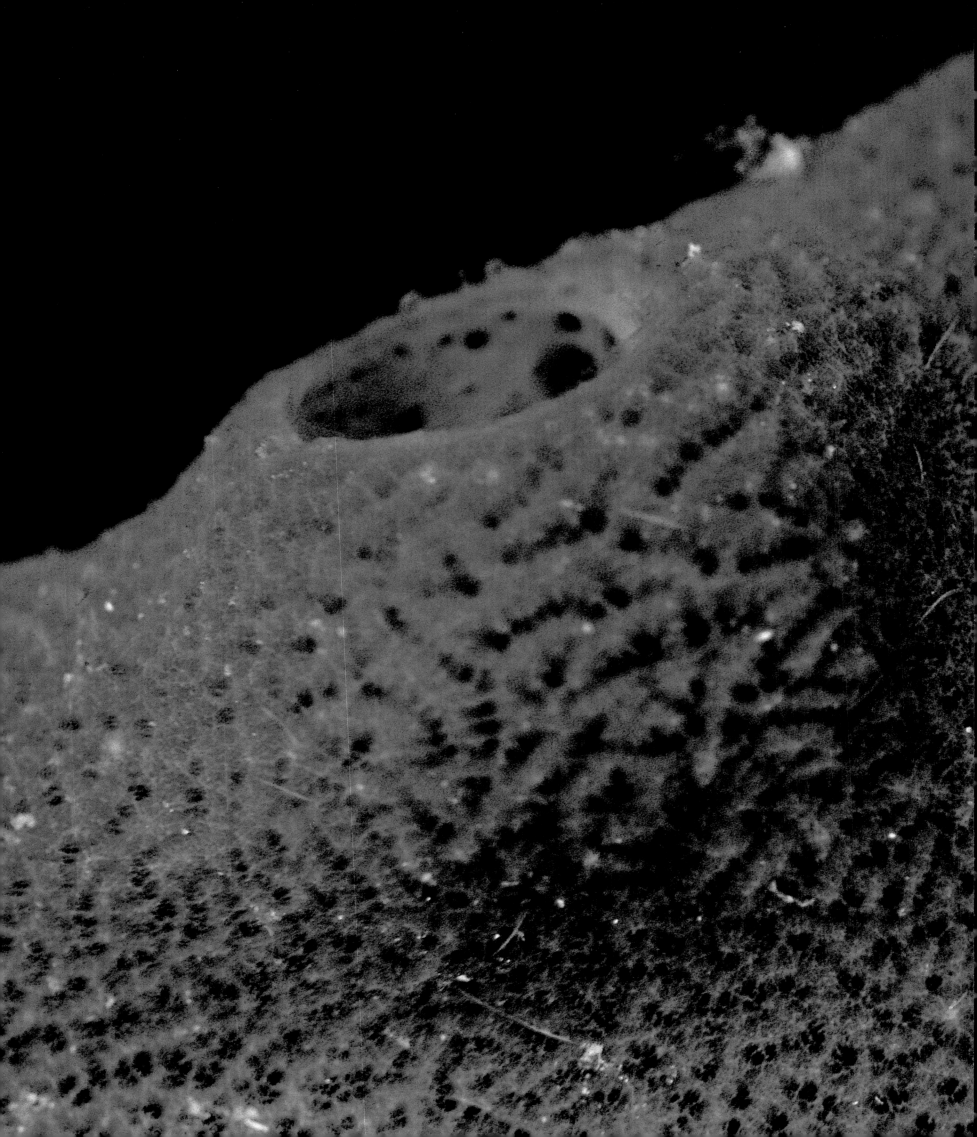

RIGHT: Kakaban Island features a landlocked lake that contains jellies and mangroves. The jellies have lost their sting through years of isolation. Until recently, such lakes were thought to be unique to the islands of Palau.

But away from the dive resorts there is virtually no management. And where there is management, the economics often make little sense to a poor country. It costs far more to catch violators than the violators pay back in fines. Scientists have concocted economic models showing how local fisherman have done sore damage to their own incomes with blast fishing. The reefs can't withstand the wanton punishment, and there are soon almost no fish to catch. But long-term economic tailspins and conservation don't matter much to a fisherman watching his competitors beat him to, and bombing out, a prime spot.

Though dive resorts are responsible for the few reefs that enjoy a semblance of, or complete (Sipadan), protection, divers haven't left the landscape unaltered either. No doubt, the resorts on Sipadan have saved the island's reefs from certain destruction. But they have also lowered the island's freshwater table so much that water now has to be imported, and not all the operators transport solid waste back to the mainland. Long-time divers to Sipadan have noticed the deteriorating visibility of the waters, probably from sewage and runoff. Were he still with us, Cousteau would know that this art work is no longer untouched.

The Malay people are a gentle, accommodating, and often unflappable folk. There is a Malay expression, often applied when things go wrong. *Tidak apa.* "It just doesn't matter.'" But it matters greatly.

The flashlight fish has a light organ under its eye which is used in mating, confusing predators, and finding prey. Symbiotic bacteria within the light organ produce enough light for the fish to find the plankton upon which it feeds. Different species have different ways of controlling the light. This species occludes the light organ by raising a black curtain of skin.

PHILIPPINES

In the Philippines, frankly, it will take initiative just to get off the beach. On a perfect day, as you stroll down to the water's edge and the outrigger banca that will take you to today's dive, your senses will bask in a sweep of white sand beach backdropped by delicate palm-frond rustle. Offshore, tower-stacks of blue-edged white clouds billow up into morning blue sky falling to a mirror-still plane of pale baby blue ocean. Boracay Island's White Sand Beach has been ranked one of the world's ten best beaches, but all this means was the judges never made it to this beach on which you now stroll, or the hundreds of others that dot the Philippines' 7,150-island chain.

RIGHT: A tiny clingfish lives within the arms of its host, a yellow feather star, or crinoid. Clingfish have a sucking disc on their underside, and this commensal fish probably steals food from its host's arms while gaining protection from its host as well.

OPPOSITE: A school of purple fairy basslets hovers over a lush, protected coral reef at Similan Island. The dainty, brightly colored fairy basslets can change sex from female to male.

A huge school of bannerfish thrive in the protected marine reserve of Apo Island. Marine reserves have been proven to "seed" surrounding areas with fish.

islands that man has tagged possess an appropriately beguiling singsong beauty—Bohol, Leyte, Panay, Cebu, Samar, Cabilao.

Understandable were you to wave off the outrigger banca—lined with tanks and heavy with anticipation and the day's picnic lunch—opting instead to spend the day cloud-gazing prone from the beach. But this would be a sore mistake. Because in the Philippines it's as if God laid out the terrestrial beauty as a smoke screen to distract you from the truly *maganda* world that exists below the water.

Mindoro and Palawan Islands, Tubbataha, Apo, and Basterra reefs, Batangas Bay—divers recognize these as near-paradisical dive sites. Scientists recognize them—and the hundreds of other islands and reefs— as the juncture of the Pacific and Indian oceans and the place, they believe, where marine life began, flourishing first in the triangle formed by the Philippines, peninsular Malaysia, and Papau New Guinea before leaching out into the surrounding seas. The biological short of it—marine life here has had the longest time to develop, allowing the family trees of hundreds of marine animals to prong off in hundreds of forks of their own. Making the word *varied* paltry.

In this vast archipelago much is astonishingly *maganda* (beautiful), very little is *pangit* (ugly,) and you will experience *unang na loob* (a great sense of indebtedness) simply by opening your eyes in the morning.

The Philippine archipelago is the second largest in the world (behind Indonesia), arching for roughly 1,150 miles through the South China, Celebes, Sulu, and Philippine seas. Added enticement, only about two thousand islands are inhabited and roughly two thousand aren't even named. The names of the

Scientists have classified at least 4,951 identified species of marine plants and animals along the Philippine coast and surrounding waters—410 coral species, at least 1,030 species of coral fishes alone, and hundreds of different nudibranchs. These dry numbers underscore a wonderful reality. Nature's attempts at evolution are imaginative, and the weird and wonderful are available in all their glory here. See a small explosion of sand on the bottom of Batangas Bay. Peer through your mask as the tiny sand storm drifts away to reveal nine inches of hideous goblin fish, crawling slowly across the bottom on modified pectoral fins pushing the sand like fingers, its death mask of a face focused on the task at hand. *Pangit* by superficial standards. A work of sheer evolutionary beauty to the appreciative diver drifting in twilight green waters above the sandy bottom of Batangas Bay.

And that is just one of the small things you'll probably miss, beset as you are by a flood of far more

Like trees in a forest, coral colonies compete for sunlight, which allows their symbiotic algae to photosynthesize.

ABOVE, TOP: A scorpionfish is well camouflaged among the branches of a sea fan.

ABOVE: An ornate ghost pipefish or sea dragon hovers above a sea fan. These small fish, related to pipefishes and seahorses, are not uncommon, but are so well camouflaged that they are rarely seen by divers.

LEFT: The Philippines were once home to some of the largest and lushest coral gardens in the world. Corals require clear, warm, and stable water to thrive. They are delicate animals, and are easily killed by sediment or the careless touch of a hand or fin.

obvious life. Dive Basterra Reef in the Sulu Sea—just to the south of the famed Tubbataha reefs—and you might first drift over a sandy bottom pocked with flounders, garden eels, and gobies. Then a shallow reef smothered with corals, then a fall away wall where tuna, mackerel, turtles, manta rays, hammerheads, whitetip, blacktip, and grey reef sharks drift in the blue. On a single dive, the casual diver might see fifty different species. Focus a bit more and you'll see hundreds. And much of the most abundant sea life, shy and ruthlessly efficient at camouflage, never even comes into view.

The sheer geographical scope of the Philippines raises an obvious question. Where to go? Currently (though you can bet new dive areas are being explored as you read) most of the diving in the Philippines focuses on six main areas: conveniently located Batangas Bay on the main island of Luzon, about two hours south of Manila by car, with gentle sloping reefs and mini-walls; Boracay, with beautiful beaches, shallow reefs for beginners, and deep drop-offs for the advanced. Mindoro, with sheer wall drift diving; Bohol, with a wide variety of sites; Cebu's coral gardens swarming with tropicals, and, of course, Palawan, with walls, wrecks, and, quite possibly, mantas. All of it in soothing tropical water (temps range from the high 70s to mid-80s) with equally enticing visibility. A low might be 50 feet in Mindoro or Boracay— an eye-popping high might be 135-foot plus in the waters off Cebu, Bohol and Tubbataha reefs.

It's not all blissful ease. Currents can be fierce, or morph to fierce quickly, explaining the plethora of drift dives and alert dive boat operators. Travel within the Philippines can be difficult, buffeted by labor strikes, power failures, and the like. Weather can throw in a crimp too. Roughly nineteen typhoons pass through the archipelago each typhoon season (June–September), mucking up viz and, more important, boat travel—a boat in a typhoon is a very unpleasant place to be. Generally the best, and safest, diving is had from March to May, the months between the southwest (June to October) and northeast (November to March) monsoon seasons. But there's plenty of flex

in here too, and you can trust the banca and liveaboard boat operators who, assumedly, love life as much as you do. And finding them isn't hard. There are hundreds of dive operators in the Philippines, from beach resorts to four-star liveaboards—in Batangas Bay alone there are over thirty resorts. Most diving is typically done from simple outrigger bancas, some small (powered by what amounts to a lawn mower engine), some larger, which ferry you out to the day's reef or island of choice. An added plus is that language is rarely a barrier. The Philippines is the world's third largest English-speaking country (behind the United States and United Kingdom). Should you be caught in a current beyond your scope, your cries for help will be clearly understood.

As with diving anywhere it pays to be careful, explaining why, despite the warm waters, divers who know the Philippines dive in a full suit. The tremendous diversity of Philippine waters assures the reefs are teeming with life, and some of that life has opted to cope with intense competition and predatory pressure by developing attention-getting stinging mechanisms. With a poke, the mesmerizing red and blue fire urchin can produce a sensation worthy of its name; a harmless bare-skinned brush, and the innocuous-looking, fern-like fire hydroid also bestow substantial pain.

OPPOSITE: Individual polyps of a coral colony live within limestone skeletons that they have secreted. Each polyp has stinging tentacles which capture plankton. Symbiotic algae living within the coral polyps produce food.

A pair of variegated lizardfish wait to ambush prey. These camouflaged, torpedo-shaped fish have a large mouth with long needle-like teeth. They patiently wait on sand or rock surfaces for passing prey.

There are, as you might imagine, hundreds and hundreds of spectacular dive sites—discovered and undiscovered—but there are a few that anyone toying with a Philippine dive adventure should note. Near the top of any list (in a land of such dive wealth, it would be misleading, and unfair, to rank any spot as the pinnacle) are the Tubbataha Reefs. Accessed most commonly by liveaboard boats operating out of Puerto Princesa on Palawan Island, the two reefs squat 113 miles away in the Sulu Sea. The two reefs—North and South—about four miles apart, rest on sand and slope away from depths of thirty to sixty-five feet before plunging down in glorious walls complete with overhanging caves and crevices.

Thanks to a protected status—the Tubbataha Reefs and nearby Jessie Beazley Reef collectively make up the Tubbataha Reef National Marine Park—the reefs are smothered with life. Lettuce, staghorn, table, leathery, and whip corals, trumpetfish, cornetfish, anthias, damselfish, lionfish, scorpionfish, groupers, garden eels, pufferfish, hawkfish, guitar sharks, nudibranchs, sharks, rays, turtles, red feather stars like draped feather boas—you get the colorful picture. Some believe the soft corals and pelagics are slightly better on the South Reef, but in a world this beautiful this seems like petty quibbling.

Proving how wrong it is to rank anything as the best, just to the north and south of the Tubbataha Reefs lie some great dives as well—Bancoran Island and Basterra Reef to the south; Cavili, Calusa, Cagayan, Arena, and Dondonay islands to the north.

Also of note is Balicasag Island, part of its reef a protected marine sanctuary, and its vertical walls home to hammerheads and whale sharks in December and January. The nearby Cabilao Islands also offer some of the Philippines best diving; particularly hammerhead sightings off the islands northwest, and aptly named, Hammerhead Point, again in December and January.

And for sheer weirdness and fun, you can dive Cayangan Lake on the north end of Coron Island. Roughly one hundred feet inland, separated from the ocean by limestone cliffs, Cayangan Lake is one of the few places offering climbing in full dive gear

The sharp spines of the fire urchin are tipped with venom. The urchin can inflict a painful sting, causing intense pain hours after the fact.

(the climb in to the lake takes roughly ten to fifteen minutes), and, courtesy of hot springs, a rash of clear thermoclines and a water column that heats up appreciably as you descend. At one hundred feet the temperature might be 105 degrees F. Sure it might be one of the Philippines most photographed spots, tourists snapping off pictures as if they'd never seen a lake before. But few of them plunge in the lake itself, allowing you to sink through its surreal jello layers; from freshwater to salt, crystal clear to tea brown, cool to hot tub.

Note the several mentions of marine sanctuaries. The Philippines has had, and still has, its share of serious environmental abuse. Pollutants, sometimes in staggering concentrations, pour from rivers and are dumped off beaches, and this isn't likely to improve. About 60 percent of the population lives in coastal *barangays* (villages) and cities, and if the current population growth continues unabated, the population of the Philippines will double by 2025, and waste discharge will reflect this. Out on the water, and over the reefs, Filipino fishermen have long practiced innova-

A hermit crab peers out from beneath its borrowed shell. The shell protects the crab's soft abdomen. As they outgrow their borrowed homes, they may fight other crabs for their shells.

tive, and destructive, fishing methods. They have blasted the reefs with homemade explosives, killing and gathering up vast swaths of fish, leaving rubble where reef used to be. To accommodate the growing market for aquarium fish, in the 1960s enterprising fishermen began stunning and capturing coral-reef fish with the liberal use of cyanide and other poisons. Also practiced was the sad but effective art of muro-ami—enveloping entire reefs in a huge net with one end open while boys dove below the surface and banged rocks on the reef, scaring fish into the net; often the nets were closed, killing young divers still in them. All three fishing methods are now banned, but enforcement over 1,150 miles of archipelago is not easy and so they continue, though on a much smaller scale. Divers still report hearing explosions underwater (an unfortunate few who are too close have had their eardrums ruptured)—the sound can travel for miles—and signs of blasting are often at hand. Tourism, and diving, have had their impacts too. Mining of beach sand—moving it from undeveloped beaches to the well-enhanced beaches visiting sunbathers and divers take for granted—has proliferated, in some instances resulting in major changes in the coastline.

But plenty of encouraging moves have been made, because the Philippines seems to be working harder than many of its Asian neighbors to start protecting marine resources. Marine-protected areas in Philippine waters have increased dramatically—16 in 1980 to 160 by the mid-'90s—though again, complete protection is difficult to enforce. To protect threatened sea turtles—Philippine waters are home to loggerhead, green sea, hawksbill, olive ridley, and leatherback turtles—the Philippine and Malay governments worked together to establish, in 1996, a Turtle Island Heritage Protected Area in the Southern Philippines. And the Philippines holds the distinction of being the first country in the world to conduct a nationwide assessment of coral reefs, though what this assessment has largely measured so far is a depressing decline in reef health.

But conservation-minded thought and action are in place, and with them, hope. Which is, of course, *maganda*.

ABOVE, LEFT: A diver swims past a huge coral colony in the protected marine reserve of Similan Island.

ABOVE: A parasitic clam lives on the arm of a sea star. The clam sucks fluid and tissues from the star by inserting its proboscis into the groove from which the star extends its tube feet.

JAPAN

Fewer places are buffeted more by stereotype than the islands of Japan. Japan is ultra-urbanized, ultra-rigid, ultra-polite, ultra-expensive, ultra-crowded, and, to the *gai-jin* (foreigner), sometimes ultra-surreal. A place where trains run on time, where diners covet potentially lethal fish (improperly prepared fugu, a blowfish whose organ enzymes are deadly, kills unfortunate gourmands every year), where a massive shrine to the sea (The Seagaia Ocean Dome houses a huge artificial pool complete with rolling breakers and 460 feet of white sand beach) is built a stone's throw from the sea itself.

ABOVE: In Japan, the entire coastline is owned by fishing cooperatives. Divers can only enter the water at certain locations and during certain times of the day. Izu Marine Park, two hours south of Tokyo, is one of these places. Here, divers wait in line to enter the water at the designated entry point.

RIGHT: A profusion of soft corals covers a rock wall in Japan's Izu Oceanic Park.

ABOVE: *This large lionfish was attracted to divers, investigating their cameras and masks. It was obviously accustomed to divers, and may catch small fish scared off by divers' movements.*

ABOVE, RIGHT: *This dragon moray eel is being cleaned by shrimp as it hides in a crevice. Dragon morays tend to prefer rocky reefs, rather than coral reefs.*

Each of these examples is, of course, true and real, and reflective of Japanese culture; a yen for efficiency, a love for seafood delicacies, an obsession with amusement parks, and most everything else, ruthlessly orderly and neat. Eerily clean and quiet, Tokyo is aptly described by one writer as "New York City with a muffler."

But to view Japan wholly in terms of its stereotypical images is as right minded as believing that the actors in Godzilla movies really spoke English, and the time delay was a problem with your TV set.

The real truth about Japan falls across the spectrum, and this is ably reflected in the country's diving. Yes, there are spots that are crowded with divers who wait politely in a neoprene queue just to get in the water. Just as there are dive spots bereft of divers. Yes, traveling in Japan can be expensive. But you can also find a decent hotel in downtown Tokyo for $75 a night, and enjoy a hearty bowl of udon noodles and tempura for $7. Bring your own gear, make good use of Japan's ruthlessly efficient train system, avoid weekends and Japanese holidays, and you can enjoy a won-

derful shore dive, cheaply and alone. Best to see both Japan and its diving as multifaceted; geography alone highlights the rightness of this outlook. Japan is a vast chain of islands, four major ones (Hokkaido, Honshu, Shikoku, and Kyushu) and some one thousand smaller islands stretching roughly 1,860 miles. Its latitudinal spread runs from subarctic in the north to subtropical in the south. This is a range beyond stereotype.

Japan is associated with many offerings, graceful Shinto shrines, meticulous gardens, superb dining, the spectacularly ornate theatre of *kabuki and no*, and the snow-shrouded bulk of 12,385-foot Mount Fuji, but it is rarely associated with diving. This is a shame, because Japan's sea life can be marvelous and its underwater offerings varied.

Take the Izu Peninsula. Southwest of Tokyo, Izu Hanto is a pleasant place of scenic seascapes and rural charm. On the peninsula's eastern side you'll find the city of Ito and Izu Oceanic Park.

One of Japan's first dedicated marine parks, established in 1964 by Japanese ichthyologist Dr. Hajime Masuta, IOP, as it is most commonly known, offers

wonderful diving, no secret to divers who flee Tokyo in droves from June to August on summer weekends. (In summer you can wait thirty minutes and more just to get in the water via the designated entry.) But time it right, a week day in October or November (the best months for visibility, an average of seventy-five to eighty feet), and a surprising proliferation of temperate and tropical life, minus the divers, can be yours for the gawking, thanks to a combination of currents that provide for both tropical and temperate species. During summer, the Kuroshio Current sweeps warm water up from the tropics. In winter, the Oyashio Current draws down cold water from the north. The resident sea life responds. Basalt (Japan is a highly volcanic and seismic place) outcroppings are smothered in soft corals and algae. One hundred yards from shore, the reef wall descends vertically into deep water, and the wall is festooned with kimono colors; whip corals, huge gorgonians, crinoids, and soft corals. Over, in, and around the sandy bottom and reef there are nudibranchs, pipefish, frogfish, lionfish, dragonets, dragon moray eels, and delicate endemic cherry blossom anthias, all going about their business as if man never existed. Spearfishing is prohibited within IOP, and its sea life nearly thumbs its pectorals at divers.

Added enticement, the Japanese yen for amenities sees to it that other IOP offerings include freshwater rinse basins and hot showers. Picture a liveaboard, without the seasickness and the irritating bunkmate you can never escape. Nearby Futo Harbor, nestled in

This underwater view of surf crashing on volcanic rocks reveals a rugged world beneath the waves.

the southern corner of Sagami Bay, has spring-fed hot tubs to relax in post dive. For the *gai-jin* there are romantic touches of Japan too. Time it correctly, and your entry into the waters of Izu Oceanic Park may be preceded by the basso chime of gongs from the pine-shrouded Buddhist temple above the beach. Dive off the small resort town of Osezaki on the peninsula's western side and, on clear days, the crown of Mount Fuji rises, clearly visible, in the blue sky. There are other reminders that this isn't Kansas. Izu's coastline is controlled by fishermen's cooperatives. Diving is allowed only in designated parks, and only between the hours of 9:00 a.m. and 3:00 p.m.

Seasonal timing is also important, especially in central and northern Japan. In winter, cold air from Siberia collides with moist Pacific air masses, sometimes causing massive snowfalls in Japan's west. Summer months are dominated by warm, moist air from the Pacific, so high temperatures and humidity reign. Late summer brings typhoons, with torrential rains and rough seas making for poor-to-dangerous diving. The Izu Peninsula provides a nice microcosm of this fluctuation. Divers come to Izu year-round. But in summer and early autumn they can find water temperatures as high as the low 80s and visibility as poor as fifteen feet. In winter Izu's waters become clear. Visibility ranges from forty to eighty feet, but water temperatures may drop to the mid-50s.

The Izu Peninsula is well known. But with a bit of enterprise and the right dive master, less trammeled marvels are unveiled. Even closer to Tokyo, off the Miura Peninsula, lies the tiny island of Jogashima, where a fifteen-minute boat ride in a traditional wooden fishing boat puts you before striped filefish, intricately patterned, glowing pinecone fish, and conger eels as thick as your thigh.

OPPOSITE: A triplefin blenny is well camouflaged among coralline algae and sponges.

BELOW, LEFT: A twenty-year old giant soft coral tree thrives in deep water in Japan's Izu Oceanic Park.

BELOW: Colonial parasitic anemone, dividing asexually, have overgrown a whip coral.

PAGES 174–175: *Moorish idols swim past the rocky coastline of Izu Marine Park. Moorish idols are extremely widespread across the Indo-Pacific, ranging from the cooler waters of Hawaii, Japan, and the Galapagos, to the warm waters of the tropics.*

By dint of convenience, the island of Honshu dominates Japan's dive landscape, home as it is to Tokyo. But Honshu is by no means Japan's sole dive opportunity. Far to the south, Okinawa is littered with dive sites you won't know—Hedo Point, Nago Nets, Malibu Beach (no relation), Devil's Cove, Tsuken Island—but the local dive master will. (Note: Move away from the tourist cities and English is not largely spoken. It's a good idea to make tour arrangements in advance with someone who not only knows the waters, but is bilingual.)

The largest island in the Ryukyu archipelago, Okinawa is home to substantial history too. It should not be forgotten that here, in the closing months of World War II, was fought the largest land, sea, and air battle in the Pacific. United States casualties totaled nearly 50,000. Japanese forces lost roughly ten times that number, and 150,000 Okinawans—almost a third of the population—died with them. A visit to the sobering Himeyuri Peace Museum near Itoman is a must lest we forget the sobering price of war. All is not dour past either. Okinawa's culture is unique, with contributions from China and Southeast Asia as well as Japan. To see a performance of Yotsudake, an indigenous dance, is to brush close with Eastern elegance and grace. In fact, when traveling anywhere in Japan the wise diver won't ignore Japan's history and culture, or its breathtaking terra firm beauty. The big cities dominate the headlines as cities are wont to do. But a stroll among the mountain scenery, hot springs, and waterfalls of Kirishima National Park (southern Kyushu) will convince you that Tokyo does not define Japan.

There is diving far away from it all too. Some five hundred miles south of Tokyo, and nearly as many worlds away, lays subtropical Chichijima Island, part of a larger clump of islands known as the Ogasawaras or Bonin Islands. One of these islands, Iwo Jima, is intimately familiar to even the most casual historian. Here is a place of small, neat towns, bright blue seas, rustling palms, and sunsets wholly bereft of the smoky reds and deep purples of the polluted mainland. Beneath the water swim Yuzen angelfish, spotted sweetlips, silvery schools

of amalco jacks, and pelagics ranging from nurse sharks to humpback whales.

Thanks to the legacy of WWII, the Ogasawaras are also a superb place for wreck diving. The beauty of diving and sobering history can be addressed in one fell swoop drifting through a now-silent cargo ship, smothered with brain and ryumon coral, its viscous holds littered with thousands of rounds of ammo, tins of rations, and drums of gunpowder.

The Ogasawaras offer other pleasures too. Whitetip sharks and sand sharks congregate at Shark Inlet on Minamijima Island. The Keita Islands are often visited by dolphins. December through March, humpback whales migrate past the Ogasawaras, and dive boats will plop you in the water, an unforgettable sight accompanied by a bewitching underwater symphony. Again, the smart diver books ahead, ensuring the services of a knowledgeable and decipherable guide.

Still most paths lead to, or at least through, Tokyo, and for the diver and sea lover this offers opportunity for a side foray like no other. Known locally as Tsukiji (pronounced skee-jee) for the neighborhood where the market stands, the Tokyo Central Wholesale Market, fifty-six acres of it, sprawls across a piece of reclaimed land on the edge of Tokyo Bay. Tsukiji is, far and away, the world's largest fish market. To describe it as vast is to label *The Last Supper* a sketch. The market's narrow passageways are clogged with gridlocked vehicles, trucks, bicycles, and shouting humanity. The rest of the available space is crammed with long rows of tuna, crates spilling over with tail-slapping flounder, and blue plastic trash cans brimming with squirming eels. There is no more multinational place. Eels from Taiwan, swordfish from Florida, sea urchins from Oregon, octopus from Athens, salmon from Santiago, crabs from Cartagena, the procession stretches away to an indiscernible horizon obliterated by a garish flare of noise and light. For the visitor, just as many emotions swirl; stupefied amazement, incomprehension, bewilderment and, frankly, depression. The fish begin arriving by truck convoys just before 3:00 a.m. By 8:30 a.m most of the market's contents have passed out the door. Several

This colonial parasitic anemone can divide asexually. Here, a colony has overgrown a whip coral.

A scorpionfish is seen here perched on a sponge. Scorpionfish are a widely diverse family of fishes, all of which have poisonous dorsal spines. The sting can vary from mildly painful to extremely painful, even fatal.

This tiny frogfish resembles its background of algae and rock. Frogfish position themselves where prey are likely to come along.

million pounds of seafood, sold off so fast the market has a mysterious absence of fish smell. To see the fish buyers walking through mist rising from the long lines of frozen tuna, a neatly aligned army, stilled and gape-mouthed, is to understand who is the consummate predator of the sea. Those who work in the market know this. Tsukiji has its own Shinto shrine. In the shrine's garden there is a large rock with an inscription, placed there by the Association of Sushi Suppliers. "We have pleased many humans with fine sushi," the inscription reads, "but we must also stop to console the souls of the fish." Still, the convoy of trucks never stops.

The Japanese call the market *no daidokoro,* "Tokyo's pantry," but it is unfair to blame Tokyo because the consumption of the ocean's bounty is not, of course, limited to Japan. While the market is too loud for the visitor to contemplate much of anything, later in quieter moments it is not difficult to make connections, both global and personal. The business of bringing fish to the palate has become so efficient that wholesale buyers at the Tokyo Fish Market employ agents on the charter docks in Miami, buying marlin caught by tourists, and eaten by anyone with an inclination for finely prepared fish. These are not easy times to be a fish.

It is true, Japan's environmental track record is, more often than not, poor, consumption taking a backseat to preservation. This is a nation that still actively hunts and kills protected minke whales, ostensibly for scientific purposes, though the meat is later consumed in Japan. DNA tests of whale meat from Japanese markets have also proved that other protected whales are taken by Japanese ships, then labeled as minke. Bluefin tuna, prized as sushi by Japanese and non-Japanese alike, is consumed with abandon. On any given day the floor of the Tsukiji market is lined with hundreds of bluefin tuna, stretching away like bundled cocoons in the frozen mist.

There is a Japanese saying, *Nuchida takara,* "Life is the most precious thing." But man is subjective in his definition of the life he finds precious, and a saying is merely a saying until it is actively applied.

A yellow moray pauses among soft corals. It is the commonest moray eel species in Japan, and locally it is called "brutal eel." Its brutality is only in self-defense, because it is highly prized by gourmets.

THE NORTH PACIFIC

CALIFORNIA

Thirty-eight miles transports you back hundreds of years, to a place where the elements again rule in prehistoric hush. Sea birds skim along dark, basalt cliffs. Fish jump. Seal lions poke their heads from the water—inquisitive, whiskered barristers. Damp, snorting winds ruffle the outer waters, then skip like a flat stone across vast blankets of kelp, languidly rising and falling as if in deep sleep.

ABOVE: California sea lions bask in the sun at the Breakwater, a popular and accessible diving site, in Monterey. Clumsy on land, sea lions move like rockets underwater.

PAGES 180–181: The Big Sur coast, between Monterey and Santa Barbara, has been rightly called "the greatest meeting of land and sea in the world" by landscape artist Frances McComas.

RIGHT: Shifting sunrays penetrate the canopy of a giant kelp forest. The large forests of kelp found in California are unusual in the ocean, where the majority of plant life consists of floating microscopic plants, not large forests. Kelp forests grow only in temperate waters where a suitable substrate, depth, cooler temperatures, adequate nourishment, and proper light levels are to be found.

Female sea lions are often curious and friendly. They are highly social and noisy animals, and dominant males may gather harems of twenty females or more.

one side of the curtain, a crush of humanity. On the other, glorious escape.

But the ultimate irony may be this. Life actually masses on a far greater scale beneath the waters than on the freeways. Scientists guess that the kelp beds gracing the Channel Islands—Santa Catalina, San Clemente, Santa Barbara, San Nicholas, Anacapa, Santa Cruz, Santa Rosa, and San Miguel—and most of the Southern California coast are home to an estimated eight hundred species of marine life. They guess because that's the best they can do. So much life uses the kelp forest for food, protection, substrate, and general cavorting that the numbers rocket past numbing. A single kelp plant—again a scientific guesstimate—may support more than a million individual organisms. Granted, most of them are microscopic, but the point is simple. California's waters are rife with life.

For the diver this is wonderful, and problematic. Sink down into the crackling green-blue waters off Santa Barbara Island, and in a finstroke you may be confronted with dozens of life forms worthy of gawking. A silver flood of jack mackerel, a grey smear of fast-moving sea lion, spinning through the water like a piscine hula dancer; or, squatting almost imperceptibly at the center of a kelp blade, a tiny nudibranch of vivid orange.

Charles Darwin once observed that "the number of living species of all orders, whose existence intimately depends on the kelp is wonderful." This was a man not easily impressed by biological diversity.

Diving off California's islands and inshore waters is often defined by the phantasmagoric kelp forests, whether you are descending off the Channel Islands, Santa Cruz, or Monterey. Forgetting for a moment the life that inhabits the place, enjoying the kelp forest's stand-alone beauty is worth the price of admission. Any diver who has ever finned through the hushed forest will gush forth a torrent of adjectives, and they'll all be spot on, and, frankly, woefully inadequate. Few things rival the sight of California sunshine piercing the kelp canopy, foggy spears of light revolving slowly in greenish-blue elevator shafts, like floodlights on opening night. And it's not just the sight, it's the

Thirty-eight miles to the east, Los Angeles stews in a bouillabaisse of call waiting and congestion. Here, just off the craggy shoreline of tiny Santa Barbara Island, one of the world's largest urban blemishes simply ceases to exist.

Water, as any diver knows, is a marvelous buffer, and no place exhibits this better than California, whether it's a boat trip to the Channel Islands, and some of the best diving in the world, or a simple step-plunk right off the beach at La Jolla Shores. On

feeling. There is a theory that holds that dolphins leap from the water because they enjoy the surrounding silence. Moving through these quietly swaying forests may produce the same carefree euphoria.

Tropical reefs can be brighter and more conspicuous, but many divers believe there is far more to see in the kelp beds, plus you never know what's going to turn up. Diving off Point Dume near Malibu, a primal warning bell might turn your attention from a tiny bluebanded goby to the migrating grey whale blotting out the sun above you, the majestic giants migrating from Alaska to Baja, Mexico, in the late fall to mate and give birth, then northward again in

the spring. Impossibly beautiful jellies waft up from nearshore submarine canyons, basking sharks swim their way, mouths agape, through the Santa Barbara Channel. Life in other oceans is limited by available nutrients. Not so here. During spring and early summer, prevailing north-northwest winds blow inshore surface waters out to sea, and colder, nutrient-rich waters surge up from the deep. Add to that the California Current bringing cold, nutrient-rich water down from the Gulf of Alaska—powerful waves and currents spooning that planktonic soup in close to shore—and you have a many splendored food web, and a feast for the diver's eyes.

The Pacific white-sided dolphin lives only in the cold temperate waters of the Pacific Ocean. They often engage in bow-riding and acrobatic leaps out of the water. Thousands of these dolphins were being killed annually in high-seas drift-net fisheries for squid, tuna, and billfish. A United Nations ban on this type of fishing in 1993 has alleviated this problem.

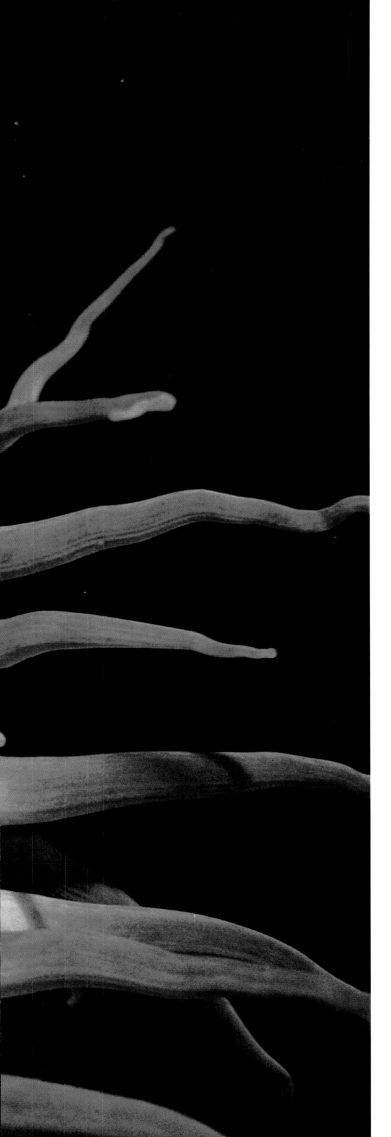

Immune to its host's stinging tentacles, a painted greenling rests among a rose anemone's tentacles at night.

Yes, the water, more often than not, is cold, especially along the northern and central California coastline where the down-swinging California Current hugs the shore far more closely than it does in southern California. And there's a reason why, even in sun-splashed southern California, Gidget and her surfer buddies were always running for beach bonfires looking goose-pimply. It's hard to generalize, since there can be plenty of temperature variation, but here are some general parameters. Surface water temperatures in northern California typically range from 50 degrees F. during winter to 59 during late summer, and that's at the surface.

Drop through a thermocline off Monterey and the water can be as low as 45 degrees. Southern California's waters are warmer, ranging from 59 in the winter to as high as 70 in the summer, but still cool enough to scare plenty of divers off to the tropics.

A shame. First, there is plenty of exception to these temperatures. Diving off Monterey can indeed be cold, damp, and wind-raked. But dive Monterey's waters on a sunny, windless summer day with eighty-foot visibility and you'll be sorely tempted to cap the dive by tossing "Captain Bill's Guide to Caribbean Hot Spots" overboard.

BELOW: The mantis shrimp is a primitive crustacean which digs burrows in sandy bottoms, lines the burrow with shells, and uses a particularly well-sized shell to seal up the burrow during periods of inactivity. Its main claim to fame is the ability to strike out with stiletto-shaped front claws, which is said to be the fastest movement in the animal kingdom.

This giant pelagic jellyfish, *Chrysaora melanaster*, was discovered by divers off the California coast in the early 1990s. Jellyfish are floating worlds, each with their own community of crabs and fish which make their home within the bell, protected by the stinging tentacles of their host.

This diver has happened upon a salp chain, a bizarre member of the tunicate family of invertebrates which possesses a notochord and a nerve cord similar to the backbone of vertebrates. Most tunicates are bottom dwellers, indistinguishable from primitive sponges. This tunicate makes its living by floating in the open ocean, gulping down quantities of water through its wide mouth and filtering it for food particles.

Variety? California is an enormous chunk of coastline—roughly 1,260 miles —and its offerings are appreciably vast, from a short, easy swim to the submarine canyons one hundred yards off lovely La Jolla beach to a rugged cliff descent down to Big Sur's beautiful Jade Cove. Amazing dives can be had right under civilization's appreciably sized nose (Point Loma, right in the heart of San Diego, offers two terrific wall dives and beautiful kelp beds), and in places where civilization still takes an appreciable back seat (California's redwood-silent, sealife-rife, North Coast near the Oregon border). You can beach dive, boat dive, and if you aren't careful with your footing (see Jade Cove), head-first cliff dive. You can be jostled by swarms of divers, or dive alone. Monterey, the Channel Islands, and the submarine canyons off La Jolla steal much of the ink. But it is equally true that the kelp forests and reefs of central and northern California provide some incredible diving, usually without the crowds. To say there is something for everybody in California's waters is understating the case.

For diving purposes it's easiest to divide the state in two, though not in half. Point Conception, just to the northwest of Santa Barbara, separates the calmer, warmer waters of southern California from the rougher, cooler waters to the north. North of Point Conception, where waters are more exposed, it can get indeed wild and woolly—rough, cold water and heavy currents. All this water milling about can dim visibility too. As a general rule, visibility south of Point Conception is often ten to fifteen feet greater. But the beauty of diving in particular, and Nature in general, is that there are glaring exceptions to this rule and every other. And it would be foolish to turn your back on any of California's largesse just because you can't dive in a shorty.

The Channel Islands are certainly one of the gems of California diving. The underwater diversity of the islands, sprinkled off the coast from roughly Santa Barbara to San Diego, are rivaled by only a few places on the globe—the Galapagos, portions of the west coast of Australia, and a few other locales. Eight distinct ecosystems are separated by roughly a finger's

length of map, and here's why. The Channel Islands sit smack-dab between cold, nutrient-rich water steaming down from the north, and warmer, clearer water humming up from Baja California. So the northern islands (San Miguel and Santa Rosa) are dominated by cold-water species, the southern islands (San Clemente, Santa Barbara, and Catalina) feature warmer-water denizens, and the islands in between (San Nicholas, Anacapa, and Santa Cruz) are a mix of the two. Comparing the sea life of San Miguel with that of Catalina might be equated to comparing the musical styles of Mick Jagger and the Mormon Tabernacle Choir. And the two islands are only a little over one hundred miles apart, offering wondrous diversity and good news for divers who prefer a short boat ride to the experience of grueling plane trips and rude customs clerks.

Because the islands are offshore, removed (though not altogether) from the worst of southern California's substantial urban runoff, the visibility is usually far better at the islands too. While you might hope for— and get—50-foot visibility on a San Diego shore dive, visibility at the islands can commonly be 50–70 feet. On rarer, but not unheard of days, especially in the

Harbor seals, gentle and playful like puppies, are frequent visitors to Monterey waters.

PAGES 190–191: This hermit crab has found a home in a jeweled top shell.

OPPOSITE: An anemone has captured a bat sea star with its stinging tentacles, and is drawing its prey to its mouth.

BELOW: This sea otter is eating an abalone, a habit that has not endeared it to fishermen. Yet the presence of these animals has been proven to create healthier kelp forests. The sea otter's main food items—sea urchins and abalone—are kelp grazers. The sea otter's voracious appetite controls these populations, thereby creating larger and healthier kelp beds, and thus, larger fish populations.

PAGES 194–195: This striking design appeared on a white-spotted rose anemone's foot. The tentacles of this large anemone can subdue and hold onto larger prey such as crabs and sea stars.

fall, visibility at the islands can reach 100–150 feet, providing sun-splashed cathedrals of kelp and sea life of stupefying variety housed in fall-away waters.

Though civilization is easily forgotten while rocking on a dive boat off Santa Barbara Island, it is a mistake to think that civilization has ignored the islands. Distance buffers the islands, but only to a degree. Before the Channel Islands National Park (which includes most of the waters ringing the islands) was established in 1980, scientists asked that Congressional decree establishing the park also call for a long-term monitoring program of the islands' underwater health. That request was granted, which was a wonderful thing, except that most of what researchers have monitored is the steady, and sometimes shocking, decline of many marine species. Abalone, the meaty little mollusks that once peppered nooks and crevasses off the islands (and the mainland), have been sorely overharvested, in some cases, nearly to extinction. Giant sea bass, once plentiful around the islands, were nearly wiped out by spear fishermen and line fishermen (though they appear to be slowly rebounding since a 1982 ban made it illegal to catch them). Pacific angel sharks, once common, are hard to find as a result of overfishing. Perhaps

most disconcerting, the island's kelp beds seem to be taking a hit, too. In some spots, entire luxuriant fields of green are gone, reduced to barren scrabble littered with sea urchins. The dwindling of the kelp beds is, of course, particularly troubling since it is the fabric on which the survival of many other marine species rests.

Another California gem is, of course, Monterey, a place whose jaw-dropping shoreline seascapes are easily eclipsed by the beauty that drifts, darts, blooms, and sways a stone's throw from the cliff edges. Monterey's best dive seasons are fall and winter, when plankton growth is lowest and visibility highest; but spring and summer shouldn't be discounted either because in these seasons upwellings bring up nutrient-rich waters and a potpourri of food chain-gobbling life. The famed diving off Point Lobos State Reserve (four miles south of Carmel) is everything it has been made out to be— an explosive tapestry of reef colors, kelp forests, solitary pinnacles, and myriad marine life, from tiny armies of day-glo nudibranchs, to the rare, but not inconceivable, sighting of forty-foot basking sharks. Off Monterey you can cavort with harbor seals, yellow labs reincarnated as bug-eyed projectiles that playfully nip at your fins. Or, in fall, you might drift stupefied amidst mass blooms of pulsing, hypnotic jellies, transparent intricacies of breathtaking beauty. Also not to be missed, some of the world's best tidepooling.

Off Monterey too, lies a world you won't see, a place where, frankly, the mind has a hard time finding any kind of footing. The Monterey Canyon could swallow the Grand Canyon. Could you throw decompression limits to the wind, you would descend first through the familiar water column, then on down through blue-black darkness with stars rushing past; marine snow, tiny bits of dead plankton and decomposing fish, like staring up into nighttime snowfall, only more silent. Then down into cold blackness, a place of weird lantern-slung, fang-toothed, bulbouseyed creatures that makes Alice's Wonderland seem mundane, and long stringy things that look like mucous necklaces, undulating slowly—siphonophores, dense with stinging tentacles and, the dots along these strings, dozens upon dozens of waiting stomachs that

Wolf eels are closely related to small fish called blennies and can grow to a length of six feet. They mate for life and can usually be found around the hole or crevice they call home. The wolf eel's teeth are large and strong, adapted to crushing their diet of clams, sea urchins, and crustaceans. They look ferocious but are docile animals and divers' favorites.

The blue shark, an open ocean predator, is among the most abundant of temperate-water sharks. It has been implicated in attacks on shipwrecked humans, but is a rather slow-moving, predictable shark. Due to human slaughter of shark populations, diving charters to see these sharks in recent years have seen markedly fewer large animals.

can stretch to 130 feet, longer than a blue whale. In the black waters, spotted ratfish and the longspine thornyhead, the latter now fished and sold as rockcod or red snapper, delicious yes, but the end of the line for a fish that can live for one hundred years. On the bottom, delicate deep-sea mushroom corals, ghostly white, and predatory tunicates that resemble translucent Pez dispensers, filter feeding with gaping mouths.

It is a weird, wild, and wonderful world, and it is at our mercy. For anyone who loves the ocean, the waters off Monterey bear witness to both sadness

and hope. Here, unchecked industry wiped out the sardine fishery. Here, in this deep canyon, lies unknown possibility. Scientists have identified about 250,000 different species in the ocean. They estimate that the deep ocean could be home to 10 million more—creatures who could help unlock secrets ranging from alternative energy sources to cancer cures. A place, say deep-sea scientists, where we are afforded a rare second chance to study and understand first, before setting the wheels of harvest and exploitation spinning.

The humpback whale is perhaps the most familiar of the great whales, known for its acrobatic leaps (breaches) out of the water and its haunting songs. The humpback whale undertakes an impressively long annual migration, from feeding grounds in high latitudes to the tropics, where they mate and sing.

THE SEA OF CORTEZ

Moments you might—or might not—experience in the wilderness known as the Sea of Cortez.

The languorous—

Vast curtains of fish, falling through the water like fat, silver raindrops, parting suddenly, swept clear by a graceful Pacific manta, the edges of its wings curled like lace curtains in a soft breeze, its movement so graceful as to appear an afterthought.

The violent—

Floods of baitfish, pinched into a whirling, frantic ball while sailfish and striped marlin slash through the bait like merciless fencers on speed, the floating fish bits picked off by gobbling tuna and dolphins.

The eye-popping, iridescent and eerie—

Hundreds of scalloped hammerhead sharks, back-lit by the sun, their shadowy, muscular forms undulating slowly. Seamounts sprouting veritable gardens of Panamic green morays, as if Medusa had turned herself to stone. Nighttime schools of Humboldt squid, sleek torpedoes pulsing beautiful currents of red and white beneath translucent skin, special effects Hollywood couldn't duplicate.

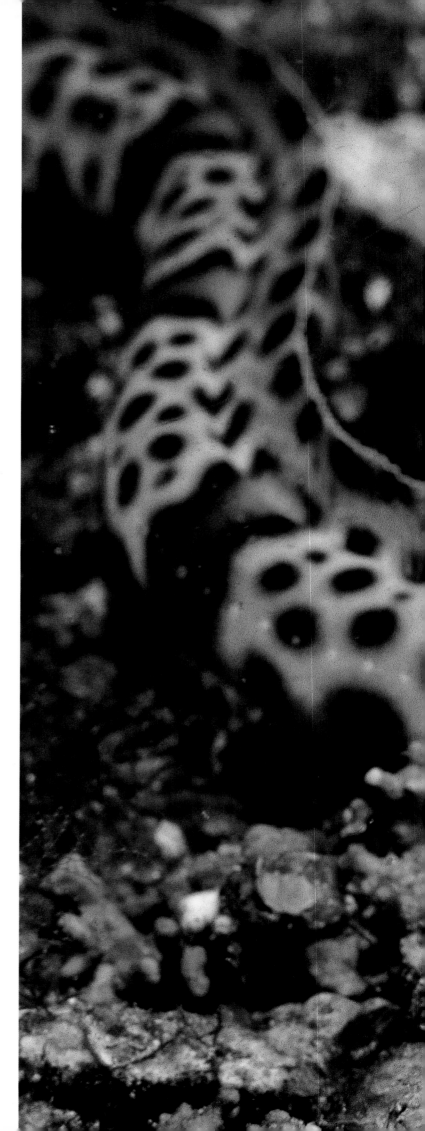

PAGES 198–199: *Redbanded snake eels are supremely adapted to burrowing through sand and coral rubble. They quickly find any source of food, such as crustaceans and other fish, and are rarely seen by divers.*

LEFT: *A wandering anemone and its probable clone have taken up their home upon the stalks of soft gorgonian corals, killing the part of their host where they have settled.*

OPPOSITE, TOP: *Sailfish can reach speeds of fifty miles per hour. Their large sail-like dorsal fin is probably used in demonstrating territoriality, attracting a mate, and even to herd schools of fish.*

OPPOSITE, BOTTOM: *Land's End is a fitting name for the huge granite outcroppings at Cabo San Lucas, at the very tip of the Baja California Peninsula. In between the rocks is a picture-perfect sand beach. One side opens to the Pacific Ocean, and the other side faces the Sea of Cortez.*

PAGES 202–203: *The color pattern of the longnosed hawkfish may help to hide it in the sea fan in which it perches. Like all hawkfish, the longnosed is an ambush predator, scooting from place to place and remaining in position on top of a sea fan or coral head.*

The Sea of Cortez, known more dryly as the Gulf of California, has been called a colossal fish trap, one of the most unpredictable dive spots on the globe, the likeliest place to encounter Big Fish and North America's last underwater frontier. Sums a long-time charter boat captain, "You could spend five lifetimes here and not come anywhere close to seeing everything."

First a little geology, so that you might better grasp the place. Spanning roughly eight hundred miles, the Sea of Cortez is one of the world's deepest gulfs, falling off to a depth of over two miles at its southern end. Its formation was tectonically simple. Mexico was once a solid land mass, no mainland, no Baja. Then the Pacific plate began to move inexorably in a northwesterly direction, tearing loose a thin sliver of Mexico and leaving a vast, watery gulf in its wake.

An added benefit for the diver is that Baja, and much of mainland Mexico, is a harsh and forbidding place, explaining why civilization has come slowly.

Even though tourist resorts now string portions of Baja's coast, a paucity of freshwater and an abundance of torching heat have seen to it that vast tracts of land bordering the Sea of Cortez remain undeveloped. Until the 1970s—with the construction of three airports and the completion of the 1,059-mile Transpeninsular Highway—getting deep into Baja was an exercise in spleen-jolting roads, prolonged sailing, or adrenal flight. As naturalist Joseph Wood Krutch aptly put it, "Baja California is a wonderful example of how much bad roads can do for a country."

Not that people weren't coming to the Sea of Cortez. Spanish conquistador Hernando Cortez first explored its waters in 1539. Missionaries came too, though their observations were somewhat suspect. In 1602, one Father Antonio Ascension, gazing at the mantas flooding the waters, concluded, "Their motion is scarcely perceptible, but when its prey is near it moves with great speed and enfolds and squeezes it. It is a very rare man who can save his life even though he is armed to strike out and defend himself." John Steinbeck, who visited the Sea of Cortez in 1941 and was swept away by the place, was more accurate: "The real picture of how it had been there and how we had been there was in our minds, bright with sun and wet with sea water and

A jewel moray eel opens its mouth to breathe. Moray eels have an undeserved reputation for ferocity. They may bite if provoked, but are otherwise docile.

blue or burned." Diving in the Sea of Cortez is about far more than diving. Bump along in a panga off a remote guano-stained island, watching pelicans plunge to the water and baitfish ruffle the surface— the sound like a brief squall of fat raindrops—all beneath a vast arc of blue water and sky, and you can't help but be touched by the wildness of the place. But the underwater world can steal the show. Even Steinbeck might have found himself without words had he been able to drop below the water's skein.

The Sea of Cortez is mostly a place of contrast, and the wise diver should note this. Generally speaking, the northern reaches of the gulf house greater numbers of fish, while there are more species in the

Anemones are cnidarians, related to jellyfish and hydroids. They have a central mouth and gut surrounded by a ring of stinging tentacles. Some anemones are able to reproduce by cloning themselves, thus taking over areas that might otherwise be lost to other species. These aggregating green anemones are probably all cloned from a single ancestor.

south. Dive guides will inform you that at times the waters to the north can be quite cold (mid-50s), and the waters to the south tropical, at times nearly sweltering (as high as 91 degrees F. in the summer). The same guides will tell you that diving is generally best from late June until early November, when upwelling brings clear water into the gulf and winds, discounting the summer hurricanes, are relatively calm (versus winter with its strong winds and currents and viz-clogging plankton blooms).

All of this is largely true, except when it isn't. In the Sea of Cortez winds blow when they aren't supposed to, water turns over suddenly, plankton blooms in June. And if you commit yourself to diving in summer, understand that you will miss the whale sharks that congregate almost every spring off the coast between Cabo San Lucas and La Paz. Or the gray and blue whales that congregate around the Baja Peninsula in winter—the grays to calve, the blues to feed.

Don't expect guarantees, while keeping in mind that unpredictability has its rewards. See the diver who has laid out hundreds of dollars to dive the famous El Bajo seamount near La Paz to see mantas, and seen none because they have been largely fished out. See him finning disappointed back to the boat, when a gray form catches his eye. Slowly the fish turns, a forearm-thick bill materializes, and the animal's bulk grows inconceivably powerful as it drifts to within four feet of the stunned diver for a closer look. What does a six hundred-pound blue marlin have to fear?

The Sea of Cortez has its famous spots, and they deserve the recognition they've garnered. At the northern end of the gulf there is the Bahia de los Angeles (ten hours south of San Diego), its summer waters filled with invertebrate life. Also in the north, there's the wreck of the *John Elliott Thayer*, huge chunks of a great sailing ship that burned at anchor in 1858, torched by a disgruntled crew member who may have objected to the ship trafficking in guano.

Moving south, La Paz is gateway to the Big Three—Los Islotes, Salvatierra, and El Bajo—and plenty of other magic the right dive operator may reveal (because many of the dive spots are several hours

PAGES 206–207: A king angelfish, yellow-tailed surgeonfish, and rainbow wrasse swim among corals at Cabo Pulmo. Pulmo Reef is perhaps the only place on the west coast of North America where one can drive to a place, get out, and snorkel among corals.

by boat, the typical dive schedule is a two-tank, all-day trip). Salvatierra is a sunken ferry loaded with fish and yellow-polyp black corals, about ninety minutes out of La Paz, and a mile south of Isla Espiritu Santo.

Los Islotes (also roughly ninety minutes by boat) is famous for its sea lion rookery, which, in late summer and fall, when the pups and yearlings are cavorting, is the equivalent of frolicking at the Happy Valley Preschool playground after all the students have been given excessive doses of caffeine. Diving with these whiskered, twirling, darting creatures has brought joy to thousands of divers, and served its purpose for sea lion young too. It's their way of prepping for the serious battles of dominance they will wage as adults—to the quick and the agile goes the choice breeding territory, and mate.

And, of course, there's El Bajo. Eight miles northeast of Los Islotes, designated on charts as Marisla Seamount, El Bajo consists of three underwater peaks, their summits pronging to within fifty feet of the surface. And they are magnets for all manner of wondrous sea life. Here you may see a dozen sailfish. Or, yes, soaring mantas. Some ichthyologists reckon El Bajo is home to more moray eels than any dive site on the globe. But the place is best known for schooling hammerheads, and the distinct possibility of marlin, sailfish, and manta, sometimes in droves. In short, one of the best spots in the world for big animals.

Again, important to realize this is a gathering spot for wildlife, and not an Epcot exhibit. Big fish may be there, and they may not. It can also take some

OPPOSITE: Octopii have complex brains, eyes that resemble our own, and the ability to alter their shape and color at will. Here, a tiny Fitch's pygmy octopus hides underneath a sea fan.

RIGHT: A giant jawfish makes its home in a burrow in sand. Male jawfish brood eggs in their mouths until the eggs hatch.

Spotted sharpnose puffers keep close to a sea fan for protection. With a body shaped like a ping pong ball, puffers cannot use their lateral body muscles to swim as most fish do. Instead, their pectoral fins propel them through the water, waving like helicopter rotors.

BELOW: This California sea lion, surrounded by a school of baitfish, frolics in the shallow waters off Baja Mexico.

wiles to best see them. No one is certain why hammerheads sometimes circulate around El Bajo in jaw-dropping masses. One theory proposes that the seamount,
rich in metals, may modify the geomagnetic field such
that the sharks are attracted to it. Science also believes
the sharks come for a more rudimentary attraction.
Cinematographers Bob Cranston and Howard Hall
witnessed the first documented sighting of hammerheads mating off El Bajo, a coupling apparently so
attention-consuming that one mating pair—pressed
belly to belly—nearly dropped on Cranston's head.

When not so focused, hammerheads are actually
quite skittish. Cranston and Hall were able to approach
them closely because they were using closed-circuit
rebreathing systems that didn't give off bubbles, but
a diver's bubbles are apt to send them bolting.

There are unsung spots too. Just outside the
fishing village of Loreto (to the north of La Paz) lie
the islands of Coronado, Carmen, Danzante, and
Monserrate, and a marine reserve with a variety of
stellar dives, from deep, manta-strung walls to sea
lion colonies. Loreto boasts an international airport,
and many of the comforts of tourism, but for some
reason tourists have overlooked the place.

At the Sea of Cortez's southernmost tip are Cabo
San Lucas and San Jose del Cabo, which have not been
overlooked—an explosion of all that's best and worst
about tourism. But there's great diving a drive or short
boat ride from here, most notably Banco Gorda—a
seamount, and big fish magnet—and Pulmo Reef—
an eye-stroking assemblage of green and gold coral
clusters, and one of few places in North America where
you can get right out of your car and snorkel among
stony corals.

That once sleepy villages like Cabo and San Jose
del Cabo are no longer sleepy, or for that matter separate (they are nearly strung together by tourist shops,
theme restaurants, and sprawling resorts), has led many
newcomers to lament the recent despoiling of Baja and
its sea. Truth is, man's hand touched the Sea of Cortez
long before the most recent planeloads of turistas
arrived. Yes, the unchecked development that, over the
past thirty years, has transformed towns like Cabo and

*ABOVE: A guineafowl puffer shows
the remnants or beginning of a
yellow color phase. Puffers are so
named because they can swallow
water to swell up like a balloon as
a defense against predators.*

*Highly social common dolphins form
herds of tens to many hundreds.
They often ride the pressure wave
in front of a moving boat.*

A true monster of the deep, the Humboldt squid flashes red and white in excitement as it pursues prey. Five feet long and weighing up to sixty pounds, these squid are frighteningly efficient predators. Their tentacles are lined with suckers, which in turn are lined with razor-sharp teeth. The squid will attack and feed on anything in their frenzy, even each other.

La Paz, has dumped fertilizer, pesticides, industrial waste, and worse into the water. Yes, twenty years ago Jacques Cousteau was alarmed by the overfishing he saw. But Steinbeck saw this plunder too. "They cruised slowly along in echelon with overlapping dredges, literally scraping the bottom clean," wrote Steinbeck, observing a Japanese fleet dragging nets in 1941. "Any animals which escaped must have been very fast indeed, for not even the sharks got away."

Science has now put a figure on these numbers; it is estimated that for each pound of shrimp, nets drag up 15–25 pounds of by-kill. On the written page, this is a dry, featureless number. But waste is something to behold. The Sea of Cortez has an active longline shark fishery. To see a shark hauled from the water, its fins summarily sliced off, and the jerking, living remains dropped back into the sea is a sight never forgotten. If you are unlucky the water will be clear and you can watch the spasmodic jerking continue as the shark, apex predator of the sea, sinks for the bottom, unable to control its swimming. Mantas too, docile and trusting, are harpooned or pulled from the sea in nets. Toss in lobster, yellowfin tuna, sardine, anchovy, and marlin fisheries, all of them largely unregulated due to poor cooperation among government offices and vast, unpoliceable expanses of empty sea, and the depletion adds up.

The irony is that the wildness of the Sea of Cortez is masking what some see as dire circumstances. "New divers who come down here are overwhelmed by the abundance of life," says a diver with thirty years logged in the Sea of Cortez. "But it's nothing compared to what it once was."

All is certainly not lost. Though slow to move, the Mexican government recognizes the value of tourist dollars, and plenty of tourists come to enjoy the impressive beauty that remains. From any boat, on any given patch of this majestic sea, you can watch pelicans plunge to the water like feathered footballs, bait fish boil the surface, and pods of dolphin split the surface, while beneath the water's skein a primal world plays out a timeless game. The ocean and its infinite possibilities replete under a dome of blue sky.

THE REVILLAGIGEDO ISLANDS

Here they come, rising through water so blue it might as well be Montana sky. They come up slowly, curious and in no particular hurry, swelling in size, gumdrops becoming half dollars, half dollars becoming balloons, balloons becoming yellowfin tuna, solid, glinting silver, bullet-shaped and nearly as fast, able to accelerate to forty miles an hour in a wink.

ABOVE: Tiny Roca Partida, miles from any other land, rises straight up from hundreds of feet of water. Rocky outcrops and seamounts (undersea pinnacles) are gathering places for marine life, attracting the ocean's largest and most exciting animals. The volcanic seamounts of the eastern tropical Pacific are famous for their concentrations of life—manta rays, hammerhead sharks, and tuna.

RIGHT: A floating log attracted this huge school of baitfish. Floating objects have a magical attraction to fish. A log the size of a door may have a school of fifteen hundred tuna underneath it.

and so the Revillagigedos are a place where fear and fascination mingle. In *Heart of Darkness* Joseph Conrad wrote, "We are accustomed to look upon the shackled form of a conquered monster, but there, there you could look at a thing monstrous and free." Assuming Conrad found this pleasing, he would have immensely enjoyed these islands.

In diving circles the Revillagigedos—Socorro, San Benedicto, Clarion, and Roca Partida—have gained near mythical stature. But on Nature's map they are little more than four bits of rock scattered by a disinterested child's hand over a vast reach of Pacific Ocean some 220 miles south-southwest of Cabo San Lucas, Mexico. The largest of the islands, Socorro, is nine by eleven miles. The smallest, Roca Partida, is a mere rock sticking out of the water, taking fifteen minutes to swim around at the surface, but several dives to see everything underwater. More than three hundred miles of roiling waters separate San Benedicto, the northernmost island, from Clarion; San Benedicto and Socorro, the two most popular dive sites, are forty miles apart. For those with a geologic interest, the Revillagigedos are the last visible remnants of an ancient volcano; and their dry land terrain—bleak, rugged, and rocky (no beaches or dive resorts here)— reflects this. For divers they are fish magnets, undersea pinnacles lurching up from the ocean's depths, combed by storms, upwellings, and a swirl of nutrient-rich water. Grand Central Station for a mind warp of wild creatures, moving through water where visibility can stretch to 150 feet (100 feet is common).

Cabo San Lucas has its sweeping Land's End arches. But the Revillagidedos can seem like the World's End. Which, of course, is their beauty—a place both spooky and magnetic. All but one of the islands are uninhabited, at least by man. Dry land home to several rare and threatened birds, including the Socorro mockingbird and green parakeet, as well as unique plant species, the island chain has been called Mexico's little Galapagos. It's a twenty-four-hour boat trip from Cabo —1,730 miles round-trip from San Diego—and a journey with potential thrills of its own. Divers have plopped overboard in the

This foursome halts their drifting ascent thirty feet from the surface. With a casual flick of powerful tail, they disappear behind a cobalt blue curtain that yaws open to hundreds of miles of vast Eastern Pacific Ocean.

At this moment, yellowfin tuna, some of the biggest in the world; at any other moment, most any other large pelagic fish. The Revillagigedo Islands swarm with them—hammerhead, Galapagos and tiger sharks, sailfish, marlin, whale shark, bottlenose dolphin, tuna, and the languorous, surreal Pacific manta rays. There's no telling what will appear when;

OPPOSITE, TOP: Isolated Socorro Island in the Revillagigedo Archipelago is a gathering place for marine life, renowned for diving encounters with manta rays.

OPPOSITE, BOTTOM: San Benedicto Island, the remains of an old volcano, is well-known for its population of docile giant manta rays.

RIGHT: An underwater view of Roca Partida shows that it is a sheer needle of rock climbing up to the surface. Because seamounts are pinnacles of rock sticking up out of deeper water, they provide shelter and a settling place for invertebrates, algae, and other small animals. These animals provide the basis for a food chain.

PAGES 218–219: A trio of octopi engage in a mating ritual on a seamount. Two males extend sperm-tipped arms to the one female. Their specialized arms are cast off when mating takes place, and the female carries them and their contained sperm around with her until she fertilizes her eggs.

open ocean with pods of sperm whales. The islands themselves are stark, not surprising given their volcanic origin. Beneath the waves, the topography mirrors what's found above—an underwater landscape both stark and dramatic; with giant boulders, lonely pinnacles, and rippled lava flows.

The islands' remoteness keeps the crowds down, serving up another oddity. The Revillagigedos denizens, for the most part, go about their business snubbing convention and paying little deference to man. Tiger sharks sweep through shallow waters at any time of day, ignorant of the scientific body of literature that relegates them to deep offshore waters during the day. Socorro spiny lobsters, the base of their antennae bright robin's egg blue, strut about in the middle of the day. Reclusive in other environs, Panamic green morays lie out of their crevices when they please.

In the waters off the Revillagigedos, man is viewed as a curiosity to be ignored or explored. In other parts of the world, sharks usually keep their distance. Here they can be nosier than paparazzi, cruising within arms reach and closer; disconcerting for divers expecting standoffish behavior. On occasion, divers have been chased from the water by aggressive sharks, too. But, for the most part, like the rest of the Revillagigedos citizenry, the mass of sharks that weave

about the islands serve up more opportunity for fascination than fear. Huge schools of hammerheads weave through the waters—this schooling behavior an undeciphered mystery to scientists, but proven magic for the diver gazing up at a flood of sinuous forms backlit by the sun.

This laissez faire attitude, exhibited by an even larger Revillagigedos denizen, serves up one of diving's most bewitching experiences; the chance to swim with the docile and curious Pacific manta ray. Like the hammerheads, the rays, some with wingspans approaching twenty feet, are a puzzle to scientists—lifespan unknown, gestation unknown, gypsy nomadic or a distinct home range, unknown, population size, unknown. Let the scientists work that out. For the diver, the manta's impact is clear. To see these enormous creatures soar through the water column is to feel your heart do the same. This joy might be defined by the manta's grace, their playful curiosity, or their near opiate-producing Zen calm—if defining such things didn't ruin them altogether. Best to just sit back in awe.

Swooping languorously through the water column, the manta rays are drawn to the seamounts, where, hanging motionless, they allow themselves a parasitic cleaning courtesy of floods of jacks and bright

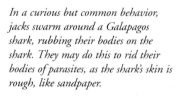

In a curious but common behavior, jacks swarm around a Galapagos shark, rubbing their bodies on the shark. They may do this to rid their bodies of parasites, as the shark's skin is rough, like sandpaper.

Many manta rays encountered in the waters around the Revillagigedos have two large remoras, or sharksuckers, attached to them. The remoras attach to the mantas with suckers on the tops of their heads. These remoras have attached so strongly that their suckers have left marks on the manta's rough skin.

A clarion angelfish approaches a manta ray to clean it at this seamount in the Pacific Ocean. The mantas are apparently drawn to this site by the prospect of a cleaning. The larger fishes allow the cleaners to swim all over their bodies and even within their mouths to rid it of parasites.

RIGHT: The docile, approachable manta rays at the Revillagigedos are unique for their diffidence to divers. These same mantas, famous for allowing divers to ride on their backs, used to be seen in the Sea of Cortez, but due to overfishing they are now rarely seen there. The Revillegigado Islands, due to their remoteness from the mainland, is currently the best place to encounter these gentle creatures.

orange clarion angelfish. They are equally prone to hover beneath dive boats, waiting for divers; and hover directly above divers' heads, enjoying the caress of their hands and their bubbles on their rough undersides.

Over one hundred mantas have been catalogued at San Benedicto alone—identified by individual distinctive black and white patchings—and one of their favorite gathering spots is a seamount-cum-manta-magnet known as The Boiler. Just west of San Benedicto's north end, it's not unusual to have a half dozen mantas hanging just off this pinnacle like stalled magic carpets, waiting their turn to be serviced by cleaner fish. And, yes, it is possible to ride on the backs of mantas—divers have hitched rides of thirty minutes and more—though some dive boat operators are discouraging contact these days. Still, many divers believe the mantas enjoy the contact, if they are approached slowly and alone. Drop twenty divers off a boat, and have half of them fin madly for the manta and watch it disappear in a swoop. But come to the manta slowly, place your hands flat on its vast spread of back and you can experience an incomparable thrill, swooping through the water, feeling, through the palms of your hands, the slight sandpaper scratch and the mass and flex of powerful muscle.

Touch or no, there's no shaking the odd feeling of bonding; two pairs of eyes—one pair wide, the other inkwell black—gazing at each other. It's true, mantas do

A diver glides along with a giant manta ray at a seamount off San Benedicto Island. If approached quietly and with respect, these mantas will often let divers get close to them and touch them. Pacific mantas, close relatives of sharks and stingrays, swim through tropical seas feeding on plankton. Because of their horns and strange appearance (the name "manta" is Spanish for "blanket"), manta rays were once feared by fishermen and native islanders, who called them the devilfish. Divers, however, have discovered that these huge animals are actually quite docile and gentle.

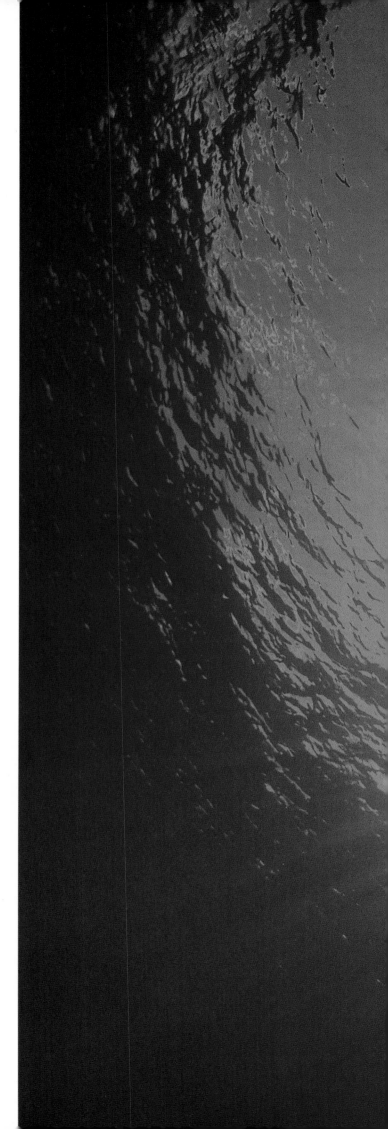

have large brains—larger than any fish—but scientists believe evolution has directed the focus of this brain toward supremely heightened senses, not to communicating telepathically with burbling bits of neoprene. Still many divers swear that they feel a connection with the animals, and if that's part of the magic, what right-minded diver would let science stand in the way?

Nowhere else will you encounter mantas as docile and as large, and so the mantas get much of the ink. But the fact is the Revillagigedos teem with all manner of life—bluefin trevally, green jack, tiger reef eels, Moorish idols, Socorro wrasse, redtail triggerfish, masses of parasite-picking clarion angelfish. Assuming you have the presence of mind to count (strong currents and the possibility of anything morphing out of the blue make focusing difficult), it isn't unusual to see forty different species in one dive. Under a single floating log, you might find juvenile yellowfin tuna darting through massing baitfish like madcap footballs, while dozens of Galapagos sharks sample from among great swirling balls of chub and jacks. The food chain sandwiched into a Tokyo subway car.

Plopped in the open ocean, waves and currents around the islands can be substantial; large ocean swells sweep the archipelago, and the surge on the north side of the islands can be particularly heavy. It is not always a hospitable place. More to the point, the islands can be a nexus for nasty weather. But the dive operators who make the journey out know the best season (the islands are generally best accessible from November through March), freeing you from the concern of a long swim in.

The islands' isolation is both boon and bane. Cruise ships won't overrun the place any time soon. But, 350 miles from mainland Mexico, it is also a difficult spot to police. In 1994, likely recognizing the Revillagigedos' commercial as well as ecological value (it's estimated that eco-tourism at the islands generates roughly $2 million a year), Mexico declared the chain a biosphere reserve. Spearfishing and sport fishing are allowed on a limited basis; commercial fishing vessels aren't allowed to navigate within 12 miles of the islands. Killing a manta—their flesh used primarily for shark bait in the lucrative shark finning trade—can bring a $10,000 fine.

The biosphere was established in 1994 after two American sailors videotaped two Mexican fishing vessels using nets, baited hooks, and harpoons to catch and kill anything they could. Among the more memorable footage, dozens of sharks being finned and tossed overboard, sinking, unable to swim, to the bottom, and the fishermen hacking off a manta's wings with axes. *No mas*, said the Mexican government after the video aired on various television stations, bringing public uproar.

Unfortunately not everyone has gotten the word, or perhaps they are willing to accept the risks. In April of 2000, divers watched a fleet of seven seventy-to-ninety-ton Mexican drift gillnet boats drop their nets, some within a mile of shore. The boats spent five days hauling up bulging netfulls of sea life, some so heavy the boat winches couldn't pull the nets from the water. The actual numbers will never be known, but the divers who watched estimated that 2,000–4,000 sharks were killed, plus mantas, tuna, turtles, and other by-catch. For two days after the fishing vessels left, one dive boat operator claimed his divers didn't see a single shark; unnerving, when the normal tally of shark sightings would have been in the hundreds.

Mexican officials have admitted that poaching is a problem, but they have also pointed out, rightly enough, hat it is difficult to police. In the case of the April 2000 massacre, the Revillagigedos themselves may have meted out justice. One of the fishing vessels purportedly sank in rough weather.

Such incidents are often written off as a poorer country's inability to police its own. Interesting to note that in a 1965 book a former president of the National Geographic Society describes the pleasures of manta hunting off the Bahamas. Mantas are rarely seen in the Bahamas today.

Still the Revillagigedos remain a place where you might swim with manta and bottlenose dolphin while, sonaring in from the blue, come long wails like the distant creak of a slowly opening door: humpback whales, singing.

Redtail triggerfish often gather in huge schools around the Revillagigedo Islands. Its other name, the crosshatch triggerfish, is perhaps more appropriate because males have red tails and females have bright yellow tails.

THE HAWAIIAN ISLANDS

The islands of Hawaii have been made out to be many things by many ad agencies. But simply put, they are a sensuous place. Rain comes down in sheets, smashing and slapping at dank walls of vegetation. Thick rainbows sprout from the ocean and waterfalls drop from impossible heights in thready wisps.

ABOVE: Hanauma Bay on Oahu is one of the world's most popular snorkeling spots.

RIGHT: A diver pets a wild moray at Molokini Crater off Maui. Moray eels, ferocious in appearance, have been taught by many divemasters to accept food and to tolerate petting by other divers.

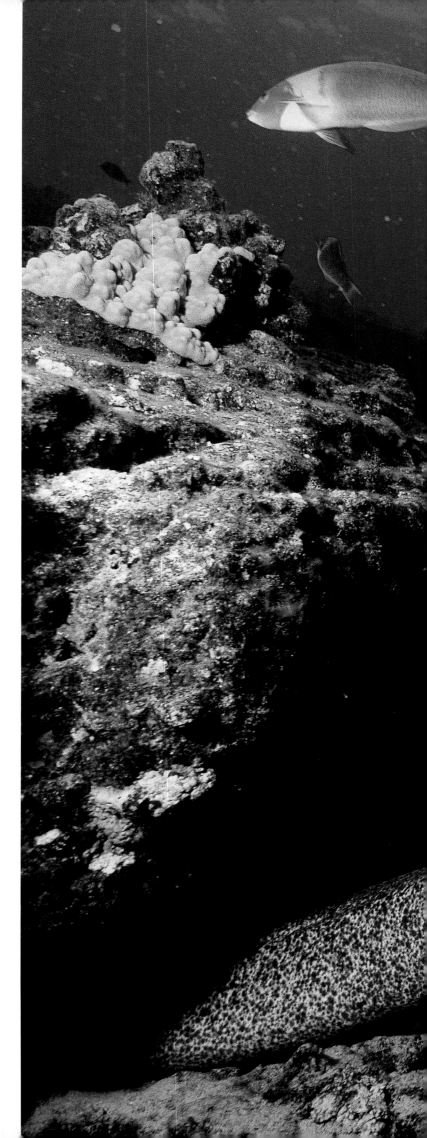

It is a place of lush extremes. Tropical rainforests, grassy savannahs, black lava moonscapes, pastures smothered in high altitude fog. And, of course, skin-splayed beaches radiating heat. Small wonder about 7 million tourists come to the islands each year, making them the world's most popular tourist destination, and a happy cornucopia of sunburnt faces, tacky postcards, garish shirts, and cool trade wind breezes.

Ironically, the Hawaiian islands are also the world's most isolated archipelago, 2,400 miles from the nearest continent (North America). But for the diver—or anyone else who doesn't relish sharing a cooler-size square of sand with three coconut-scented couples from Racine—the good news is most visitors never leave Waikiki; the beach-shopping-hotel clot still accommodates half of Hawaii's visitors. For divers who like to keep note of such things, most visitors come to Oahu, followed by Maui, the Big Island of Hawaii, and Kauai.

But even in the most popular of destinations, there are wonderful surprises smack dab in the center of congestion, or just through a side door. Sure, Maui's Molokini Crater—the partially submerged volcano rim jutting up in the Alalakeiki Channel between Maui and the uninhabited island of Kahoolawe—is swamped with snorkelers and divers, especially in the inner waters enfolded by the (dormant) rim. But that doesn't detract from Molokini's hypnotizing blue waters, where fish life explodes thanks to the crater's status as a preserve. And step just slightly off the beaten track, around to the backside of the crater, and you'll find one of Hawaii's best dives. The aptly named Back Wall is brushed by rainbow swirls of fish and cruised by reef sharks and other large pelagics; in early winter, whale sharks are even a possibility. Even on Oahu, just minutes from downtown Honolulu, Hanauma Bay may groan under the weight of divers and snorkelers, but they are there for a reason. Snorkelers and

The lemon butterflyfish is found only in Hawaii, while the black durgon (a triggerfish) is found throughout tropical oceans.

228

beginning divers can explore the beautiful inner reef, advanced divers can explore the outer reef and the points, and the bay is a reserve, swarming with fearless, in-your-face fish.

In Hawaii it doesn't pay to be elitist and snotty, unless you want to miss out on the fun. Hawaii is home to fall-away blue waters, not to mention nearly five-hundred species of nearshore fishes. The islands' waters also contain the highest percentage of endemic fish on the planet—you won't see white spot damsels, lemon butterflyfish, psychedelic wrasse, or titan scorpionfish anywhere else. Reams of other interesting sea life too, from hawksbill turtles and spinner dolphins, to humpback whales and the rare and endangered Hawaiian monk seal.

One thing you shouldn't come to Hawaii for are vast spreads of coral. Reefs do exist, especially in the northwestern islands. But at the southeastern end of the Hawaiian island chain, where virtually all the diving takes place, cool winter water temperatures make life difficult for polyps, and waves the size of buildings conspire to pulverize what does take hold. The Hawaiian islands are volcanic in origin; their birth, and continuing growth, a fascinating process that involves heaping, oozing dollops of molten earth, not the massing of delicate coral polyps.

Grasping the ongoing genesis of these volcanic islands will help you as a diver better appreciate what you see beneath Hawaii's waters. Divers new to Hawaii are sometimes disappointed by the lack of coral, and the plethora of barren, puddled rock. The place looks like a meltdown in a brown crayon factory. But if you understand what you are seeing, the once-dull basaltic rock becomes a vivid picture of Hawaii's fascinating geology, and a philosophical reminder of the impermanence of all things.

The endangered Hawaiian monk seal is often seen in the remote French Frigate Shoals. These seals are found only in the Hawaiian Islands.

PAGES 230–231: An endangered green sea turtle is cleaned by reef fishes. Yellow tangs and other reef fish pick algae and food particles off the turtle's back. Green sea turtles have come back dramatically since they were designated as endangered in 1978.

A frogfish, resembling a sponge, sits in wait to ambush prey.

Flounder are well known for their ability to change color to match their background. They start life looking like normal fish, but as they grow one eye migrates to the other side of the head, and the fish starts swimming on its side with the eyes topmost. This peacock flounder's eyes act as periscopes as the fish lays covered in sand.

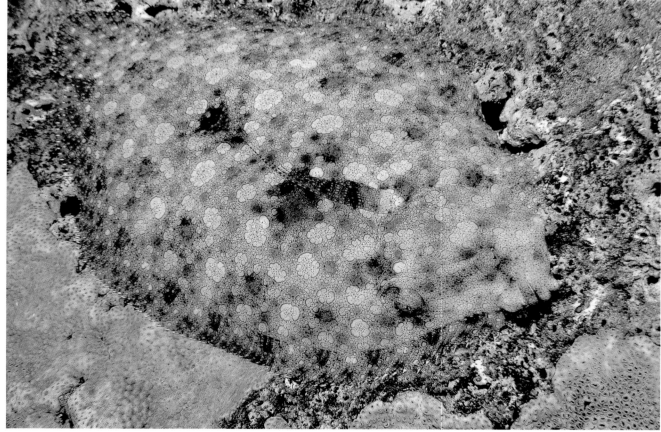

Hawaii's islands are individual basaltic volcanoes, formed, in marching order, by a single hot spot beneath the ocean floor. Over the past 70 million years the hot spot has remained stationary. But above it, the crust of the Pacific tectonic plate has been sliding northwest. Each island formed as it sat above this hot spot. Each stopped growing as the movements of the Pacific plate pushed it off the hotspot, and a new island took its turn—a kind of assembly line volcanism.

Today's visible string of islands stretches across more than fifteen hundred miles of central Pacific Ocean, from the Big Island of Hawaii in the southeast to Kure Atoll, French Frigate Shoals, Midway Island, and others in the northwest. Continuing away from the still visible Midway and Kure, stretching for thousands of miles beneath the ocean, is a vast chain of now submerged islands, their day in the sun done.

The more familiar islands in the southeast—Maui, Kauai, Oahu, Hawaii—are the youngest islands. The youngest of all is the Big Island of Hawaii. Hawaii's Kilauea volcano, the most active volcano in the world, currently squats directly over the hot spot. Since 1983, Kilauea has oozed forth over 1.5 billion cubic yards of molten magma from its spout, adding over 550 acres to Hawaii's shoreline.

If you're not much for geology or philosophy, no matter. An underwater world rife with huge caverns, massive arches, and twisting, sponge-encrusted lava tubes is simply a cool place to swim around in. These surreal basalt formations, and their attendant colorful sea life, are everywhere. On the Big Island there's Place of Refuge, about twenty miles south of Kailua, easy shore access to a hazy blue world of sea turtles, and tropical fish. While much of Hawaii's waters can be wild—read waves and currents—Hawaii's Kona coast, sheltered for the most part from prevailing waves and winds, offers the islands' calmest conditions, with dozens of shore dives. On the North Shore of Oahu, just to the north of Waimea Bay, there's Three Tables, another shore dive with surreal topography, though not in winter, when some of the biggest surf in the planet shakes the North Shore. There is even opportunity for divers to see these rock gardens form. As of

From underneath a breaking wave, Hawaii's pounding surf resembles fierce, rolling topside storm clouds.

this writing, at least one enterprising dive outfitter in Hilo is offering divers the chance to watch lava as it snaps, belches, and cools itself in the sea.

There are dozens on dozens of these underwater basaltic drip castles, and any one of an equal number of dive outfitters will help you find them. Another advantage to diving Hawaii is simple. It is tropical diving minus the expansive reefs yes, but also bereft of the hassles of travel in less developed countries. No questionable demands at Customs. You can drink the water. Dive outfitters pick you up at your hotel. After that, all you have to do is step in and out of vans and on and off of docks. Another of Hawaii's allures is its predictable weather, generally sunny and warm with frequent but brief rain showers. There is no bad time to dive Hawaii, though in winter massive waves close the northern dive sites.

In the islands, shore diving on your own is an option—especially along the sheltered Kona coast. But it pays to go with local experience, even when shore diving. Weather in the islands can change quickly, and local divers know where to take you when it does, sparing you the inconvenience of being swept out to sea by rapacious currents or diced to sashimi in pounding shore break.

Waterfalls are common among the lush hillsides of Hawaii.

The oceanic whitetip shark is a stunning shark, seen only above the deep waters of the open ocean. It can be aggressive toward humans and is often seen following pods of pilot whales, where it may feed on food scraps left behind by the whales.

BELOW: The short-finned pilot whale is a common small whale in the tropics. Its bulbous forehead is used to emit sonar waves that it can use to detect prey and survey its surroundings.

Boat trips open a vast world of options. From Maui, boats lead to the magic of dozens of sites rimming Lanai and Molokai, and Molokini Crater. A boat can get you to Moku Ho'oniki Island, just east of Molokai, and possibly schools of hammerheads and more fish than anywhere else in the islands. On the Big Island, boats ferry divers out to South Point, the southernmost tip of the United States, a wild place where currents collide, and humpback whales, whale sharks, and pilot whales might swim. A boat will also take you to Niihau—the forbidden island—off Kauai. Privately owned, Niihau's terra firma is closed to outsiders. But its spectacular dive sites, many of the best in Hawaii, are open to divers. Pinnacles, coral gardens, and sheer wall drop-offs where you might see swarms of blacktip, grey reef and whitetip sharks, spinner dolphins, mantas and possibly the endangered Hawaiian monk seal (exposed to the full brunt of northeast winds, the island is pretty much undiveable during winter months).

Hawaii also has some of the best night diving in the world, nocturnal critters skittering out of caverns and fissures to fill the nighttime waters with flame orange, scarlet, and lemon yellow. The night manta

The false killer whale is a very social species which sometimes strands en masse. They consume a large variety of fish and cephalopods, and they have been seen chasing and attacking smaller dolphins and even larger whales.

OPPOSITE: A humpback whale breaches in an acrobatic display.

This spotted dolphin has reason to jump for joy. Regulations now prohibit tuna fishermen from encircling these dolphin with nets in order to catch yellowfin tuna.

ABOVE: Tropical counterpart to the great white shark, the tiger shark is the most feared predator, and responsible for 90 percent of all fatal shark attacks on humans in the tropics. They are among the largest and most dangerous of all sharks, and are often described as indiscriminate predators that gobble up cans of nails, license plates, turtles, seals, and humans with equal enthusiasm. Here, a ready and waiting tiger shark attacks a fledgling albatross.

dives off Kona are world-renowned. Day or night on the Kona coast, nowhere are your odds better, with the possible exception of Yap, of seeing mantas regularly.

Hawaii isn't all idyll. Ever since Captain James Cook arrived in Hawaii in 1778, man has lain his hand heavily on this paradise. Thanks to the grazing of introduced game animals and livestock, many of the plants discovered by Cook's botanist will never be seen again. In the water, the introduction of alien fish species, the practice of shark finning, severe depletion of fish stocks, and derelict fishing gear are major environmental concerns. The matter of fishing gear— dumped overboard or lost by purse seiners, gill netters, and trawlers—is emerging as a big problem in the largely undeveloped islands in the northwest, where vast quantities of fishing nets have been found snagged on reefs and beaches. It's estimated that millions of tons of fishing gear may be dumped or lost by large commercial fishing fleets working the waters in the North Pacific, currents then sending the gear drifting into the islands. These same islands, many of them protected reserves, are remote and difficult to patrol. There is plenty of evidence that these wild refuges aren't just being inadvertently netted, but are also being purposefully fished for sharks (and fins), aquarium fish, lobsters, pearl oysters, and large food fish. The number of monk seals, endangered and found nowhere else, continues to decline despite their protected status, possibly because commercial fishing vessels in

BELOW, LEFT: Goose barnacles attached to an abandoned fisherman's float feed by filtering out food particles from the water with their legs. Barnacles are crustaceans, like crabs and lobsters. They settle onto a floating object as larvae and eventually fuse to their floating substrate with their heads.

BELOW: Butterflyfish are known for their bright color patterns, and are perhaps the best known of all reef fishes. Their coloration may serve as a signal, warning others of the same species to stay away. Most of the species feed partly or exclusively on coral polyps. The Tinker's butterflyfish is found only in deeper waters, past 100 feet.

ABOVE: The wedge Picasso triggerfish, or humuhumu nukunuku apua'a, *eats sand and filters it through its gills.*

RIGHT: Butterflyfish usually patrol a coral reef either singly or in pairs, feeding on coral polyps. They form mated pairs which can last for their lifetimes.

OPPOSITE, BOTTOM: The longnose butterflyfish forages among the cracks and crevices of the coral reef for its food. It seems to prefer nipping off the tube feet of sea stars and sea urchins. It can be found by itself or in groups, often swimming upside down in coral caves.

the northwest islands are fishing up the lobster, octopus and fish the seals need to survive.

There is good news, too. Green sea turtles have come back dramatically since they were designated as endangered in 1978. One of the largest green turtle nesting sites in the Pacific is on the sandy islets of French Frigate Shoals. The numbers of endangered humpback whales has also increased dramatically, the majestic giants coming to the islands between November and May to give birth and rear young, filling the waters with their hypnotic song.

And in the far northwest, wilderness, in all its amazing glory and brutality, survives. Each June, around the edges of diver-less French Frigate Shoals (in the northwestern islands, sport diving is currently limited to Midway Island), tiger sharks vector in from the deep. Their swift dark shadows waver through the shallow waters, rising to pluck fledgling albatross that have dropped to the water, and so failed their final lesson in flight.

Nature is sensual and sudden, and the sea is forum for both.

OPPOSITE: A guineafowl puffer puffs up its body as a defense against predators. Puffers have the unique ability to inflate themselves by gulping down water. As a further defense, most puffers are poisonous to eat. Puffers possess one of nature's most potent toxins, tetrodotoxin, which has been known to kill a human in five minutes.

The slate pencil urchin is found on many Hawaiian reefs. Its spines are stony, and they are often used for wind chimes.

COSTA RICA

Anyone would be forgiven a momentary bout of neck-prickling concern, a feeling that somehow, through some heretofore-impossible wrinkle, you had slipped back in time. Surface through vast clouds of fish to thundering tropical rain. The chop slaps at your face, the surge of open ocean swells jerks your body to-and-fro like an antic dance partner. Across the mist-water, an island rises from the sea, its peak hidden in grey clouds, the rest falling to the sea in a wild, lush green tangle, thready waterfalls arcing down from its cliffs. Below you, the sea teems with resplendent life, life that, during your time below, ignored you for the strange and inconsequential presence you are, going about their eternal business of survival. This is not a place where happy little fish come skittering up for a frozen pea handout. They are the handouts, and so have other concerns. The density of sharks per square inch in the waters off Cocos Island are, at the same time, mesmerizing, enervating, and alarming. From where you bob, three hundred miles off mainland Costa Rica, there is no sign of man.

Whitetip reef sharks gather around a seamount off Cocos Island. This species differs dramatically from the oceanic whitetip shark in both behavior and appearance.

Undersea pinnacles are gathering places for marine life. This small pinnacle off Cocos Island had schools of squirrelfish and snapper surrounding an underwater arch. The large eyes of squirrelfish enable them to hunt for plankton at night.

Then, through the thunder-drum of rain, an insect buzz reaches your ears. The Zodiac morphs out of the mist, whapping across the bumpy waters, and you realize, with perhaps sizeable relief, that in short order you will be back on your liveaboard, sharing tales of thick schools of hammerhead sharks amidst warm, dry twenty-first-century amenities, perhaps keeping your story of momentary panic to yourself. Ha, ha. Imagine thinking you had slipped back to another time. Realize that Cocos has had the same effect on millions. Aerial footage of Cocos appeared in *Jurassic Park*.

There are few places in the world like Cocos Island. If you want to frolic at a beach resort and drift in warmth over brightly colored fish with the sun on your back, this is not the place for you. If you want

schools of big fish—yellowfin tuna, whitetip reef sharks, and hammerhead sharks—sometimes vast, vast schools of them in a wild, rough and tumble, unpredictable environment, well then Cocos Island is your place.

For the serious diver, Costa Rica means Cocos Island. Several fortunate circumstances combine to make this Costa Rican island-marine reserve (since 1992)-World Heritage Site (since 1997) a unique, magnetic draw. Distance is one. Water is God's own buffer and, should you opt to dive Cocos Island, there are roughly thirty-six hours of it between the industrial port of Puntarenas on the Costa Rican mainland and anchorage off the volcanic lump of Cocos. It's no gondola ride either. The open waters of the Eastern Pacific are tossy-turvy enough to lead even the most adventurous sorts to whining. Plying waters not far to the south, Charles Darwin spent his fair time hanging over the railing, leading him to make this peevish evaluation of the sea: "A tedious waste, a desert of water, as the Arabian calls it." Brief for Darwin. Perhaps this was penned at sea, and he suddenly didn't have time to write more.

Remoteness isn't the only thing that makes Cocos Island special. The island sits at the convergence of several major oceanic currents. These currents produce massive upwellings. They also serve as conveyor belts, ferrying small—and very large—life from distant waters. And, Cocos is one of the few places on the globe not threatened by development. (Except for a small enclave of rangers, the island is uninhabited.) Attempts have been made to domesticate this jungle-covered island. Cocos Island receives between eighteen and twenty-four feet of rain annually. During the rainy season—ironically when the diving is best—if it is not misting, raining, or thundering down, it is gearing up to do so. Club Med for earthworms and fungi.

Cocos is, however, a highly desirable destination—read the only one for miles—for denizens who aren't bothered by wet, a sort of aquatic truck stop along a long, empty highway. All manner of sea life parks here to feed, mate, clean, or be cleaned. There may be no other place in the world that provides more consistent opportunity to see hammerhead sharks. This shouldn't detract from the dozens—sometimes hundreds—of other sharks, primarily whitetip reef sharks, but also oceanic whitetips, silkies, and Galapagos sharks. If you want to see sharks, you can dispense with a lifetime of diving elsewhere and make one trip here. Nor should you forget the good odds of also encountering whale sharks, humpback whales, giant mantas, super-sized yellowfin tuna, turtles, marlin, and sailfish. That's the Big Stuff. There are also the Big Schools, of snapper, grunts, rainbow runners, and blue creole fish.

Big Rain, Big Life, Big Distance.

The diving isn't easy. Most of the dives are deep, often below one hundred feet, and often in

appreciable currents (not the place to forget your signaling device or air horn), which can kick up quick. The water may be warm on the surface (80 degrees F.), but encounter an upwelling sixty feet down and the temp can drop 15–20 degrees. In a meteorological twist of fate, the best months to see hammerheads—June, July, and August—sit smack dab in the midst of the May through December rainy season, when seas are the roughest, currents are the strongest, and water is the murkiest. Though visibility is sometimes better when you drop your face in your cereal bowl, it is often shockingly good at Cocos too, even in the face of rain and runoff from the island. As a general rule visibility ranges from fifty to eighty feet, but it can easily exceed that since, at Cocos, rules are often broken and the only constant is change. Divers have pulled up to a site during a driving rain, glanced with dismay at the brown water ringing the island, then plopped overboard to clear blue water with viz of one hundred feet or more.

For a long time—and still—Cocos was the stuff of mystery and legend. Word first got back to the dive community via sporadic reports from yachties, who casually mentioned a rock three hundred miles north of the northern Galapagos Islands of Wolf and

A trumpetfish in its golden phase attempts to hide behind a leather bass. The long, thin trumpetfish uses its body shape to blend in with branches of sea fans, and to hide behind larger fish. It can change its color and position to blend into the background, and is often seen drifting in a vertical position, head down. It is an ambush predator.

A rainbow casts an ethereal glow over this Costa Rican tropical rainforest.

Darwin that boiled with sharks and other big pelagics. But yachties weren't the first sailors to ply past Cocos. Pirates gave the island its name, calling it Isla del Cocos for its abundant coconut palms. And, depending on how far toward legend you are willing to lean, these pirates may or may not have dumped their share of loot on the island. Among the purported spoils, a life-sized statue of the Virgin Mary, gem-encrusted and made of solid gold.

Plenty were willing to lend credence to faded maps and rumors, and some dedicated their lives to finding treasure on the island. August Gissler, a German sailor, began his personal quest in 1889, tortured by his own firm belief and the occasional cryptic clue. Carved on a palm tree, Gissler found the less-than-helpful words, "The Bird is Gone." Twenty years later, Gissler left too, none the richer though more titled, having been appointed, for a time, governor of the island.

There aren't many dive sites on Cocos, but now they too have become legend. Dive mangrove-covered Manuelita Island, and you might see a school of hundreds of hammerhead sharks. Dive it a second time, and the current might sweep you through hundreds of

Schools of hundreds of hammerhead sharks can be encountered off certain tropical seamounts. Scientists believe that sharks disperse at night, then return to seamounts by following the magnetic fields created by ancient lava flows. Molten lava which has seeped through cracks in the sea floor creates ridges of magnetic intensity, which the sharks may follow like roads.

Whitetip reef sharks swarm at night, surrounding and trapping a fish under a coral mound.

whitetip reef sharks. Descend along the craggy sea-mount known as Alcyone (named after the Cousteau Society boat) and in the deeps (the shallowest portion of the seamount crests at ninety feet) you might find mobula rays, courting marbled rays, monstrous yellow-fin tuna, or a whale shark. Dirty Rock may be the most reliable site in the world for hammerhead shark sightings-cum-overwhelmings—lucky divers have seen schools of one thousand or more.

These days, many of these divers are lucky because they are also properly equipped. Divers have long approached hammerheads at Cocos, and else-where, only to have entire schools of the magnificent fish vaporize at the first sound of bubbles. Only a few liveaboards have exclusive rights to Cocos, and boats like the *Undersea Hunter* and the *Sea Hunter* have accommodated for the shark's aversion to bubbles by offering bubble-less nitrox rebreathers, and training and certification in their use during the thirty-six-hour crossing and ensuing dives at the island.

Though Cocos Island steals much of Costa Rica's thunder, the mainland offers Big Fish and little fish too, without the need to stockpile dramamine. In the north, there's the Gulf of Papagayo. In the south is the more remote Osa Peninsula. Both areas offer a nice counter to demanding Cocos. Here you *can* drift in still, warm waters over reefs (but don't expect Caribbean-quality coral; what you'll mostly find are patchy reefs heavy on cup corals with scattered bits of sponge, algae, and barnacles). Within the Gulf of Papagayo, you can spend a two-tank morning diving some of the sixty-plus local spots—Sorpreso (Surprise), Virador (Outlook), Cabeza de Mono (Monkey Head)—none more than thirty minutes away, then repair for an afternoon of lolling about on any one of a number of lovely beaches. Playa del Coco, Playa Hermosa, Playa Ocotal, and Flamingo Bay have all the comforts—resorts, B&Bs, restau-rants, dive shops and lots of easy dives—and varied marine life, from whitetip reef sharks, to snapper, jacks, Moorish idols, king angelfish, and moray eels. You won't be alone, you won't swim with hundreds of hammerheads, and when you surface you'll know

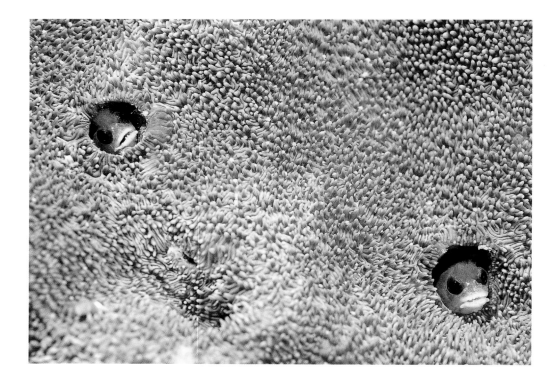

precisely what century you're in, though you may not know where you're having dinner.

If you yearn for a bit more wildness, there's a happy compromise. Divers can venture out from the gulf for day and overnight trips to the Catalina Islands and the Bat Islands. While it's unfair to niche any open ocean spot, the Catalina Islands are noted primarily for manta rays, the Bat Islands mainly for large bull sharks.

ABOVE , TOP: Two blennies peer out from their homes in a coral colony. They are using abandoned worm tubes as homes.

ABOVE: Two color phases of the guinea fowl puffer, the yellow and normal phase, are shown here.

A whitetip reef shark is being cleaned by a goby. These sharks are often found resting in caves during the day. The goby will wander over the shark's body in search of parasites.

The Osa Peninsula, jutting out at the terminus of Drake Bay at Costa Rica's southern end near Panama, is more famous among eco-trekkers than divers, and that is the diver's loss. Yes, here there is dry-land—actually decidedly moist—access to the lush Corcovado National Park. But there is also access to Caño Island Biological Reserve, home to a diverse range of marine life—manta rays, bull sharks, sea turtles, garden eels—and the best visibility (fifty to sixty feet, with peaks of eighty-plus) on mainland Costa Rica.

It is important to remember too that thousands of eco-trekkers can't be wrong. Costa Rica is one of those places where limiting your adventures to the water is a sad mistake. Terra firma magic runs the gamut, from wild rivers to howler monkeys, and Jesus Christ lizards that scurry upright across still waters as if dashing across glass. The Costa Rican government has set aside vast tracts of land in an impressive preservation system—over 27 percent of Costa Rica is protected—and outfitters have blossomed like dandelions to take you to these places. Chirripo National Park, and a chance to hike to the top of Costa Rica's tallest peak (12,600 feet). Exploring the vast cave system of Barra Honda National Park. Following the jungle trails of geo-thermically popping Rincon de la Vieja National Park, skirting vapor geysers and muddy pools—

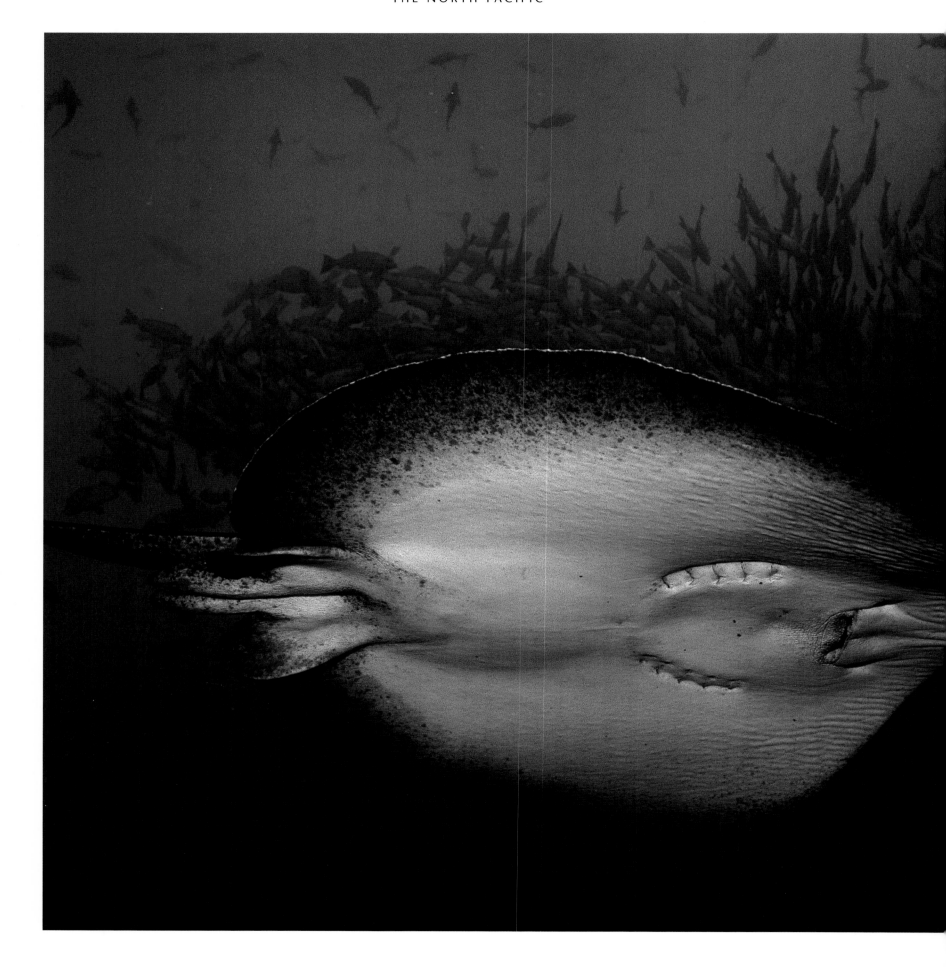

torched from below by superheated gases—that spit and bubble like pasty beans left on the stove too long. Heading into the rare and beautiful Monteverde Cloud Forest Reserve, a mist-shrouded, ephemeral place, whose beauty remains untainted by the New Agers and Deadhead castaways who have adopted the place.

There is even opportunity to explore Cocos Island, though at least one person has disappeared while doing so, so wandering off alone isn't encouraged. Cocos Island is equally wild as its underwater shores—cackling frigatebirds, plants growing on plants growing on plants, spiders, feral pigs. There's rocky shoreline to poke around. Or hike to the island's two-thousand-foot summit, which doesn't sound like much until you've personally fought your way through suction mud, thick foliage, and thicker humidity. Or wander along the river bed that meanders into Chatham Bay, gazing at the names etched in the otherwise smooth boulders, some of the carvings over one hundred years old.

Huge marbled rays are often seen around the pinnacles and seamounts off Cocos Island.

Costa Rica's mainland waters suffer from familiar problems: overfishing, uncontrolled development, water pollution, loss of valuable wetlands. And Cocos isn't untouched. Though the island was declared a marine reserve in 1992 (and a national park before that), and fishing is forbidden in nearshore waters, longliners, poachers, and shark finners have made their mark. Once plentiful, the ranks of Galapagos sharks have been sorely thinned.

It has been argued that discovery brings ruin. Taking an even more extreme outlook, physicist Werner Heisenberg claimed that to observe is to disturb. Merely seeing something affects the thing seen.

But to observe is also to appreciate. And seeing a place like Cocos Island instills in the observer a realization that in Nature, in the best of circumstances, man is nothing more than observer. Not everybody gets it. Believing he owned Cocos Island, when treasure hunter August Gissler died he bequeathed part of the island to oceanographer William Beebe. No one truly owns Cocos, or any wild place. Proof of this, and Gissler's real treasure, surrounded him.

Picturesque waterfalls like this one are what help to make Cocos Island the wettest island in the world.

THE GALAPAGOS ISLANDS

A day among the Galapagos Islands might unfold like this. See dolphins and orcas frolic in dawn's first light. Dive with rays, sharks, and vast shimmering schools of striped salema, a fish, like many in the Galapagos, found nowhere else. Watch sea lions dart about, vainly attempting to unravel stoic, imperturbable marine iguanas. Stand at a cliff's edge, swept by the hoot, whistle, caw, and shriek of thousands of blue-footed and masked boobies, waved albatross, frigate birds, mockingbirds, shearwaters, and Galapagos hawks. Observe a tortoise ancient enough to have observed Charles Darwin himself. Watch the sun purple the sky, darkening a pod of sperm whales. Slip into sleep knowing that your dreams could be no stranger. As Herman Melville wrote, "I know not whether I am not the occasional victim of optical delusion concerning the Galapagos."

A masked booby surveys a rainbow created by surf emanating from a blowhole.

252

Numerous marine iguanas bask in the sun after swimming for algae on Fernandina Island. They all turn the same way, to thermoregulate in the sun.

Endangered giant Galapagos tortoises confront each other in a territorial display.

PAGES 256–257: Seahorses are among the most bizarre of fishes. They are masters of camouflage, and use their tails to curl around branches of sea fans and coral trees. Their method of breeding is very unusual, as the male broods eggs in a pouch and actually gives birth to hundreds of tiny, swimming seahorses. This large seahorse rests among the yellow polyps of a black coral tree.

The Galapagos are not merely a dive destination. They are, as Darwin observed, a living experiment unlike any other. Here, six hundred miles off the coast of Ecuador, scattered among thirteen large islands, six small islands, forty-two islets, and innumerable rocks and pinnacles, you have the Nature Channel on the fritz. A small bird, slightly larger than a tennis ball, plops on the backs of bigger birds and pecks them until they bleed, and then drinks their blood. A gull, the only one in the world, hunts at night. Below the water amphibious iguanas that undulate gracefully with great powerful arcs, swimming from rock to rock to gnaw algal fuzz from their surface. And a fish with full, pouty, ruby-red lips, propped up in the sand on fins that look like gnarled limbs, lunges, when need be, for critters it has ferreted out with the highly developed lure in a hornlike protuberance jutting from its head. Nearly half the Galapagos birds and insects, 32 percent of the plants, and 90 percent of the reptiles exist nowhere else. Melville again: "What outlandish beings are these?"

Look beyond the Timothy Leary graphics and each creature is, for better or worse, adapted to its world, which, of course, is precisely how Darwin came to write *On the Origin of Species by Natural Selection* and how the Galapagos gained their fame. The marine iguana, *Amblyrhyncus cristatus*—poster animal for these volcanic isles—simply did what it had to do to survive. There was not enough food on the volcanic islands, so the lizards that survived moved beneath the waves where food did exist.

Such innovation makes for a magical place. Spanish voyagers would dub the islands "Galapagos," an old Spanish word for a type of riding saddle that resembled the shells of the giant lumbering tortoises they found on the islands. But they also called the islands "Encantadas"—enchanted. *Enchanted* has a serene ring to it, but make no mistake, for divers the Galapagos is a buzz of challenges. The vast array of sea life is partly the work of natural selection, but it also results from the combination of several major ocean currents that converge on this archipelago with train wreck subtlety. Colliding with the volcanic islands,

the currents sweep up from the depths, generating a massive cold-water upwelling that is broth for reams of life. Those same currents swirl and wrap the rocks with unpredictability outshone only by their strength. Depending on its genesis—equatorial sun-baked surface waters or frigid waters from the deep—and the season, the water can be warm (75–78 degrees F.) or chilling (high 50s, low 60s). As a general rule,

A colorful Sally Lightfoot crab hides in plain sight on a lava arch.

The bizarre red-lipped batfish has bright red lips, and hops around on its habitat of rubble bottom with its modified fins. It can move short distances very quickly.

This closeup view of the colorful mantle of a scallop shows its numerous blue eyes. Some scallops are free-swimming, and can propel themselves through the water by squirting water. This scallop, however, is rooted to the rock upon which it has grown.

the water is warmest at the northern end of the archipelago, and the best months for warm waters run from December through May, when the weather is oven hot and the seas are calm. Waters are typically coolest at the southern and far-western ends of the archipelago, with June through September being the coolest months. As a general rule, visibility runs from 50 to 75 feet.

As a general rule, you can throw out all the general rules, because you can experience all the above conditions in any given month, and sometimes in a single dive. Powerful currents can erase visibility from one hundred feet to three feet in the same dive. The western sides of many of the islands have colder water, courtesy of an equatorial undercurrent sweeping cold water up from the depths. So, the water may or may not be cold, visibility may or may not be good, but the currents almost always cook, and they can surprise—divers have been unceremoniously swept down to one hundred feet, then yanked back to just below the surface in a blink. This is not meant to startle, only alert. Be experienced and be prepared. For one thing, a surface signaling device is a must.

Those same currents that can toss you like the inconsequential flotsam that you are, also mix together tropical fish species from the north, coldwater species from the southern temperate waters of Peru, and Chile and Antarctica, and Indo-Pacific species from the west. And they deliver the nutrients that bring together all the players in the food web.

And a bizarre cast it is. Here on the equator there are Galapagos penguins, cousins to the penguins of South Africa, Chile, and Argentina, stout little barristers who wobble about the shore, then plunge into the water, morphing into black and white torpedoes. There are horned moray eels with yellow eyes, free-swimming Panamic Green Morays, underwater rocks festooned with grazing lizards, and the hopping, lunging, horned, red-lipped batfish. Viewing the great tortoises on terra firma, Darwin noted that the aged beasts appeared to be "inhabitants of another planet." One can only imagine his gawping had a red-lipped batfish lurched into his view.

The waters of the Galapagos are home to a host of familiar characters too. In shallow waters, sweeping schools of horse-eyed jacks and steel pompanos,

and playful sea lions. Out deeper, schools of skipjack tuna, wahoo, bottlenose dolphin, silky, Galapagos and whale sharks, manta and eagle rays, and dozens upon dozens of green turtles. And the sinuous swarming masses of hammerheads for which the Galapagos are renowned, especially around the remote northern islands of Wolf and Darwin. This combination of the endemic and the plenty makes for very special dives. Cousin's Rock, an innocuous stone sticking thirty feet out of the water, may be one of the most electrifying dives in the world, swarming with fantastic balls of endemic salemas numbering in the thousands, plundered by veering, darting sea lions, a feeding frenzy that breaks only briefly for a mid-afternoon siesta, then continues on its timeless play.

Better still, much of the wildlife exhibits an odd tameness, registering man's approach with the disinterest of a dozing porch hound. Wrought first by isolation and then by protection, many Galapagos denizens don't know to fear man. How can you be afraid of what, at first, you've never seen, and what you now see so much of, trumping along with cameras, binoculars, and wide-brimmed hats? In the interest of

science, Darwin reached into a hole and yanked at the tail of a land iguana. "At this it was greatly astonished," wrote Darwin, "and soon shuffled up to see what was the matter; and then stared me in the face, as much as to say, 'What made you pull my tail?'"

The only way to dive the Galapagos is by live-aboard (liveaboard dive boats offer land walks, too). Nature, and Man, demand it. Though many associate

The volcanic origins of the Galapagos Islands are seen in this view of Pinnacle Rock, from Bartolome Island.

Undisturbed and unafraid of humans, a young Galapagos sea lion yawns at sunset.

the Galapagos only with the larger, better known islands of Isabela, Santa Cruz, Fernandina, Santiago, San Cristobal, and Española, the archipelago—three thousand square miles of land in all— is actually a sprawling assemblage of smaller rocks, humps, and pinnacles scattered across fifty thousand square miles of Pacific Ocean. It's worth noting that two of the premier dive destinations, the islands of Darwin and Wolf, are about 110 and 90 miles northwest of Isabela, respectively, a long swim in any kind of current.

You couldn't go it alone even if you wanted to. The Galapagos falls under all sorts of preservationist umbrellas. It has been designated a World Heritage Site, 97 percent of the islands are national park, the sea around them marine reserve. For the visitor, the result is simple. Diver or no, the only way to see the Galapagos is by licensed boat with a licensed guide.

Above and below the water, this is done, of course, in the name of protection. In the beginning, the Galapagos were protected by isolation alone. The islands were far from the mainland and outside traditional shipping lanes. But with time various pirates, whalers, and navies were yanked off course, encountering the islands by happenstance, courtesy of powerful currents, thick fogs, and strong winds. They weren't overly impressed. "The islands are desert and bear no fruite," noted one English captain, but they did make a note of their location and the happy assemblage of fresh food. By the seventeenth century, visiting vessels sailed away from the Galapagos fat with provisions, their holds filled with tortoises, stacked upside down and alive.

Man's hand has weighed heavily on the islands ever since. We have, courtesy of happenstance and intention, introduced almost eight hundred foreign species to the island, not a good thing in a place where life is delicately balanced. Ships brought the goats and pigs, whose wild descendants continue to wreak havoc. Wild goats strip vegetation bare. Wild dogs kill iguanas and young tortoises. Feral pigs eat turtle eggs and hatchlings. On Pinzon Island, black rats have killed every tortoise hatched in the wild in the past hundred years.

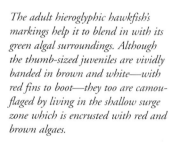

The adult hieroglyphic hawkfish's markings help it to blend in with its green algal surroundings. Although the thumb-sized juveniles are vividly banded in brown and white—with red fins to boot—they too are camouflaged by living in the shallow surge zone which is encrusted with red and brown algaes.

Man hasn't left the waters untouched either. Technically, fishing within the Galapagos waters is limited to the islands' artisanal fishermen, who fish largely with old-fashioned methods like hand-held lines. But many believe rampant corruption has government officials, for a price, turning their backs on countless illegal vessels. The numbers of sharks in the Galapagos have fallen precipitously—the sometimes unnerving swarms that greeted divers twenty years ago are no more, many of them victims of long-lining and finning. Ecuador and its neighbors are not wealthy countries. In 1992, when a prize species of sea cucumber was "discovered" littering the bottoms off the islands, a fishing frenzy saw the sea cucumber decimated, fishermen flocking out from the mainland to cash in on the Asian desire for the slug-like animal, purported to be an aphrodisiac. Even the tortoises became inadvertently involved. When park officials imposed restrictions on the sea cucumber take, irate fishermen butchered several score of the tortoises on Isabela Island. Man, apparently, is the only species that refuses to find its niche and coexist.

Many fear that even the eco-friendly hordes are having a negative impact on the islands. Tourism has increased roughly 700 percent over the past twenty years. Mainland Ecuadorians, seeing the relatively high standard of living enjoyed by their island countrymen as a result of tourism, have flocked to the islands. In 1960 the population of the Galapagos was two thousand. By 1996, it was at least fourteen thousand. So it is that a sudden downpour overwhelms an already strapped sewage system, filling the streets with raw waste that washes into the sea. Subtler processes are at work too. A liveaboard anchors off an island for the night. Its blazing lights attract insects. When the ship pulls anchor the next

OPPOSITE: A green sea turtle sleeps below a black coral tree. They are the only species of turtle that mate in the Galapagos, and are thought to be more abundant here than anywhere else on Earth.

BELOW: The Galapagos penguin is the only penguin to live on the equator. It has survived in the Galapagos because of the cold water upwelling there.

PAGES 264–265: A huge school of barracuda swims easily in a strong current. The cold-water upwellings at the Galapagos Islands nourish an abundance of marine life.

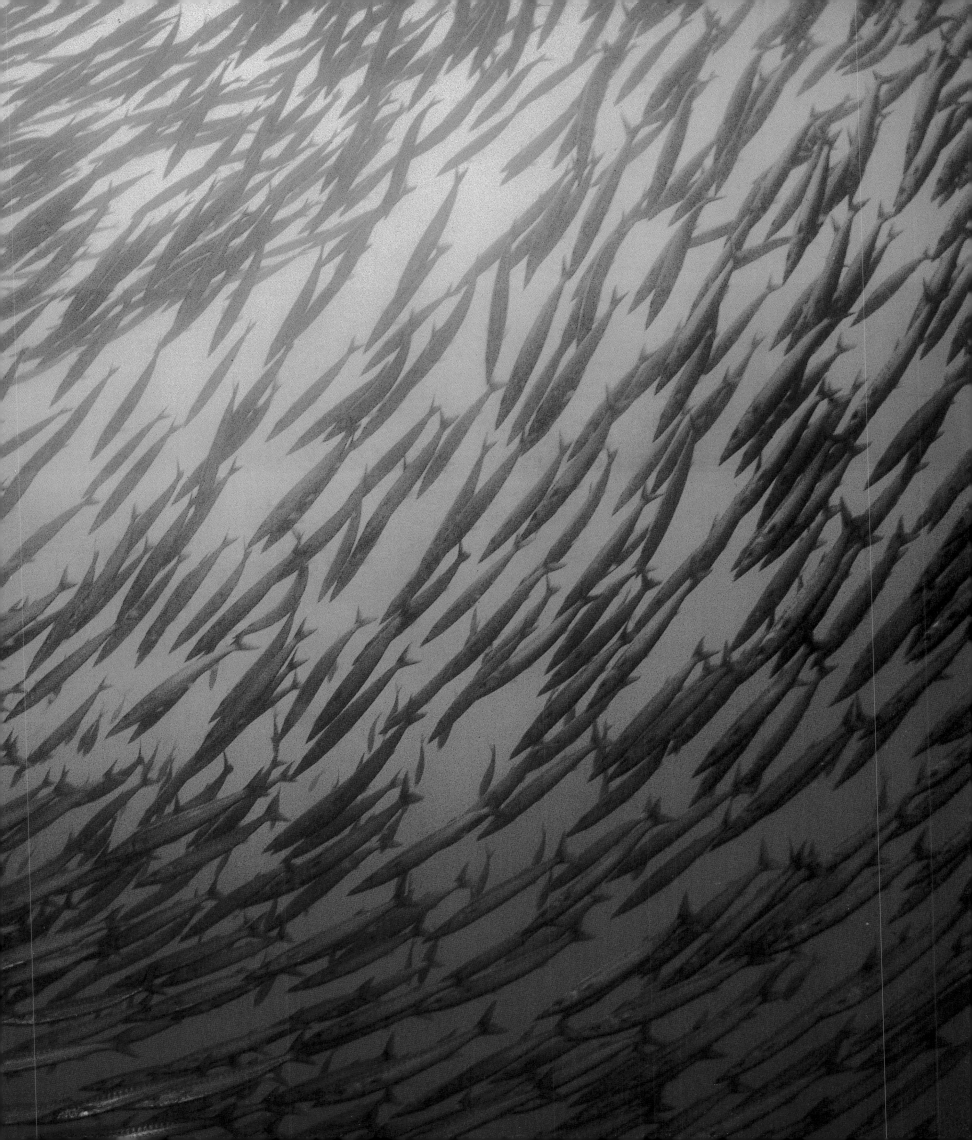

A Galapagos barnacle blenny peers out of its home in a red sponge.

BELOW: The tiger nudibranch of the eastern tropical Pacific specializes in eating other nudibranchs. It actively pursues other nudibranchs by following their slime trails, and then casts out a blue net from its mouth to ensnare its prey.

A group of whitetip reef sharks gather in shallow water, probably to mate.

PAGES 268–269: A school of golden cowrays swims into the distance.

PAGE 269, BOTTOM: The bravo clinid, a type of blenny, is found only in the Galapagos Islands and Malpelo Island, off Colombia.

morning, those insects travel on to the next island, throwing in new imbalance.

Man isn't entirely to blame for the problems in the Galapagos. In 1997–98 an El Niño clobbered the islands, causing mass casualties among much of the wildlife. But the islands are now slowly recovering, and there are other bright spots. It is true that the rats of Pinzon Island have killed every turtle hatched in the wild. But it is also true that scientists at the Charles Darwin Research Station on Santa Cruz Island have successfully collected, reared, and reintroduced tortoises to Pinzon Iisland. And in 1998 Ecuador—recognizing the islands' fragility and the importance of tourist dollars—passed the Special Law for the Galapagos. Among other items, the law restricts immigration to the islands, expands the size of the marine reserve, and increases the percentage of tourist revenue going to the national park.

Man may, after all, find his niche.

THE NORTH ATLANTIC

FLORIDA

A perfect replica—same outsize jaw, same carnivorous look, same silver needle frame, only this juvenile barracuda, perfectly formed, is four inches long. Bright youth with teeth and an attitude, it hovers in sleepy-warm mangrove water, black eyes absorbing its surroundings. When the time comes, this young buck will swim confidently from this mangrove on the backside of Summerland Key into the Atlantic Ocean a half-mile distant. For now, though, in this quiet hush of mangrove, no one is aware of its glorious existence.

PAGES 270–271: Fire coral is named for its painful sting upon contact. It is typically mustard-colored, and can assume many shapes, sometimes covering other corals. Bahamas.

ABOVE: Don Demaria, a former spearfisherman, now devotes much of his life to saving giant Jewfish swimming in mangroves.

RIGHT: Although grunts (with blue and gold stripes) and goatfish (with whiskers) are only distantly related, they often school together, thereby benefitting from safety in numbers and food items that are disturbed during feeding.

ABOVE: Caribbean manatees or sea cows come into Florida's warm water rivers and springs during cold winter months. They are endangered, threatened in Florida mainly by recreational boat traffic.

This loggerhead sea turtle was a familiar resident on an underwater wreck for many years. Sadly, fishermen have plundered the wreck and the turtle is no longer seen there. The loggerhead sea turtle is a vanishing species, now on the list of endangered marine animals.

When it comes to diving Florida, most people think of the reefs of the Keys. But the mangroves—pewter still, bathhouse warm, childhood nursery to a plethora of marine denizens—are the perfect counter to this myopic thinking. Yes, the reefs of the Keys are dazzling and a diving must. But for the diver who knows better, Florida offers a Disney-esque repertoire of opportunity. If you have never hovered motionless in sooty-golden water, eyeball to eyeball with a silver stiletto, you are missing something.

Geography ensures that Florida offers reams of diving possibility. Florida has more coastline than any state except Alaska. And diving opportunity doesn't just abound along the shoreline. Florida also has the densest concentration of freshwater springs in the world—silent, surreal, tree-shrouded pools so clear that, falling to their bottoms, you'll be yanking on your BCD tabs hoping to engage your parachute. Northern Florida's interior is honeycombed with entrances to some of the largest underwater cave systems in the world, including the Bonnet, Telford, and Peacock systems. Labyrinths of darkness and spectral sunlight, many of the caves (and springs) are centered near Branford, the legitimately proclaimed cave diving capital of the world.

There's plenty more. Moving back offshore, the Gulf Coast of Florida—from Pensacola on the Panhandle on down through Sarasota, St. Petersburg, Clearwater, Tarpon Springs, and Port Richey—offers diving in the Gulf of Mexico (mostly boat dives due to shallow inshore waters). Hopping across to the East Coast, you might drift dive off West Palm Beach, soaring in the current, crystal clarity (visibility of 250 or 300 feet is not uncommon), and marine life of the Gulf Stream where it swings in close to the coast.

Summer's calm seas see the Gulf Stream, and its warm waters, veer in closest to Palm Beach. Winter's rougher waters are colder, but it's considered the best dive time since prevailing northeast winds slow the Stream down a tad and the big pelagics—sea turtles, leopard rays, schools of amberjack and bar jack—move in closer to shore. This is a rare opportunity to touch something wondrous, a blue river of nearly

These blackcap basslets feed on plankton along deep coral reef walls.

incomprehensible mass. Sweeping past Palm Beach, the Gulf Stream carries roughly twenty-five times more water than all the rivers of the world combined.

Palm Beach is also home to one of the largest artificial reef systems in the world; in short, wrecks.

Jellies provide shelter to juveniles of many species of fish. Here, two juvenile jacks live among a jellie's stinging tentacles.

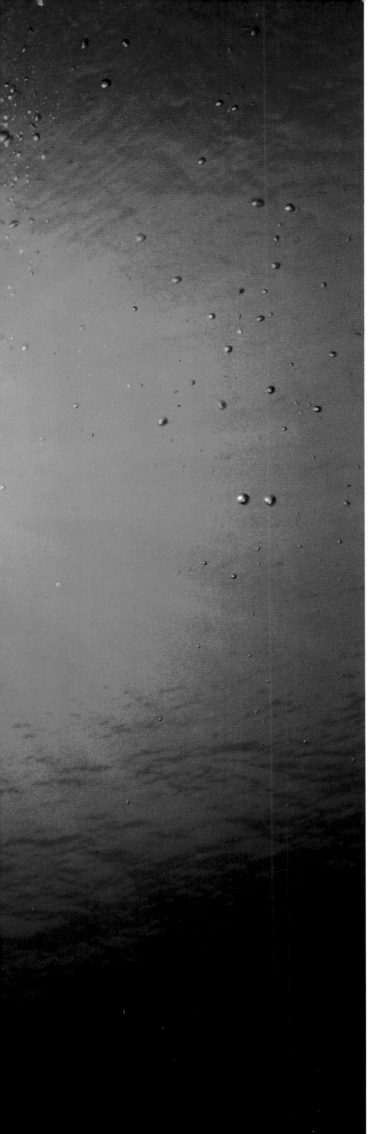

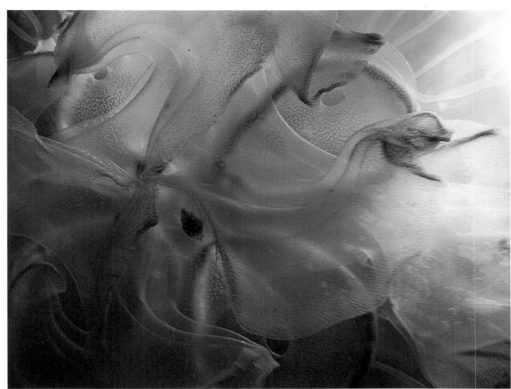

Just 1.5 miles off Palm Beach Inlet— a ten-minute boat ride—lie the wrecks of the *Mizpah* and the *Amarylis*. The *Mizpah*, a 189-foot Greek luxury liner, is a great novice wreck dive—doors and other obstructions have been removed, making it easy for divers (and turtles, groupers, and snapper porkfish)—to weave in and out of the ship.

The checklist continues. Off Fort Pierce, Florida's best spot for easily accessible beach diving (most of northern Florida's reefs lay well offshore, requiring a boat trip), three major reef lines lie within three hundred yards of shore. Off Daytona Beach, eighty-five feet down, bar and amberjack hovering along its top decks, grouper lurking inside, sits the 441-foot wreck of the World War II vessel the USS *Mindanao*. Off Miami, courtesy of the Key Biscayne Artificial Reef Site, lies a potpourri of wrecks making for some of the country's best wreck diving—the *Lakeland*, the *Orion*, the *Hopper Barge*, the *Blue Fire*. And, of course, moving down into the Keys (Key Largo), there's the world-renowned John Pennekamp Coral Reef State Park, the United States' very first underwater coral reef park (established in 1960) and still magic despite heavy use.

A moon jellyfish languidly floats in the waters of the Gulf Stream.

277

Large colonies of brain coral are common in Florida and the Caribbean.

Point is, most divers beeline straight for the Keys and, while this is understandable given what beckons, it's too bad too, because the rest of Florida offers plenty of dive magic.

Of course, the Keys are Florida's main draw for good reason. The dry stats read like this. A chain of 822 low-lying islands, the Keys stretch for over 220 miles, arcing between the Gulf of Mexico and the Atlantic Ocean. For divers, the stat of import is simple: stringing along beside these islands lies the last great coral reef system our country possesses, a soup of life. To dive the reefs of the Keys is to understand that there is no limit to shape, color or imagination.

The outer reefs of the Keys are typically separated from the islands by a shelf of seagrass beds, patch reefs, and sand expanse. A short boat ride plops you on top of them, in a place so blue at times you can't figure out whether to swim in the sea or the sky. The climate is gloriously subtropical; most of the rain falls in spring and summer, and even when it does, it doesn't steal one whit of pleasure from the islands' languid largesse. Better still, a sense of fun hangs over the Keys like one of those silly drink umbrellas. The Keys were discovered by Ponce de Leon in 1513 as he searched for the fountain of youth, and in a strange sense, he found it. And, whether you're gazing languidly at it from a white sand beach, or total-focus immersed in it thirty miles out to sea, Water is King. It fills the eyes at almost every glance, and sweeps the islands with its salt-tinged caress. In fact, the Keys barely separate themselves from the water at all. The highest point in the chain, on Windley Key, is only about twenty feet above sea level.

Each island has a different feel, from the bustle of Key Largo, the largest of the Keys, and home to Pennecamp and the Key Largo National Marine Sanctuary, to the small town torpor of Tavernier and Islamorada. Marathon Key is a well-kept diving secret; over-anxious divers stop farther north, or blow right through town in their hurry to get to Key West.

You can pick the flavor that best suits you. But offshore the Keys all share a similar riot of sea life, and the dive spots liberally sprinkling themselves from north to south have sent many a diver home dopey with glee—Northern Patch, Turtle Rocks, Carysfort Trench, French Reef, Sand Island, Alligator Reef, Sombrero Light, Pelican Shoal, Western Sambo, and Sand Key.

The Keys receive the largesse of two oceans. They are a mixing pot, and breeding ground, for Atlantic and Gulf Coast species. Hard and soft corals, sea fans, sponges, feather stars, spiny lobster, pink shrimp, snapper, grouper, cobia, red-tailed triggerfish, hulking Jewfish—they are all here, and plenty more.

Sun, sand, sin, and a sea sonnet of life. For these reasons, and others, the Keys aren't bereft of divers, or for that matter boaters, fishermen, tomato-red tourists, seekers, seers, and outright weirdos. One-tenth the size of Australia's Great Barrier Reef, the Keys host roughly ten times the number of visitors annually, and their impact on the islands, and the reefs, has been substantial. You can drive the length of Key West in ten minutes (without traffic), but the thin Key West phone book has room enough for ten yellow pages listing dive shops.

This onslaught, and the great mass of South Florida just to the north, has had serious impacts on the marine environment. The residues of South Florida, and its rabbit warren growth—6.3 million people now, a projected 12 million by 2050—wash into the Florida Bay and down to the Keys, kicking large parts of the reefs smack in the teeth. Effluent, sedimentation, algal overgrowth brought on by spikes in suspended nutrients, they all kill already fragile

corals. Fishermen—and divers—hook, spear, net, and otherwise yank tons of fish from the ocean, often before their reproductive time. Severe impacts are felt as far away as the once remote Dry Tortugas, 70 miles west of Key West and 140 miles from mainland Florida. Scientific studies have documented what divers here have seen first hand. There are fewer fish in the Tortugas, and they are smaller, too; the average grouper in the Tortugas now weighs only 9 pounds, compared to 22.5 pounds in the past.

Miami suburbanites and visiting divers aren't entirely to blame. In an unnerving and fascinating display of the interconnectedness of things, in 1993

This giant grouper is blithely unperturbed by the diver behind it and the photographer before it—it's visiting the dentist and having its teeth cleaned by cleaner wrasses.

American alligators once dominated the wetlands of the southeast. Since the 1870s, approximately 10 million gators have been killed for their hides, dramatically altering the ecology of Florida. Since protection as an endangered species, they have made a modest comeback and are now listed as "threatened."

scientists recorded a sudden drastic drop in salinity and dissolved oxygen on a small reef off Key Largo. The culprit, Midwestern floodwaters. In short, oil dumped in Chicago, fertilizer sprayed in Kansas, it can all end up in the Keys. These fragile and beautiful reefs are, in effect, just downstream from a host of dumping grounds.

Efforts are well underway to preserve the place. The Florida Keys National Marine sanctuary—government scientists and bureaucrats laboring to preserve and restore damaged reef—now encompasses 3,674 square miles of coastal ocean, a swath stretching from waters south of Miami all the way out to the Dry Tortugas. The hope is that marine life is resilient. Provide clean water, good habitat, and sound management, and the reefs will come back. The reality is that substantial damage has been done. The most miraculous management plan won't restore the reefs within our lifetime.

The Keys, however, remain a spectacular and magical place. Close your eyes and imagine finning slowly over a four-hundred-year-old coral forest in the Dry Tortugas, a crowded Hobbitt wonderland of myriad shapes and sizes—corals that resemble mushrooms and cones, corals spread as enormous plates and fans, corals that look like butterleaf lettuce and brains. Tucked within this kaleidoscopic hodgepodge, fans and anemones gently sway. In the water column, adult barracuda drift like thick, silver darts, out-thrust jaws larger now, but still as pugnacious and world-be-damned-looking as those of their juvenile counterparts swimming in the mangroves.

And that's just what you'll enjoy beneath the tangle of waves. Because as any diver knows, it's not just about diving. There is an easy natural magic to the Keys that is hard to finger, but you might approach it if you shut your eyes again, this time while standing on a boat dock, awaiting an advancing squall at no particular Key. First stillness, and the basting press of tropical sun on your pores. Then rolling thunder and the first puff of cool glancing across your knuckles. Palm fronds click, the air goes cooler, cooler, then fat, warm raindrops begin to plock down and, in the warm downpour, you are left to inhale the sweet smell of damp wood and the drumming of the rain running in ribbon-sheets across the water to ghost sailboats.

OPPOSITE: This teardrop crab has coverd its body with sponges to blend into its background.

LEFT: Don't be fooled by the fragile appearance of these finger-sized flower coral polyps. The small white bumps are armed with batteries of stinging nematocysts with which they feed on passing plankton.

THE CARIBBEAN

The fish come in torrents, a sinuous blue river of commuters flooding along the edge of the reef, jerking occasionally right or left en masse, as if a lone puppeteer has given them a single twitch. Evening coming, the water is slowly shadowing. Kick down past the end of the shallow reef and enter a vast cathedral of blue. Water as clear and warm as Indian summer nights, diving here is like floating through a viscous dream.

LEFT: A meeting of clouds and sun creates a rainbow palette over the Caribbean Sea. Saba, Dutch Antilles.

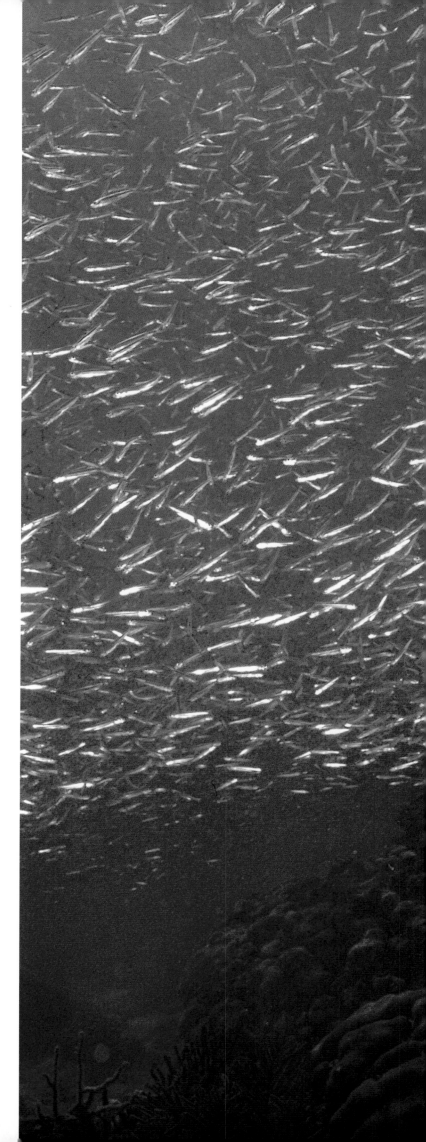

RIGHT: A school of baitfish blocks out the view over a shallow coral reef. Virgin Gorda, British Virgin Islands.

Welcome to Bonaire's Bari Reef, or for that matter pretty much any dive spot in the Caribbean, where the water is warm—84 to 86 degrees F., with the occasional cold front from October through April—and the diving is, with few exceptions, easy. Admittedly Bonaire, a tiny island fifty miles north of Venezuela, elevates diving ease to ridiculous heights. Most of the island's reefs are a few strokes from shore, and descending to them is only slightly more difficult than sleepwalking. And, like many Caribbean destinations, Bonaire's dive establishments have gone a step farther to make diving even more convenient. At the Buddy Dive Resort you can wheel your car under a palm-thatched roof, chuck your spent tanks, load up new ones, and be gone in the time it takes to read this sentence.

True, the Caribbean is not undiscovered, but this has its perks. Sailing aimlessly? In the British Virgin Islands, enterprising dive operators will meet you at your boat, provide gear and tanks if necessary, take you to choice dive spots, and return you when

LEFT: This ray hovers above a school of yellowtail snapper, providing a good view of its flattened body; the eyes are located on the top of the head, and a set of gills and a formidable mouth can be found on the underside. Stingrays are potentially dangerous animals; the barb at the base of the tail can be whipped forward with considerable force, causing great pain to a wader's unwary foot or leg. The best way to avoid a stingray barb is by shuffling rather than stepping in the surf. Stingray City, Grand Cayman.

ABOVE: Stingray City in Grand Cayman is a place where anyone with a snorkel and a mask can become acquainted with huge, six-foot stingrays looking for handouts The stingrays swarm over each diver in the group without hesitation, sometimes covering a diver so completely that the person disappears beneath their flapping wings. Stingray City, Grand Cayman.

OPPOSITE, LEFT: Divers swim along the famous coral wall of Grand Cayman. Marine life in Grand Cayman has been protected for many years, and this policy has created a virtual playground for giant groupers and other marine life now uncommon throughout other parts of the Caribbean, due to spearfishing and other activities. Grand Cayman.

OPPOSITE, RIGHT: Divers explore the waters beneath a catamaran dive boat. Virgin Gorda, British Virgin Islands.

PAGES 286–287: A pair of cleaning shrimp gain protection and food among the stinging tentacles of their host anemone. Roatan, Honduras.

done. Prefer to do it on your own? Dive sites in the BVI (and many other Caribbean islands) are clearly marked with brightly colored moorings. On Bonaire, dive outfitters leave filled tanks on the pier or beach so that if you wake at midnight with a hankering for the sea, that hankering can be slaked. Even Nature cooperates. The Cayman Islands offer some of the world's best wall-diving, and the geography of the three islands (Grand Cayman, Little Cayman, and Cayman Brac) ensures that divers can almost always find calm, protected walls to dive. Now it is not so difficult to figure why most every diver from the Midwest and East wants to dive the Caribbean, or has consummated that wish.

Familiarity may breed contempt, but looking down your nose at the Caribbean as overrun and overdived is both misinformed and a serious mistake. Certainly the names of many islands—Cozumel, Belize, the Bay Islands, Barbados, Bermuda, the Bahamas, the Caymans, Turks and Caicos—ring like overly familiar chimes. Yes, the Bahamas might feature

the glitter, schlock, and cruise ship gridlock of Freeport and Nassau. But the open-minded diver knows the islands are also home to more than a half-dozen varieties of dolphins, and Bimini and the White Sand Ridge region of the Little Bahama Banks offer the chance for stirring encounters with pods of spotted and bottlenose dolphins, and possibly the magical opportunity to observe mating, feeding, and cavorting in the wild. (Note the term "chance." Several dive operators offer these dolphin encounters, but they wisely make no promises.) Yes, Grand Cayman's Stingray City has received more ink, and more visits, than Graceland, but the wingtips of a southern stingray still move with the delicate grace of lace curtains tousled by a slight breeze. Prefer to encounter stingrays somewhere else? In June and July schools of as many as fifty eagle rays swoop along the walls of South Caicos. And on Gibb's Cay, operators from Grand Turk have developed a feeding area similar to Stingray City, where divers and snorkelers can enjoy stingrays. Sure, the U.S. Virgin Islands are over-

ABOVE, TOP AND BOTTOM: The granite boulders of The Baths on Virgin Gorda surround Devil's Bay. Snorkelers in sandy areas like this can find peacock flounders, flying gurnards, sand dollars, and a host of other animals which make sandy bottoms their home. Virgin Gorda, British Virgin Islands.

shallows, snorkelers are not left out. Roatan alone, the largest of the Bay Islands (a collective archipelago thirty-five miles off the coast of Honduras), has hundreds of shallow, snorkel-friendly fringe and patch reefs. Playa Kalki, Lagun, Cas Abou, Pelican Beach—on Curacao, snorkelers can enjoy the ocean in all its glory. Fat mushroom corals resembling collapsed drip castles, rainbow explosions of fish, and delicate seahorses clasped, black-eyed and stoic, to swaying sea fans can all be found in shallow waters close to shore.

The Caribbean has dozens of other offerings too. Fresh water cave diving (the Dominican Republic); the world's second longest stretch of barrier reef off Belize (outdone only by the Great Barrier Reef); Belize's famous Great Blue Hole (1,000 feet in diameter and 440 azure-feet deep); sheer vertical walls (the Cayman Islands); shark dives, dolphin dives, stingray dives, wreck dives. Within the vast spread of the Caribbean, the point is simple. Seek, and ye shall often find.

The Caribbean has its share of out of the way places too, plenty of them with terrific diving. Jutting three thousand feet out of the eastern Caribbean, high enough for a clear gander at the tourist spots of St. Maarten and St. Barts, the tiny island of Saba was barely accessible to the outside world until the 1960s, when a narrow airstrip was cleaved into a cliff. Today Saba remains an authentic dose of Caribbean life, where family graveyards dot back alleys, goats wander the streets, and nobody is in much of a rush to do anything. Book a dinner reservation at a local restaurant and the woman who picks you up at your hotel in a dented minivan may very well be the proprietor. Diving? Saba has some of the best and most varied diving in the Caribbean. The sheer steeps of the island above the water are mirrored below, with thrilling dives over towering cliffs smeared with colorful invertebrate life. Diamond Rock, a shallow pinnacle, is easily circumnavigated in a single dive, and during that dive it's possible to see nearly every type of Caribbean animal. Peruse the sandy bottom, and you'll have your best chance in the Caribbean of spotting the beautiful flying gurnard, a relative of the sea robin, endowed with enormous pectoral fins that it flares when alarmed.

commercialized and overrun. But on Virgin Gorda, in the far quieter BVI's (British Virgin Islands), you can enjoy an ethereal experience at The Baths, a granitic garden of giant boulders and shadowed tidal pools, the result of ancient volcanic upthrust.

No, it doesn't pay to be snotty about the Caribbean because its offerings are many.

Traveling with a loved one who doesn't dive? They won't feel left out. With plentiful warm, calm

ABOVE: *The Blue Hole in the Belize Barrier Reef, 1,000 feet across and 440 feet deep, is an ancient cave system which has collapsed. Belize Barrier Reef.*

A juvenile Spanish hogfish cleans two creole wrasse of parasites. As the hogfish matures, it switches its diet and its role on the coral reef. Ambergris Cay, Belize.

Also good news, on many of the smaller Caribbean islands if you don't like where you are a short jaunt will put you somewhere else. Most of St. Lucia's resorts are clustered to the north around the main city of Castries. There is fun diving here, but the island's best diving is in the south in the Soufriere region. Plenty of Castries-based dive boats give you the best of both worlds. St. Lucia is just twenty-four miles long. Boats from Castries reach the southern dive sites in a mere thirty to forty-five minutes.

Any assessment of Caribbean diving would be incomplete without mention of shark diving. Plenty of controversy broils around the practice, leaving two main schools of thought: shark feeding dives are unnatural and dangerous to divers and sharks, creating an armada of sharp-toothed predators conditioned to actively seek man's handouts, and if handouts

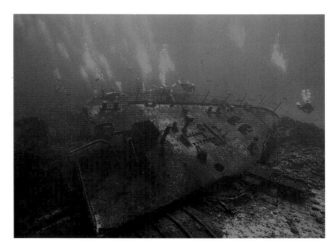

OPPOSITE: A school of grunts find shelter on the Sugar Wreck in the Bahamas.

ABOVE: Sunken vessels often become artificial reefs. The Sugar Wreck in the Bahamas is a haven for marine life, including schools of grunts and a couple of old loggerhead turtles. Bahamas.

LEFT: Shipwrecks become havens for marine life, and hold a curious attraction for some divers. The wreck of the Oro Verde, Grand Cayman.

aren't available, man himself; and, shark feeding harms neither shark nor man, and any opinion to the contrary is bunk and its disciples deserve to be fed to the sharks.

Let's leave the dickering to the many groups only too happy to get involved. Man's natterings aside, few things are as exciting as watching dozens of black-tip, Caribbean reef, hammerhead, and lemon sharks swirling before you, a ballet of clean lines, classic beauty, and attention-getting power. To see an eight-foot shark, jaw extended, tear loose a chunk of chumsicle is to intimately appreciate Nature's physical design, and Man's lowly place and prowess in that pantheon.

Tentacles of a giant anemone carry a venomous sting. San Blas Islands, Panama.

Two of the best-known shark feedings take place at Walker's Cay (a one-hundred-acre private island in the Abaco chain of the Bahamas) and Stuart's Cove on New Providence Island (also home to the Bahamian capital of Nassau). The success of those enterprises has fostered others. Grand Cayman now offers a shark dive at Shark Alley, a reef just outside the South Channel off the island's east end. Nor are the dives simply opportunity for mindless gawping. Some dives are preceded by educational sessions on topics ranging from shark behavior to physiology.

Whether shark feedings come or go will likely depend on the political results of debate. In Florida, the Florida Fish and Wildlife Conservation Commis-

sion has already voted to ban all fish feeding by divers in the state.

Also worth noting, and sadly, sometimes ignored by myopic divers, the Caribbean is an out-door adventurer's delight above the waterline too; a cornucopia of thick jungles, hidden waterfalls, swift rivers, quiet coves, and eye-popping wildlife. To say that the Caribbean possesses a variety of climes and offerings is to say that Shakespeare scratched out a few sonnets. Hike in Bonaire's Slagbaai National Park and witness a desertscape edged with beautiful, and empty, beaches. Hike Saba's Sandy Cruz trail and you follow ancient footpaths nearly smothered by tree ferns, vibrant wildflowers, and lichen-mottled mango

trees. In the Dominican Republic, just twice the size of Vermont, you can climb the highest mountain in the Caribbean (10,400-foot Pico Duarte), bicycle through alpine meadows, explore caves decorated with Indian pictographs, and windsurf in some of the best conditions east of Maui. Dominica, located in the center of the eastern Caribbean, boasts one of the region's largest rainforests, as well as a full-day hike to Boiling Lake, an enormous, bubbling cauldron of volcanically heated water. It is also home to 365 rivers, an impressive tally for an island fifteen miles wide and twenty-nine miles long. On tiny Tobago you'll find what may be the greatest diversity of plants and animals of any island in the Caribbean, except for

Cuba. Hundreds of butterflies call Tobago home, not to mention such bizarre creations as the fish-eating bat and the jumping wabbine, a freshwater fish that travels overland, locomoting by, you guessed it, in its search for new habitat.

Getting off the beaten track, of course, is also a chance to fall full bore into local culture, whether it's sharing a cafecito (zippy coffee served in small cups fat with sugar) with farmers in the Dominican Republic's Cordillera Central, or enjoying the taste, and potential side effects, of iguana soup. ("A bowl of iguana soup can work wonders for a healthy gentleman," explains a Curacao local, "though it can make women bothersome.")

Bristleworms, also called fireworms, are a type of polychaete worm. They possess stiff hairs that can sting fiercely. Saba, Dutch Antilles.

ABOVE: An arrow crab is an odd-looking crab with long spindly arms around a central arrow-shaped body. It uses its long claws to pluck at algae and invertebrates growing on coral reefs. Roatan, Honduras.

OPPOSITE: This colony of yellow clump corals usually opens only at night. Corals are colonies of stinging invertebrates closely related to jellyfish and anemones. They have a hard limestone external skeleton with stinging polyps that catch plankton in currents. Dutch Antilles.

PAGES 296–297: Dolphins have always held a special fascination for humans. Stories of their intelligence, their altruism, and their physical abilities abound as myths of the sea. The truth is that these animals can be as brutal toward their own kind as other animals. This male is asserting his dominance toward two mother-calf pairs. Bahama Banks.

To think that you can't escape the cruise ships and the casinos is silly. The Bahamas alone consist of more than seven hundred islands.

The Caribbean is certainly not untouched. For many of the islands, tourism is their lifeline, and now it's their problem. Many Caribbean islands face problems familiar to island resorts everywhere. Rampant coastal development destroys reefs, beaches, and critical mangroves. In many areas scientists have documented alarming long-term declines in coral communities, losses attributed largely to coastal development, pollution, and artificial beach construction. Simply getting rid of tourism's detritus is a serious problem. On Providenciales, the most populated of the Turks and Caicos Islands, there are no solid refuse treatment facilities. Trash is burned in open sites, and the ensuing air fouling is impressive. In the water, designated marine protected areas have been set up on many islands, but often these protected areas exist only on paper. Life before tourism was no Eden either. Many Caribbean islanders are not exactly environmentally conscious. Tossing off trash anywhere and everywhere is often part of the local fabric.

But there are happy examples of preservation and hope. Marine national parks have been established on many islands, and on some they are well protected. One of the Caribbean's oldest marine parks, Exuma Cays Land and Sea Park, established in 1959, serves as an example of what can go right when man's hand intrudes on man's ills. Nassau grouper, sorely over-fished in many areas, thrive within the park. Their egg production within park boundaries has been measured at six times that of the Nassau groupers outside the park. While conch have been wiped out in many parts of the Caribbean, the concentration of conch inside the park is about forty-seven times greater than any-place else in the world.

What is cliché is also fact. As soon as paradise is discovered, it is in danger of being lost. In the Caribbean, paradise, long-discovered and newly dis-covered, still exists. Its survival rests on another simple cliché: To see is to understand, and appreciate.

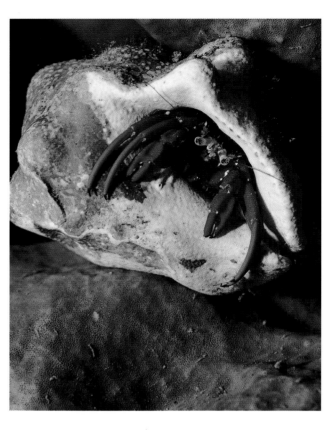

A red reef hermit crab has pulled back into its shell as a defense. It will reemerge when it no longer feels threatened. Saba, Dutch Antilles.

BELOW: The Caribbean reef shark is the most commonly seen shark at shark feeding sites in the Caribbean. Some sites will feature hundreds of these sharks, all making close passes to diving tourists. The sharks are interested in the food, not the divers. Bahamas.

A Nassau grouper in the Hol Chan marine reserve surveys divers curiously. Fish in protected marine reserves grow larger than their counterparts in fished areas; if they are not pursued as prey by divers, they will approach divers closely. Ambergris Cay, Belize.

ABOVE: *Two blue chromis, members of the damselfish family, compete for territory and, ultimately, a mate. Roatan, Honduras.*

LEFT: *A group of featherduster worms trap plankton with feathery gills. These polychaete worms settle on coral heads and secrete a tube that kills the coral polyps underneath. The worm lives permanently in its tube, with only the brightly colored, feathery gills protruding. Roatan, Honduras.*

OPPOSITE: *A fairy basslet swims above the convoluted pattern formed by a brain coral colony. These tiny, brightly colored fish feed on plankton, keeping close to crevices and caves for safety, and often swimming upside down. They look like tiny jewels floating above the coral reef. Roatan, Honduras.*

LEFT: *Two brittle stars emerge from an azure sponge at night. Brittle stars are close relatives of sea stars, but differ in several respects: they can move with astonishing quickness, and many glow with bioluminescence at night. Roatan, Honduras.*

RIGHT: *The spiny lobster is the largest Caribbean lobster. It is nocturnal, and at certain times of the year will migrate in long lines across the sandy ocean bottom. Dutch Antilles.*

RIGHT: *The upside-down jelly,* Cassiopea xamachana, *is named after Cassiopeia, the beautiful but haughty Ethiopian queen who was placed head downward in heaven by her enemies, the sea nymphs, to teach her a lesson in humility. Caribbean.*

PAGES 304–305: *The flamingo tongue, a type of cowry, feeds on the purple sea fans on which it is found. It leaves behind dead black swathes on otherwise vibrant purple living areas. Dutch Antilles.*

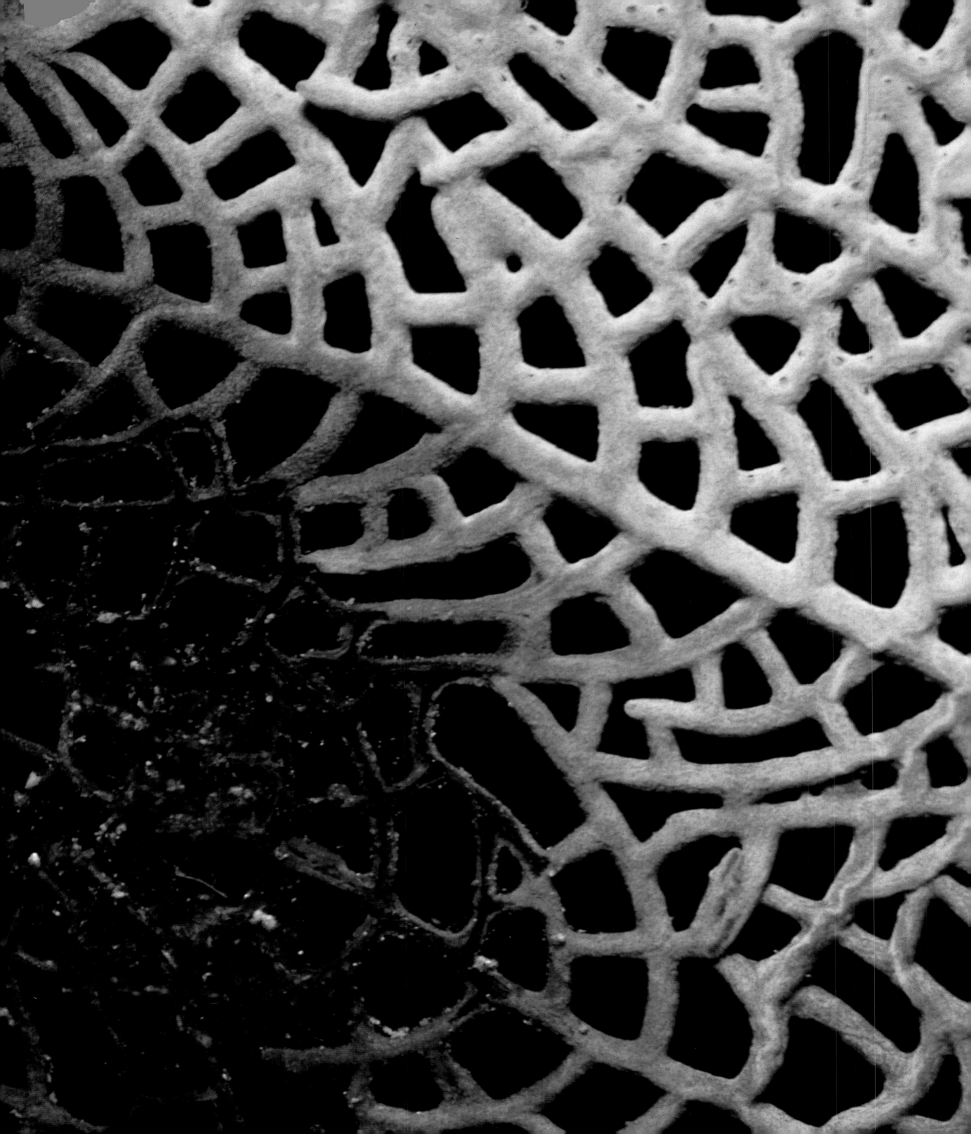

THE INDIAN OCEAN

THE RED SEA

The book of Deuteronomy calls the Sinai a "great and terrible wilderness." But really it's unfair to single out the Sinai. The same could be said for the interior of any of the countries bordering the Red Sea. March inland from, say, the coastline of Sudan, or Saudi Arabia, or Yemen, and you immediately find yourself in a torched, lunar landscape bereft of life, except for your own daft and dehydrated self.

ABOVE: A narrow sea of blue in a vast desert, the Red Sea boasts coral reefs that are renowned for their colors.

PAGES 306–307: A school of masked butterflyfish and schooling bannerfish rests in a coral reef near Hurghada.

RIGHT: A spider, or icicle, crab feeds at night among the polyps of a soft coral tree. These crabs hide within crevices in the coral reef during the day. At night, safe from the eyes of predatory fish, they find a position in the current, usually at the top of soft corals or sea fans, and pluck food particles from the water.

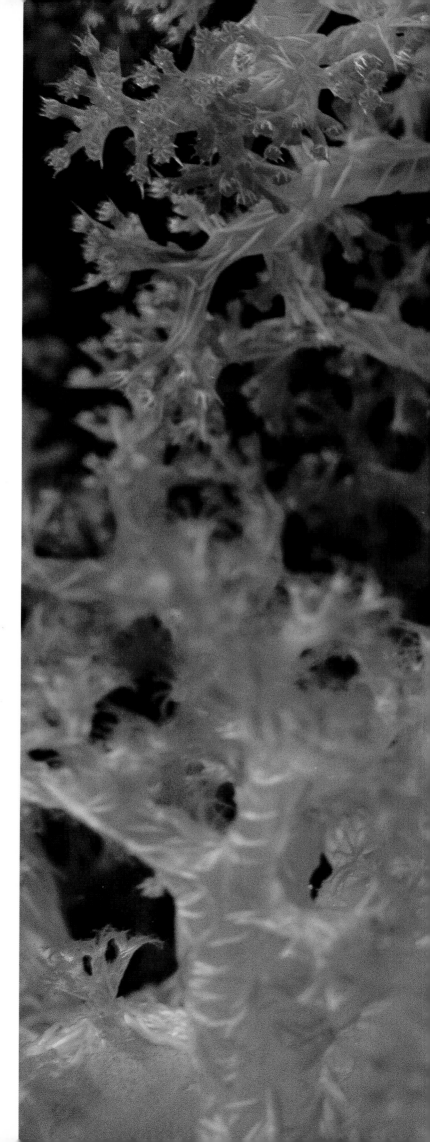

ABOVE, TOP: A male fairy basslet hovers over a coral head. They are found in huge numbers around coral reefs and, like some other sea basses, change sex from female to male according to how many males are in a group. Males usually control a harem of six to thirty females.

ABOVE: A female jewel fairy basslet, part of a harem, shows its bright colors. Male basslets are females that have changed sex.

God surely must have a sense of humor. Because if you turn your back to the deserts of Africa and Asia, stepping instead into the waters of the Red Sea, you will descend into a place where the density and diversity of life is, to put it mildly, astonishing. Name a coral, and you will likely find it here. Delicate, flowerlike *Dendronephthya*, gorgonian sea whips, and black corals, fire coral, *Acropora*, and xeniid soft corals. Life? Within a thirty-mile radius of Egypt's famed Sharm El Sheikh, a shipping port—and diving epicenter—near the tip of the Sinai Peninsula, there

are over one thousand species of fish, five hundred hard and soft corals, and roughly one thousand different kinds of invertebrates. Numbers? No scientist is foolish enough to count. Forget trying to list the colors. Confronted with a Red Sea reef, Matisse would have thrown his palette out the window and turned to macrame. Here you have a place where you might question if you are awake.

That's the biology. The diving accouterments are equally impressive. Well-preserved wrecks (courtesy of strict hands-off policies), sheer vertical walls festooned with explosions of coral, shallow coral gardens featuring the same. Water temperatures? Cooler than you might expect, peaking at 80 degrees F. in the summer and dropping into the 60s in winter. The Red Sea is also notorious for its high surface winds and aggressively choppy waters, but so what, if the visibility on a fair day is one hundred feet?

There are reasons for all this glory and glamour, the overriding one being that the Red Sea is basically the world's largest aquarium. At the northernmost end you have the Suez Canal, a thread of water so shallow and thin it barely counts as a connector to the eastern parts of the Mediterranean Sea. To the south you have the slightly wider, though still pinched, strait of Bab al Mandab, connecting the Red Sea to the Gulf of Aden, and then to the Indian Ocean. What water that does pass from the Indian Ocean into the Red Sea is largely boon—namely a rich supply of larvae that explodes in a riot of joyous growth. No rivers dump into the Red Sea, so there are no sediments for coral polyps to choke on, and no haze for divers to peer through. Evaporation approximating a Hoover vacuum—removing as much as six feet of surface water a year with virtually no freshwater to replace it—makes the Red Sea a salty place, conditions some scientists believe provide the perfect medium for burgeoning life. Unique conditions, and no easy access in or out, also explain the wealth of endemic marine creatures—one-fifth of the species are found nowhere else.

What else could you ask for? How about convenient geologic happenstance? The Red Sea is basically a huge crack in the desert floor, a flooded rift valley in geologic terms. Its sides, especially in the north, plunge down steeply almost right from shore. With no extended continental shelf on which to locate, corals form right next to the shoreline. Drop-offs start as little as a few feet out, falling away immediately to deep, open, plankton-laden waters that bathe the inshore reefs and bring in big fish. Disneyland right at your doorstep. Should you travel to Sharm El Sheikh, the hardest decision you'll have to make is whether to dive on a day boat, hop on a liveaboard, or just drive to a reef in your rental car. A hellish business.

Most of the diving in the Red Sea is done out of Egypt, and the action centers around Sharm El Sheikh and, to the south, the formerly sleepy fishing village of Hurghada. Egypt quickly figured the value of the dive dollar, and so moved quickly to become a leader in marine conservation. The most visible sign of this is the vast Ras Muhammad National Marine Park, a strictly no-take enclave established in 1983 in the South Sinai region that encompasses a host of spectacular life and reefs.

Though shore diving and day trips offer up plenty of magnificence, most of the prime sites throughout the Red Sea, north and south, are accessed by liveaboard boats out of Sharm El Sheikh and Hurghada. This is because Egypt offers something many of the Red Sea countries do not—political stability. Looking at a map, it certainly makes more sense to travel to the southern reefs from Sudan or Eritrea. But only a cursory historical review of these war-torn countries is enough to convince you of the wisdom of a long boat ride. Or, at the very least, in the case of Sudan where dive outfitters do exist, check on the current situation.

There is plenty of good diving right out of the Port of Sudan, including the *Umbria* wreck—possibly one of the world's best wreck dives—and Sanganeb atoll, a huge tower of pristine coral rising up from the blue depths that some regard as the best diving in the Red Sea. But as of this writing, Egypt has the most professional and greatest number of dive facilities, as locals aren't distracted by the unseemly

task of simply staying alive. Though it has remained relatively safe to travel in Egypt, remember too that the Sinai Peninsula has seen a long history of war. Experienced travelers don't cavort on that pristine and empty beach without first checking with locals concerning the possibility of unexpended land mines.

Ironically it was Sudan that brought the Red Sea to the world's attention. In the late 1950s, Jacques Cousteau, intrigued by the idea of underwater living, dreamed of building an underwater habitat in which men might live and work for an extended time. No

Fish sleeping at night can be approached very closely. Here, a flash-enhanced close-up of the tail fin of a sleeping parrotfish reveals dazzling colors, which may be muted in the bluish light of day.

PAGES 312–313: Many groupers start life as females, changing sex later in life. Like many fishes, this small grouper can mute its hues to match its mood or surroundings.

one else was intrigued enough to pony up funding, so Cousteau determined that he would fund the project himself and hopefully pay it off with a film. It was a gamble, but Cousteau chose to build his two underwater dwellings just off Port Sudan, largely because he reckoned the Red Sea was a whiz-bang amphitheater for a film. He was right. *The Silent World* and *Le Monde Sans Soleil (World Without Sun)* paid for the project, and introduced a world of slack-jawed divers to the Red Sea. Dive Sha'b Rumi, the reef about twenty-five miles northeast of Port Sudan where Cousteau undertook his 1963 Conshelf II experiment, and you can still see the remnants of a tool shed, a hangar, and fish pens. The actual habitats, which rested at thirty-three and eighty-two feet, were yanked from the sea when the successful experiment ended.

Politics aside, passing through Egypt offers another advantage—access to dry-land magic. Because coming to the Red Sea shouldn't just be about *rhats, maya,* and *samak* (Arabic for "diving," "water," and "fish"). To miss the Sphinx, the Nile, and the pyramids at Giza, to deprive the ears of the muezzin's call to prayer, to skip standing on a Cairo street corner inhaling the smells of roasting mutton and the shrieks of cursing drivers is to walk unseeing past the Grand Canyon to buy postcards at the visitor's center.

Pointing out highlights, and by inference lesser standards, in the Red Sea is a bit like singling out bright lights at a Mensa convention. But some dive spots do deserve mention.

Starting in the north, in the Sharm El Sheikh area, are the stellar wall dives of Ras Muhammad, with corals, reef fish, and, riding in on sweeping currents, big pelagics, including hammerheads and grey reef sharks. Also within the National Park, not far from Sharm El Sheikh Bay, is Ras Ghozlani, a neglected site that some say offers some of the best diving in the Sinai. There is stunning diving in the Straits of Tiran, courtesy of four large seamounts, fat with color and life, which plateau just beneath the surface at the entrance to the Gulf of Aqaba. Moving south, off Hurghada, there are the Giftun Islands, the wreck of the *Salem Express* (a three-hundred-foot ferry) and the near-mythical Elphinstone, a long, cigar-shaped coral mountain one thousand feet long with sheer vertical walls and sloping shoulders. Farther south, Brothers Islands, known locally as El Akhawein—which might as well mean Yet-Another-Reef-Plastered-With-Life—are actually the exposed tips of two massive reef pillars. Huge shoals of fish descend on them en masse, and their walls are steep; free-falling down their coral slopes is an unforgettable experience. (Be aware that strong downcurrents can develop off Big Brother's walls.) Far to the south, there are lovely reefs off Masamirit Islet and, near the strait of Bab al Mandab, reefs off Jabal Zugar Island.

Really though, it's silly to highlight Red Sea dive spots. Each dive operator will bend your ear about the glories of their favorite places, and they'll all be right.

It is worth noting some differences between the waters of the north and south. Most of the steep, coral drop-offs for which the Red Sea is famous are found in the north; the continental shelf extends well away from land in the south. The water to the south is typically warmer, and a little less clear, though really this is being nitpicky. An intriguing note, too, regarding the

The Spanish dancer, the world's largest nudibranch, grows to over a foot in length. This nocturnal animal swims by undulating its body.

BELOW: A group of masked butterfly-fish, endemic to the Red Sea, rests around a coral head. They are more active in the late afternoon, and feed on soft and hard corals.

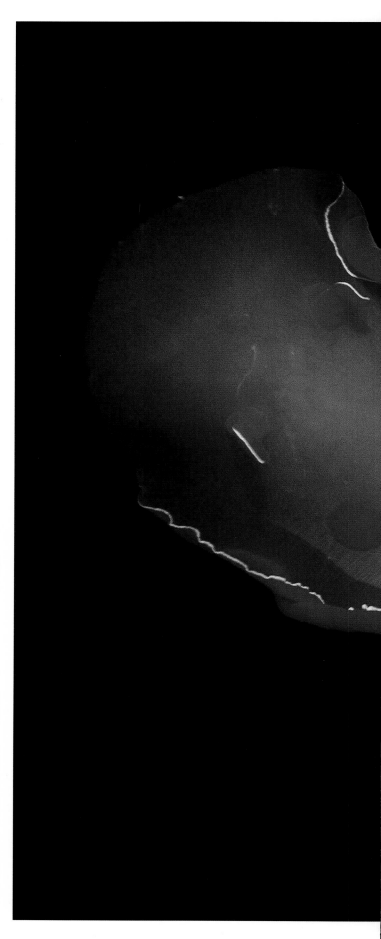

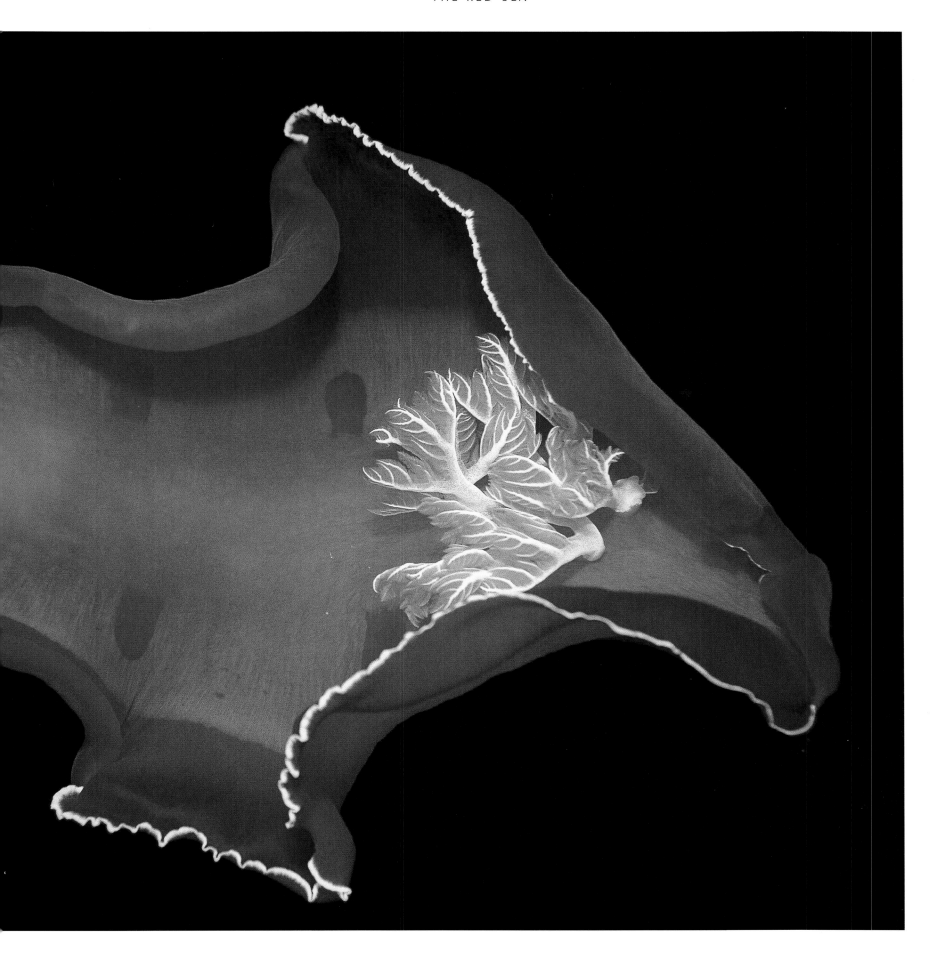

The blue-spotted stingray has round pectoral fins and a mouth on its underside that it uses to dig in the sand for food. The stinging barb on its tail deters predators.

southern Red Sea. As recently as 1987, two scientists concluded unequivocally that the fringing reefs for which the north is famous ringed the entire circumference of the Red Sea. They were, of course, wrong. This isn't pointed out to be petty, but to highlight a point. It wasn't so long ago that the southern waters were "maya" incognito, and to a large extent they remain that way.

From a diving, and environmental, perspective, it's also happy news that man has gained little or no foothold on a large portion of the Red Sea's shores, especially in the south. No man, no pollution; another reason why the Red Sea waters remain remarkably pristine. Fishing too has stayed at sustainable levels. Not that the Red Sea is unblemished. Where civilization is entrenched, more often than not it is civilization without proper sewage disposal, resulting in localized damage to reefs. In the north, the Gulf of Aqaba dumps phospate, manganese, and polluting bauxite minerals into the Red Sea, and the Suez Canal contributes its share of oil and petroleum gleck. But overall, outside of the ports and cities, the Red Sea remains markedly untouched. A gem ensconced, happily, in a great and terrible wilderness.

A school of Anthias, or fairy basslets, crowds a wall lined with soft corals. Explosions of colors like this characterize Red Sea reefs.

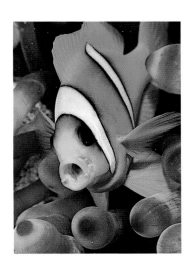

ABOVE: The relationship of the two-band anemonefish and the bulb-tentacle sea anemone is symbiotic. In exchange for protection among the anemone's tentacles, the combative fish threatens passing butterflyfish that might chew upon its host.

THE SEYCHELLES ISLANDS

They are harmless plankton feeders, docile giants, and often quite shy. But they are also the largest fish in the sea, reaching lengths of forty feet and more. Suspended beneath the surface in the waters of St. Anne Marine National Park, 27,000 pounds of whale shark cruising toward you, mouth agape, a yawning black hole five feet across—well, the brain stem experiences a primal jolt of both fascination and momentary doubt. Then the majestic creature sweeps past, leaving you first in a tumbling shock wave of backwash, then in an even more powerful glow of unforgettable memory.

ABOVE: The whale shark, the world's largest shark, is truly a gentle giant. All whale sharks are harmless plankton feeders, which feed by opening their huge mouths and inhaling vast quantities of water. Very little is known about the whale shark's population or behavior.

RIGHT The granite outcroppings of the Seychelles slide beneath the water, providing unique diving opportunities.

318

A school of larval fish keep within the shelter of a coral cave during the day. At night, they disperse to feed on plankton.

in you go, heart-in-mouth, senses alight to join Nature right on stage.

And there's plenty more magic to be had in the Seychelles. One hundred and fifteen islands scattered across 386,000 square miles in the western Indian Ocean, the Seychelles are a repository of treasures both real and, possibly, imagined. Hung in 1731, French pirate Olivier de Lasseur paid the price for his sins, but he didn't feel obligated to cough up the location of the treasure he looted from a Portuguese ship and purportedly buried somewhere on Mahe, the largest of the Seychelle islands.

More certain is the fact that isolation (the Seychelles are roughly a thousand miles east of African landfall) has culled a strange, wondrous, and staggeringly beautiful place. When British general Charles George Gordon visited the Seychelles in 1881, he concluded that Praslin, the second largest island in the chain, was the Garden of Eden. Gordon was not being poetic, he was being literal. He based his conclusion largely on the presence of the strange coco-de-mer, at forty-plus pounds the world's largest, and most suggestively shaped, seed. This curious nut, bearing a remarkable resemblance to a woman's nether regions, had previously washed up on odd beaches around the globe, leading beachcombers to conclude that the parent tree grew underwater. Having found the seed and its massive parent tree on Praslin and the nearby island of Curieuse, Gordon concluded that he was in Eden, gazing upon the naughty forbidden fruit of Genesis.

Though the coco-de-mer's shape and size command attention, there's plenty more novelty, below and above the water, to occupy the eye. The Seychelles are home to some of the rarest, and strangest, plants and animals in the world. Giant tortoises, close to a century old and weighing in at upwards of two hundred pounds, are a common sight during nature walks on Cousin Island—the Seychelles and the Galapagos are home to the last of these stately ancients. There's the carnivorous pitcher plant (a scaled-down version of the star of Little Shop of Horrors) and the fingernail-sized pygmy piping frog. The Seychelles kestrel (a diminutive falcon) and the Seychelles white-eye, a

Little is known about the wanderings of whale sharks. They are found worldwide in tropical and temperate seas, but precisely how they arrive here in the Seychelles—one thousand miles east of Zanzibar—remains a pleasant mystery. But arrive they sometimes do, sweeping through these equatorial waters in August and November to inhale plankton blooms, a stew of stinging plankton and ctenophores, and

small, greyish bird that is one of the rarest and most endangered species in the world, inhabit the Seychelles, and no place else. Yes, a rainbow coalition of over nine hundred species of fish flits through the offshore waters, often in massive concentrations. But it pays to dry off now and again, and explore the islands themselves; Cousin Island's bird sanctuary or, on Mahe, Morne Seychellois National Park.

Even the geology is striking. Granted, geology can be a nap-inducing topic, but here it deserves a mention, both for its beauty and its impact on diving. Keeping it brief, forty-one of the Seychelles islands are granitic (the rest are coral atolls). These granite humps poking up out of the middle of the ocean are the visible remnants of ancient and grand forces. When

Africa and India parted more than 650 million years ago, separating the vast continent of Gondwanaland, the Seychelles are what got left behind.

This makes for memorable scenery, above and below the water. On dry land, massive outcroppings of smoothly sensuous granite stand sentinel beside often desolate white sand beaches of astonishing beauty, explaining why the islands have long been popular with European honeymooners whose displays of public affection can make the coco-de-mer look like a buttoned-up school marm.

The same granite walls slide beneath the water, providing surreal, wavering blue-water canyons and granite block homes to white gorgonians, fields of huge plate anemones, spiny lobster and shrimp, eels,

A candy-cane sea star brightens up this Acropora coral. Sea stars are echinoderms, a class of animals that features radial symmetry and includes sea cucumbers and sea urchins.

PAGES 322–323: A lone soldierfish swims among a school of squirrelfish in a coral cave. These fish spend the day in caves within the coral reef. At night, they come out in great numbers to feed on plankton. Their large eyes are adapted to see at night.

LEFT: An emperor angelfish shows its striking coloration. In many angelfish species the colors and patterns of juveniles differ markedly from the adults. As the juveniles mature and change their coloration, other adults chase them off their territories so that the food supply is maintained.

RIGHT: A ghost crab wanders along the beach of a remote atoll in the Indian Ocean at sunset. A scavenger, it will feed on almost anything— detritus on the beach, baby turtle hatchlings, and seaweed.

and masses of fish. Clusters of boulders yield dense pockets of life, including golden cup coral, sea whips, and gorgonian sea fans. Granite pinnacles prong up from the depths, wrapped with schooling parrotfish, wrasse, fusiliers, and blue-lined snappers, and, of course, larger pelagics—sharks, turtles, manta rays, and, in season, whale sharks.

The three largest islands in the Seychelles chain—Mahe, Praslin, and La Digue—comprise almost 50 percent of the land mass of the 115-island chain. Ninety-nine percent of the Seychelles seventy-seven thousand residents live on these three islands, leaving roughly three hundred people scattered among the 112 islands that remain. If that kind of emptiness sounds alluring, you'll love hopping a liveaboard boat and diving the outer islands in the Seychelles chain—Assumption, Astove, Cosmoledo, St. Pierre, and Aldabra—one of the world's largest coral atolls and home to the world's largest population of giant tortoises (Aldabra is a World Heritage Site). Many of the islands are bereft of man, others have just

enough of man to provide what the diver needs. On Ile des Roches in the Amirantes chain, an hour flight from the main Seychelles group, ghost crabs scuttle along empty beaches, turtles poke their heads above the surface of mirror lagoons, groupers, sharks, and

BELOW: A closeup of the patterns of an emperor angelfish shows the brilliant colors of this species. Colors underwater are often used to attract mates or warn of the possessor's venomous nature.

Two porcelain crabs sit between an anemone's stinging tentacles and its foot. Protected by their host's tentacles, the crabs throw out finely meshed nets, modified third legs, to filter plankton out of the water.

turtles wheel about pinnacles a few hundred yards offshore. The only human inhabitants of the island are the guests and staff of a small lodge.

Not surprisingly, most of the dive resorts—and divers—operate out of Mahe, home to the capital city of Victoria and roughly 88 percent of archipelago's permanent citizenry. The resorts are first-rate, watched over by the detail-minded Seychelles Ministry of Tourism, and there's plenty of good diving off Mahe too, most of it a ten- to twenty-minute boat ride from shore. L'Ilot, a granite pinnacle poking up sixty feet from a sandy bottom at the tip of Beau Vallon Bay, offers the chance to dive with eagle rays and floods of flashing jacks—and, in November, the possibility of

ogling whale sharks. Though currents can be strong, L'Ilot is also a great night dive. Lit by your dive light, floods of Spanish dancer nudibranchs, attended by opaque and ghostly symbiotic shrimps, show their true, and brilliant, colors. Another fun night dive—at the south end of Beau Vallon Bay at Whale Rocks—offers the chance to drift over feeding spotted snake eels which burrow under the sand during the day. Five miles northwest of Mahe, Shark Bank, a massive granite plateau in about one hundred feet of water, is home to large stingrays, sharks, and cowfish, a fish rarely seen in Mahe's nearshore waters. And just to the east of Mahe are the six islands that comprise St. Anne Marine National Park. It's true more than 25 percent of all the tourists who come to the Seychelles go to St. Anne to snorkel, dive, or discover the reef through glass bottom boats, but the whale sharks don't care, and you shouldn't either.

Moving down the three main islands—Mahe, Praslin, and La Digue—the crowds tailspin rapidly. But the diving and snorkeling remain the same—warm water (temps rarely drop below 80 degrees F.), with great visibility that typically peaks during April and May and again in September, October, and November. However, the diving is good year round, though it's worth noting that the wettest months are December and January, when monsoons can dump substantial amounts of rain.

Before you pony up airfare, a very important note. In the spring of 1998 the Seychelles chain experienced massive coral bleaching that killed over 50 percent of the corals off many islands, and, in some instances, devastated entire reefs. On the inner islands the branching coral species—staghorn, elkhorn and table corals—were particularly hard hit. This massive bleaching and die-off will have a long-term effect on not only the Seychelles reefs, but will likely drive off some of the fish life that depends on the corals for habitat. Scientists aren't sure of all the causes—coral bleaching is often caused by a complex interplay of events: pollution, sediment, fertilizer runoff, and high temperatures—but an intense warm water spike, resulting in the warmest water temperatures ever recorded in the Seychelles, was certainly largely to blame. Proving that Nature enjoys throwing science for a loop, some of the reefs that fared the best, just off Mahe, were exposed to heavy sediment runoff. Some scientists guess that the silty waters acted as a cooling cover from sunlight.

The islands' isolation, especially in the outer chain, where there is very little fishing and pollution impact, will probably aid in recovery, but recovering from devastation this severe is not an overnight process. On an optimistic note, the inner islands have their timeless underwater granite base, and this will continue to provide home and shelter for marine life. On the outer island reefs with steep wall formations,

local divers have found that bleaching hasn't been as severe, probably due to frequent cold water upwellings along the walls.

The Seychellois also have some hard decisions ahead. The people have adopted a conservation bent, eco-tourism being a critical source of income. About 15 percent of the islands' reefs are protected as marine

A diver swims above a coral cave filled with squirrelfish, which keep to the darkness of caves during daytime.

parks or the like, and in 1999 the Seychelles imposed what amounts to the world's first environmental tourism visa. Every visitor to the Seychelles, age twelve and up, must pay a one-time one hundred dollar entry fee, the money going to preserve the Seychelles' marine and dry-land wonders. Once paid, the "Seychelles Goldcard" allows lifetime access to all the state-run land and marine reserves.

But visitors bring with them not only cash but needs: airports, hotels, roads. With mountainous interiors, the three main islands have very little flat land. On Mahe, developers are claiming large areas of reef to build the perks that tourists expect. Well-intentioned visitors readying to shout about these losses should keep in mind that their ability to visit the Seychelles is founded on reef pave-over. Until 1971, and the completion of the International Airport on Mahe, the only way to reach Mahe was by boat from India or Mombassa Kenya. The airport's runway was built over an area of shallow reef. Once the Garden of Eden is discovered, there are never any easy answers.

At twilight, waves lap against coral sand beaches and the granite formations of the Seychelles.

BELOW: Gobies live on a wire coral. They will not live on other hosts.

THE MALDIVE ISLANDS

Sunrise, the east side of Felidhu Atoll. The air is heavy with warmth and promise, the waters of the Indian Ocean lay silken smooth reflecting burnt orange and red. The Maldives are about timing and tides, and at this particular juncture both are right. This place is called Miaru Kandhu in the language of Dhivehi, the sing-song dialect of the Maldivian people. Shark Channel.

ABOVE: The larvae of many reef fish are planktonic, with unusual shapes. When they settle onto a reef, the juveniles become recognizable. Although small, these juveniles can pack a powerful wallop.

RIGHT: As strikingly beautiful as these anemonefish and magnificent sea anemones are to our eyes, they are probably even more so to themselves. Recent studies have discovered that certain reef fishes can see colors well beyond our visual spectrum.

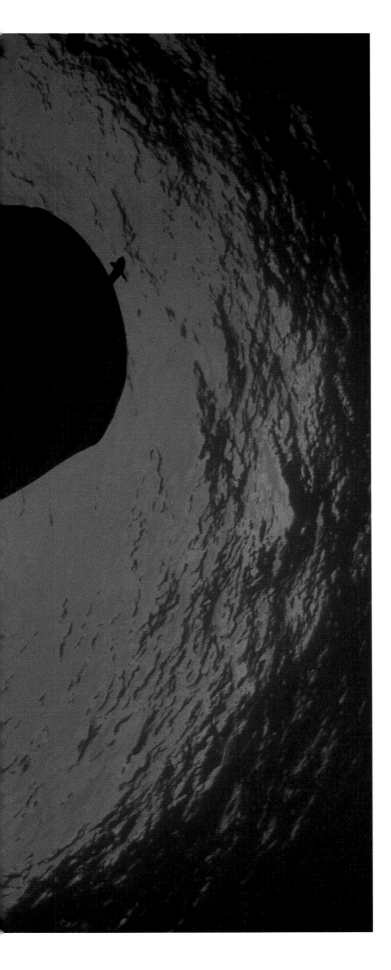

Beneath the surface the water is electric blue. What you note first is the vast doorway—nearly 330 feet wide and 100 feet deep—that serves as passage from the atoll's inner lagoon to the open ocean. Located off the tip of India, stretching 540 miles from north to south, the Maldive Archipelago numbers roughly 1,120 islands, and these are grouped into twenty-six atolls. Each atoll rings a lagoon. Some atolls are small, a little over a mile in diameter. Some are vast. Huvadhoo Atoll, just above the equator, measures forty-five by fifty miles, one of the largest atolls in the world.

Whatever their size, the atolls hove to the same dynamics. The inner lagoons are fat with fish, and when the tides begin to run out through the channels between the islands, the fish go with them. The big predators know the schedule. As the tide runs out, they drift in from the open ocean—sleek patrolling tuna, barracuda, great schools of grey reef sharks, cruising hammerheads. On the east side of Felidhu Atoll you can hover at one hundred feet, watching the predators sweep back and forth, patient as time, while the reef fish mass at the channel entrance, frantically backpedaling curtains of explosive color.

The geology of the Maldives dictates the diving, and, utilizing the local language, there are actually three options. Kandu is diving the channels between the islands as the tides sweep in and out of the lagoons. An exciting buzz and a great chance to see big predators, though it helps to be comfortable drifting alone, as water is sucked through the channels at an appreciable rate and divers have been known to get separated from the group. A second option is Maa Kandu, diving the outer reef of the atoll in a (sometimes) milder current. The final option, Thila, is the Dhivehi term for a small submerged reef, sometimes hunkered in the middle of a current-swept channel, and, happily too, often located well inside the atoll's lagoon where the current is nearly nil and reef fish mass like Tokyo commuters. The mid-channel *thilas* offer wonderful opportunity to see big and small life alike—prowling barracuda, elegant clearfin lionfish, leopard morays, mantas hovering languidly as cleaner-

Whale sharks are powerful animals but are not aggressive. Large as they are, whale sharks are somewhat timid. When diving, it is usually better not to touch the sharks, as they will usually swim around divers and will tolerate their presence much longer if they are left alone.

ABOVE: Urchin cardinalfish find safety within the long spines of a sea urchin.

A school of reef squid lazily hover above a reef.

OPPOSITE, BOTTOM: A single sea jelly may harbor dozens of juvenile fish within the protective confines of its stinging tentacles. This large scyphozoan is safely transporting juvenile filefish and batfish within its tentacles.

fish dash into their mouths and gill cavities to provide a cleaning, and, if you're lucky and your timing is right, whale sharks, mouths agape working the thermocline for plankton.

Don't get bogged down in terminology. Kandu, Maa Kandu, Thila, they all provide eye-popping opportunity. The atolls brim with color and life. More than twelve hundred species of coral fish have been identified in the Maldives and they mass, dart, hide, feed, clean and cavort over some 187 known species of coral. In twenty meters of casual finning you might pass over forty different kinds of coral—iridescent orange, blue, and yellow soft coral, black coral trees, reams of branching *Acropora*. The Maldives are very nearly a place removed from the rest of the world.

The Maldives squat beneath two distinct weather patterns—the southwest and northeast monsoons—and these play an appreciable role in the diving experience, especially in the northern islands, where almost all of the diving takes place. The brunt of the southwest monsoon falls from roughly April to November, and the weather can be turbulent—torrential rains and strong winds. The northeast monsoon, characterized by relatively calm, dry weather, lasts from roughly December to March.

It's true that the Dry Season may be the very best time to dive, with light winds and currents from the northeast that gather clear open-ocean water and superb fish life from the east and sweep them into the northern atolls. During this season, visibility, which generally averages a healthy sixty-five to one hundred feet in the Maldives, can spike to a jaw-dropping, and not unusual, two hundred feet (water temps range from 80–86 degrees F. year-round). But Nature, and so diving, is never black and white. Know where to go and the Wet Season serves up magic too. The southwest monsoon creates plankton blooms—typically on the eastern side of atolls—and the plankton blooms bring in mantas and whale sharks. Ocean currents generated by the southwest monsoon can also sweep in clear open-ocean water, making for magic dives along the windward western edge of some atolls. Visibility can vary by the day, too, incoming tides bringing clear water into the atolls, outgoing tides being nutrient rich and sometimes murkier.

Tidal variations, seasonal variations, variations to those variations—the most critical factor when diving the Maldives is a knowledgeable guide. Most of the best diving is done off a boat. Find an operator that knows the little nuances, and be enthralled. Miss the right boat and drift at sea with a guide who is apologetic, but uninformed.

Diving is currently restricted to about half of the Maldive's twenty-six atolls. Not surprisingly, the majority of the dive sites are located in the northern islands, especially near North Male—home to the capital (Male), the international airport, and one-fourth of the entire island chain's population. Most of the resorts are on North Male or on the islands a short boat trip away. Ditto for fantastic and now famous dive spots like Rasfari (at the northwest edge of North Male itself), Girifushi Thila (in the channel between Girifushi and Himmafushi islands), Madivaru (hammerhead point) on tiny Rashdu Atoll, and Miaru Kandhu on Felidhu Atoll.

Not that the place is overrun. The first tourist resorts in the Maldives didn't open until 1972, and for a long time the islands were mostly a playground for Europeans. That has changed. In 2000 an estimated four hundred thousand visitors descended on the Maldives, an impressive number but one that pales a bit with the seven million tourists who visit the Hawaiian islands each year. The Maldives have been spared this kind of onslaught largely because it takes some effort to get there. Unless you choose to swim from Bombay, there is no quick, direct line. Fly from Los Angeles, and you have to go to Singapore first; from New York, Europe. Either way, it's a lot of travel.

Be prepared, too, for a few potential quirks and discomforts post-arrival. Day and night, the weather can be stifling hot. The people of the Maldives are

lovely and gracious. Many are also devout Muslims and frown upon the imbibing of alcohol, though not the laws of supply and demand. Some divers have found themselves on boats without beer, wine, or air conditioning, and bottled water at five dollars a pop.

These are minor discomforts that pale in the face of an engaging fact—the Maldives still dwell

ABOVE: Nurse sharks are usually seen resting in coral caves during the day. They feed on crustaceans, urchins, and other animals which they detect using a pair of barbels above the mouth. Although they look harmless, they do have teeth which they may use on divers who harass them.

PAGES 336–337: *A brittle star moves across a sea fan at night.*

OPPOSITE: Goldman's sweetlips are the only sweetlips with diagonal rather than horizontal stripes. Sweetlips are in the same family as grunts, and are closely related to snappers.

BELOW: The powder-blue tang, like all surgeonfishes, has a sharp knife-like scale at the base of its tail. Tangs are herbivores which feed primarily on algae on the coral reef. The blades at the tail are used only for defense.

largely in the past. A blue, sun-spackled place where fishermen fish for tuna with pole and line, and track the fish by watching sea birds. The capital of Male is a rambunctious place with colorful markets and exotic sounds, but move off North Male Atoll and man's imprint evaporates slowly, then disappears entirely—a vast chain of beaches and atolls that resonate with silence. Only about two hundred islands in the Maldivian chain are permanently inhabited.

But beauty of this sort is an alluring enticement, and the numbers of tourists descending on the Maldives is increasing exponentially. New and upgraded resorts are sprouting on the developed islands. And the charming emptiness of much of the island chain ensures that the islands that are developed are heavily impacted. Nor is there much to begin with. International airport, capital, seventy thousand-plus inhabitants, tourist resorts—North Male Atoll is one square mile in all. Small islands have a limited capacity to deal with tourist waste, much less the direct physical impacts of visitors. It is no coincidence that reef studies have noted a significant decrease in the condition of reefs around many resort islands. And when you build resorts, you use the materials at hand. Coral mining has damaged reefs; sand for cement

is scooped from lagoons. The impacts of coral mining aren't brief; surveys of mined reefs have shown few signs of recovery twenty years after mining has ceased.

Nature has dealt the Maldives its blows too. The widespread coral bleaching, which leveled reefs around the world in 1998, hit the Maldives particularly hard. When ocean temperatures jumped 3 degrees Celsius between late April and May of '98, in some shallow reef-flat areas up to 100 percent of the coral was killed. Hardest hit were the reefs in the resort areas, since healthy reefs are better able to withstand threats.

While fish life still thrives, local fishermen are upgrading their equipment to take more fish and responding to the lure of foreign markets. Exports of live grouper (usually to Hong Kong and Japan) have increased as much as ten-fold. When local fishermen discovered the value placed on sea cucumbers by markets in China, Singapore, and Hong Kong, these plump little fellows nearly disappeared from the lagoons where they are easily harvested. Shark fishing—and finning—is up. A researcher noted that a single shark live is worth three thousand dollars generated annually from divers, compared with thirty dollars dead for export, but dive dollars don't go into a fisherman's pocket.

There's plenty of good news too. The reefs that were heavily bleached are coming back, thanks in part to fast-growing corals like *Acropora*. Coral mining is now strictly monitored, and permitted only at specific sites. Environmental impact statements are now required for new resorts, and plans are underway to protect certain dive sites.

But the biggest problem facing the Maldives is much broader, namely staying above water. Sea level rise is an understandably hot topic in an island chain where 80 percent of the land area is less than three feet above mean sea level. And here, the fate of the Maldives is in other hands. As one author of a global warming study noted, "The Maldives can probably do little to influence the western nations largely responsible for the increasing emission of greenhouse gases, climate change, and impending sea-level rise."

Truth is, no place is, any longer, worlds away.

THAILAND

Stand at the edge of a riot of green foliage, toes digging into sand white and soft as confectioner's sugar. Vines sprouting purple flowers and sweet scent lace across the sand toward the Andaman Sea, china blue beneath a squinty-bright equatorial sun. The nine islands of Thailand's famed Similan Island chain are often referred to by number. This island, Ko Miang, is Island Number Four, a tag as apropos as dubbing the Sistine Chapel "Mural Number Three."

LEFT: Dramatic limestone formations are a prominent feature of Phang Nga Bay.

RIGHT: A lionfish, proudly displaying its venomous spines, hovers among soft coral trees in the Similan Islands. These brilliantly hued soft coral trees inflate with water during periods of food-bearing current.

OPPOSITE: A divemaster has fed sharks on the Burma Banks for several years. These nurse sharks came to know him well and learned to take food from Ohis mouth. In recent years, probably because of the fishing of sharks for their fins, almost no sharks have been seen at this site.

Above and below the waterline the Andaman Sea is an astonishingly beautiful place, though neither the Andaman Sea nor the Similan Islands are untouched. Here on Ko Miang, home to Similan Island National Park, there are tent campgrounds, a clearing of tin-roofed bungalows, and the acrid smell of smoking wood that promises additional clearing and civilization. But step down the short path that cuts across Ko Miang, and man's clatter disappears. Smoky beams of sunlight pierce the forest canopy, velvet butterflies flutter, and, high in the trees bats hang like rotted black plums.

Odd thing is, this sense of serenity pervades whether you are on a dappled path on Ko Miang or in downtown Bangkok. As any world traveler knows, graciousness and genuine warmth are not always in fat supply, and, diver or no, this is one of the great joys of discovering Thailand. Buddhism, Thailand's dominant religion, encourages a temperament steeped in serenity and gentleness, and this sense of serenity hovers over Thailand, as palpable as the hot sun. Thai people are

A Buddhist monk surveys the beach scene at Phuket, a popular destination for tourists from Europe and North America, and the jumping-off spot for dive boats to the Similan Islands.

both gentle and gracious in their dealings with each other and with *farangs* (foreigners), possibly because Thailand is the only Southeast Asian country that never suffered the yoke of colonial invasion. The Thai people are both proud and humble, a rare combination anywhere these days.

This pleasantry and plenty of others have led divers to discover Thailand, and Thailand has, in turn, discovered divers. Over seventy dive operators work out of Phuket Island alone (an hour's flight from Bangkok), ferrying divers out across the Andaman Sea to the Similans and beyond, so that famed spots like Richelieu Rock can resemble Miami Harbor. But Nature is adept at blotting out man. Nine islands comprise the well-visited Similans, but some 155 islands dot the Andaman Sea. Many of them are remote and uninhabited, and the right liveaboard can deposit you there.

The Malay Peninsula—including the countries of Malaysia, Thailand, and Myanmar (formerly Burma)—neatly divides Thailand diving into two distinct regions, the Andaman Sea to the west and the Gulf of Thailand to the east. There are plenty of dive sites in the gulf, and along both the east and west coasts of mainland Thailand. But the coastal and gulf reefs pale in comparison to the reefs and pinnacles of the Andaman Sea. While the Gulf of Thailand boasts its share of numbingly beautiful islands and beaches, it also serves as the repository for runoff from twenty-one Thai rivers alone. Malaysia, Vietnam, and Cambodia also contribute their share of runoff. What is common knowledge to river scientists might be news to divers. Southeast Asia has the world's most turbid rivers, responsible for supplying roughly 25 percent of the oceans' suspended matter. Some of it stays in the Gulf of Thailand.

There is a reason dive operators cluster like subway commuters in Phuket (and to the north at the quieter port of Ban Khao Lak). The eastern Andaman Sea is Thailand's best diving—better still between November and April when effects of the southwest monsoon have blown over. Easily accessible sites close to Phuket— places like Shark Point and Anemone

Oriental sweetlips school in the Similan Islands. The juveniles of this species look completely different from the adults.

ABOVE: *The three spindle cowries on this sea whip are extremely well-camouflaged to match their host. They even have phony "polyps" on their mantles, which can be seen clearly in this photograph, as the sea whip has retracted its polyps.*

PAGES 346–347: *A closeup of the crown-of-thorns starfish shows its venomous spines. These spines can cause a painful sting if they puncture a finger or carelessly placed knee.*

Reef and nearby islands like Racha, Phi Phi, and Koh Doc Mai—offer good marine life and soft corals. But the true scene-stealers lie offshore. To the southeast of Phuket, the sea is dotted with limestone islands and lovely reefs, among them the deservedly famous, and aptly named, Hin Daeng and Hin Muang (Red and Purple Rocks), host to explosively colorful colonies of soft corals and anemones. Roughly fifty miles north-west of Phuket lie the Similans. Onward and upward from there, Tachai Island, Richelieu Rock, the Surin Archipelago (offering some of Thailand's most devel-oped hard coral reefs), and the mystery of Myanmar waters. As of this writing roughly twelve dive boats have permission to enter Myanmar. Until 1997 Myanmar's waters were closed to foreign visitors cour-tesy of a repressive government whose human rights abuses outshone Atilla the Hun's. But impoverished and hungry for tourist dollars, the government has loosened some reins. For divers, Myanmar and the eight hundred-plus islands of the Mergui Archipelago represent a rare treat in trammeled times—a chance to be one of the first divers to fin over a reef.

Liveaboard diving isn't the only option, but it is far and away the wisest one. Traveling between islands, days blur, daybreak lifting the veil on islands plush with vegetation and topped with mushroom stacks of dawn-pink clouds (as a general rule, best to travel during the dry season from November to March). The names change—Ko Bon, Ko Tachai, and Ko Turlina (*Ko* is Thai for "island"), Richelieu Rock, the Burma Banks—but the explosion of life remains constant. Hard corals pile upon each other in a hobbit forest jumble. Stonehenge blocks of granite serve as palate for soft coral murals and tantalizing swim-throughs. Big schools of barracuda move casually in the current, needlefish dot the surface like silver shavings, torrents of rainbow runners and bigeye jacks pour down the sides of the pinnacle and reefs in flashing waterfalls, cuttlefish hover, their fins undulating like lace curtains moved by the most delicate breeze. Lionfish group in masses; Indian headdresses flared out in a strong wind. Life is everywhere, big and small. Harlequin ghost pipefish meld with sea fans, tiny Pegasus fish flare

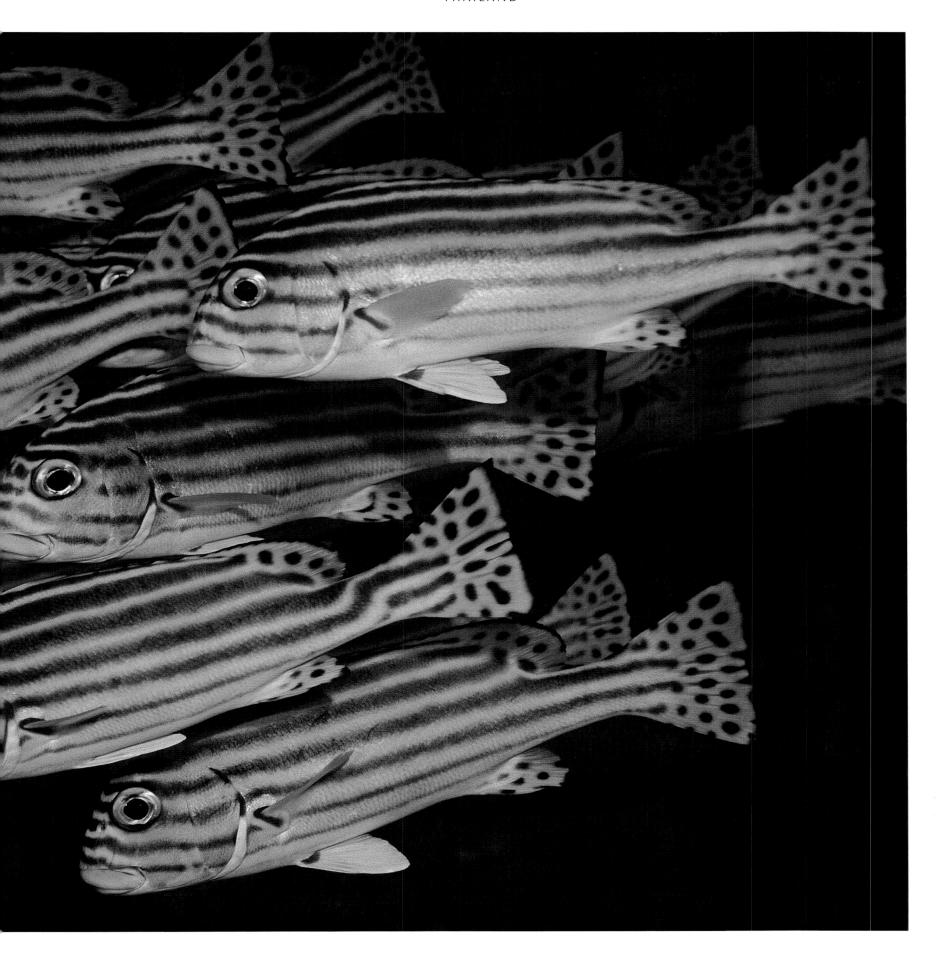

Whale sharks can reach lengths of forty feet. Richelieu Rock, near the Similan Islands, has often been a good place to see these gentle giants. Like most sharks, the bottom of a whale shark's body is lighter in color than the top. This "countershading" may serve to hide the animal from view in the open ocean.

their Tinker Bell wings, and endemic Andaman sweet-lips and blue-spotted jawfish live on the reefs. Out in the crackling blue (many Andaman sites are sur-rounded by fairly deep open ocean) barracuda drift, along with wahoo and dog-tooth tuna. Become absorbed with a purple dragon nudibranch, and miss the zebra shark tracking gracefully over the reef in slow leonine movement. Life has made a home here, and in many instances flourished, and a diver's heart can't help but swell with joy.

The Andaman Sea, of course, is also renowned for whale sharks, placid giants going about their gape-mouthed business, bestowing upon the diver, in one casual pass, adrenal rush, lifetime memory, and a firm grasp of personal insignificance. Much ado has been made about whale shark sightings in the Andaman Sea, especially at Richelieu Rock, which, during the

months of February, March, and April offers among the world's best odds of seeing the ocean's largest fish. It's true, at times whale sharks have frequented Richelieu with such regularity that spoiled and sated divers started ignoring them. During one period, the giants went so far as sparing divers the need to travel to Richelieu, congregating right off Phuket. Dive opera-tors offered daily whale shark tours ("Guaranteed whale shark sightings! Boat leaves at 2PM"), and, if that wasn't good enough, you could have a gander at the creatures via parasail. But whale sharks are both mysterious and migratory; where they go, how many there are, these simple truths still elude scientists. Whale shark sightings in the Andaman Sea have dropped precipitously in recent years. Ten years ago, it wasn't uncommon for a dive operator to spot sixty whale sharks a season. In 2001, one of Phuket's top liveaboard operations encountered two. It's possible this reflects a flux in migration patterns. But it is also sobering to note that this may reflect the clamor for shark tofu. The soft meat of the whale shark is coveted by many Asian palates, especially the Taiwanese who dub the shark *tofusa* (tofu shark). Whale sharks are killed elsewhere in the western Pacific and Indian oceans just for their fins in order to supply an Asian shark fin soup craving, a despicable practice that now occurs in all oceans and seas. The sharks are protected in Thailand, but that does them little good when their migratory urges lead them elsewhere. The gentle giants aren't particularly keen on boat traffic either, and that might also explain their absence at Richelieu Rock, where it is not uncommon now to see eight dive boats drifting about the tiny protrusion of Richelieu's tallest limestone pinnacle. Richelieu is still a world-class dive fat with sea life, but at the moment whale sharks are not among the entourage. Some divers intimately familiar with the Andaman Sea believe this is due to a natural flux. Some believe hunting has ensured that many whale sharks will never see the waters off Richelieu again. "There's big money in it," says a local dive master. "The sharks are going to be killed."

The waters off Myanmar offer both hard lesson and hope. Here the Andaman Sea—and recently discovered sites like Three Islets, High Rock, Twin Islands, Fanforest Pinnacle, and the Burma Banks (a series of undersea pinnacles)—offer lush diversity and world-class diving. But there are tremendous environmental pressures too. When Myanmar first opened its waters, dive boat operators making the first exploratory forays did so with tingling honeymoon anticipation. Their expectations were met with a yin and yang of reward and disappointment. In spots the diving was glorious, a magnificent stew of variety and surprise. But many of those same spots bore ample evidence of heavy fishing, including highly destructive blast fishing.

The Myanmar Navy takes a dim view of illegal blast fishing, especially when practiced, as it often is, hit-and-run style by commercial boats from Thailand. "They'll shoot first and ask questions later," says one dive master. But the waters are vast, and the fishermen are resourceful. It's well-known that the Myanmar navy stays ashore on certain holidays. Out on the water, blast fishermen mass in an explosive celebration of their own.

Myanmar is at a crossroads, and a single dive can neatly illustrate this. Descend off Three Islets—rocky crags swept by white-breasted sea eagles—and you might find six differently colored harlequin ghost pipefish, brilliant golden wentletrap snails, Spanish dancer nudibranchs, and yellow-lipped sea kraits making their sinuous gravity-free way up the rock walls. Fat schools of silver-blue squid hover in the water column. From a cavern in the pit of the largest islet, four grey reef sharks, thick-muscled lords, vector out of the recess and circle casually in the blue. The ceiling of another cavern is hung with a school of fat copper sweepers, hovering in the dim light like golden teardrops.

Reeling in the face of this rampant life, you still won't miss the sharp basso reports, distant, foreign, but not indecipherable—dynamite explosions.

Thailand's coast and waters suffer other problems too. Mangroves, once the dominant feature along much of Thailand's coastline, and an important nursery for many marine species, have been

Two cuttlefish engage in a mating ritual off Richelieu Rock. When mating, cuttlefish can be approached closely by divers.

decimated, filled in for development or ruined by shrimp farming. Highly profitable, shrimp ponds not only serve as nursery for plump shrimp, they also eventually turn acidic, forcing shrimp farmers to abandon their ponds and hew again into pristine mangrove to create another. Huge expanses of abandoned shrimp farms line the Thai coast. In the early

OPPOSITE: A tiny coral goby, so small that it is almost invisible, watches for passing food particles while resting on a colony of coral.

LEFT: The mudskipper ventures out of the water in search of prey. Its modified gill structure allows it to breathe air while on land.

BELOW: Nudibranchs are shell-less snails found in all the world's oceans. The colors of this nudibranch are stunning, even underwater. Scientists theorize that the bright colors advertise the fact that many nudibranchs are poisonous, and terribly untasty.

A banded coral shrimp services a pair of moray eels in a crevice on the Burma Banks. The banded coral shrimp can often be seen waving its antennae about and dancing on top of a coral head in an attempt to attract a client to a cleaning.

BELOW: Dozens of spiral-gilled worms, also called Christmas tree worms, extend their feathery feeding appendages from their homes in a coral head. At the slightest hint of danger, such as the water pressure from the approach of a diver, the entire array of worms will disappear, leaving an empty coral head. The colorful worms will reappear in a few minutes if the water is undisturbed.

1960s, mangrove forest covered 36 percent of the shoreline of the Gulf of Thailand. In thirty years, development and shrimp farming had halved that.

On offshore island reefs, both in the gulf and the Andaman Sea, rest the detritus of heavy fishing, abandoned wire fish cages and snagged nets. In shallow waters, fishermen hunting shellfish trample reefs. Eco-tourists mete out their share of damage too. Snorkelers trample shallow reefs as effectively as shellfishermen. Demand has seen to a profusion of dive boats, but demand hasn't supplied them all with holding tanks, and this pollution is a growing concern.

Man has crafted an imperfect world, and this merits concern and attention. But just as it is a mistake to proclaim Nature untouched, it is silly and pessimistic to ignore the beauty at hand. Moored somewhere in the Andaman Sea, the lucky diver feels the wind sweep warm across the water, chasing leaping dolphins while purpled islands sleep on the horizon like great dinosaurs.

Harlequin shrimp attack and feed on the venomous crown-of-thorns starfish, itself a voracious predator on coral.

CONSERVATION ISSUES

SAVING OUR SEAS

It's easy to distance ourselves from the ocean, a remote, implacable, and still mysterious place.

A baby boy contracts cholera in Bangladesh. The mother feels her child's suffering. Scientists note an increase in cholera in Bangladesh in late spring and summer. These spikes coincide with spikes in sea surface temperatures in the Bay of Bengal. Warm water and feverish infant are inextricably linked. The warm sea encourages the growth of zooplankton that carry the cholera bacteria. Monsoons drive the water into estuaries where the bacteria contaminate local water supplies. The baby boy dies, a mother grieves.

PAGES 356–357: Fish traps crush coral reefs through their sheer bulk, and abandoned and lost fish traps can continue to trap fish for years. These traps were deployed near Similan Island in the Philippines, in a marine reserve. Reserves are often ineffective if they don't have a continued enforcement presence. Philippines.

LEFT: A sign off the Breakwater in Monterey, California, a popular diving site, warns of a beach closure due to a sewage spill. Sewage spills and uncontrolled runoff during storms are major sources of pollutants in coastal ecosystems. California.

RIGHT: Giant waves pound Oahu's North Shore in the winter months. Hawaii.

358

Ocean currents absorb heat from the tropics and distribute it around the world. If the Gulf Stream and its extension, the North Atlantic Current, should veer, northern Europe could become a gray, icy land. Scientists no longer debate the existence of global warming, only its future effects. Some oceanographers predict large-scale disruptions in ocean currents, such as the Gulf Stream—a very chilling possibility.

Living coral reefs cover 360,000 square miles, an area slightly smaller than British Columbia. An innocuous splotch on the globe? Corals secrete calcium carbonate—limestone—on a scale so massive it affects carbon dioxide levels in the atmosphere, and the very health of the planet.

ET-743 isn't a particularly catchy name, but it could possibly become a joyous household word. Derived from a sea squirt (or tunicate), ET-743 has been found to slow or halt the progression of cancer tumors. It is being tested on patients with advanced breast, colon, ovarian, and lung cancers, and sarcomas. As you read this, researchers are working to find drugs that may do things that nobody thought drugs could do. Coral, sponges, tunicates, and mosses have already yielded compounds active against inflammations, asthma, heart disease, leukemia, tumors, bacterial and fungal infection, and viruses, including HIV. The oceans are home to more than two-thirds of the world's species, and nearly as many possibilities of providing life-saving biopharmaceuticals.

Cast a look back. The plants in the ancient oceans breathed forth the oxygen-rich atmosphere that brought the land to life.

The ancient Greeks believed that the ocean flowed around the Earth and into eternity. Before it does, the ocean flows into all our lives. And just as intimately, our lives flow into the ocean.

Consider this near Twilight Zone scenario. In the Midwest, farmers apply tons of chemical fertilizers to corn and other crops. Feedlots for cattle, hogs, and chickens generate improbable amounts of methane, ammonia, and nitrogen.

Iowa suburbanites spray their rose bushes. Rains and snows wash this nutrient-rich and pesticide-laden brew into the Mississippi River, whose watershed drains 41 percent of the continental United States into the Gulf of Mexico. This massive flow of freshwater fans out across the surface of the saltier and denser gulf waters. Warmed by spring and summer sun, fed by a fantasy buffet of nitrogen and phosphorus, algae bloom like kudzu. Tiny crustaceans and other pinhead-sized creatures feed on the algae. The pinheads die, the algae die, and improbable quantities of both waft down to the sea floor of the gulf. There, in a voracious feeding frenzy, bacteria suck up this detritus of death, and oxygen too. Their greed overrides their own survival. In a final feeding frenzy they consume the last remaining oxygen, suffocating themselves.

Beneath the Gulf of Mexico, in spring and summer, there is a dead zone roughly the size of New Jersey. No oxygen. No life. The surface of the gulf sparkles prettily. Just beneath the happy skein, shoals of fish flick and dart. Sink deeper, and you pass through a hazy shimmering layer. Below that, stretching to the horizon and beyond,

A diver swims past the lush coral reef of Apo Island, Philippines. Left alone, sea life in many marine reserves has made a remarkable comeback. The life in reserves "seeds" surrounding areas, providing benefits to fishermen and others who use resources from the ocean. Philippines.

Algae covers a once-thriving coral reef in Maui, Hawaii. Algal "blooms" due to agricultural runoff and other sources (in this case, probably excess nutrients from golf courses) threaten coral reefs and other coastal ecosystems. Hawaii.

FAR RIGHT: Plastics in the ocean can wreak havoc on marine life. Sea turtles, used to a diet of jellyfish, often mistake plastic bags for jellies. Eating a plastic bag can kill a turtle. Here, a plastic bag caught on a coral head in Indonesia has tightened and twisted on the coral in the current. Indonesia.

empty murk and muck. The gulf is not alone. The Black Sea has a dead zone too.

Poisoned runoff is not unique to the Gulf of Mexico. In Los Angeles environmentalists call the first big storm of winter "the first flush." Trash absently tossed into streets and storm drains, oil and grease dripped onto the freeways, chemicals sprayed on the tiny lawns, all of it rushes into the sea. In 1999 the waters off Huntington Beach—Surf City USA—were closed for most of the summer due to dangerous bacterial counts. All the while the water sparkled prettily. Water is a pretty mask.

The oceans look fine, but they are not.

"There is no part of the ocean not feeling the heavy hand of society," says oceanographer Richard Barber.

It's hard to know where to start. Roughly 70 to 80 percent of worldwide marine fish stocks need urgent intervention to halt population declines and rebuild species depleted by overfishing. Fishery disasters have stunned New England (cod), the Pacific (Chilean sea bass, orange roughy, and salmon) and Canada. Fisheries are being shut down or virtually shut down everywhere: salmon off Washington and Oregon, red king crab off Alaska, cod off New England.

A discarded fishing net has become entangled on a reef in Thailand, smothering corals, sponges, and other reef organisms. Thailand.

Sensitive to the smallest changes in their environment, coral reefs are buffeted by pollution and increased water temperatures brought on by global warming. In a fuse-lit flash, fish bombs turn ancient coral to rubble; cyanide fishermen stun the live fish they are after, and thereby poison the reef. Sediment from coastal development overshadows the coral's life-sustaining sunlight; choking agricultural runoff spawns plankton blooms and explosions of coral-hungry crown-of-thorns sea stars. In a final insult, eco-tourists stand on the delicate organisms, crushing them underfoot or wiping away their critical protective coating. Some scientists warn that nearly three-quarters of the world's coral reefs could lie in ruin within fifty years. The

Indonesian and Philippine archipelagos—some 21,000 islands—contain nearly one-fifth of the Earth's coral reefs. Fewer than 10 percent of Indonesia's reefs remain in prime condition. In the Philippines, the figure is less than 5 percent.

Trawlers, used to catch more than half the world's fish, drag nets anchored at their base with heavy chains, tires, and steel plates, scouring life off the bottom like a razor mowing stubble, and scooping up wasted bycatch by the truckload. Some estimate that a dozen pounds of sea life, much of it juvenile fish, may be sacrificed for each pound of shrimp taken. The National Marine Fisheries Service estimates that the U.S. shrimp bycatch is close to one billion pounds a year. Whatever the

ABOVE, LEFT: Corals are fragile animals, easily killed by the careless touch of a fin. Here, an unknowing snorkeler is damaging the corals he is standing on. The Australian tourist industry has found that a few minutes spent educating snorkelers during the boat ride out to the Great Barrier Reef markedly changes their behavior. Palau.

ABOVE: A massive road being built on Babeldaob Island in Palau has brought numerous adverse environmental effects. Sediments washing into the ocean have smothered coral reefs and muddied previously clear rivers, the island's main source of drinking water. Seagrass beds and mangrove forests— important nurseries and filters—are being filled in and dredged to accommodate the road. Palau.

OPPOSITE, TOP: Fishermen in some poor countries use bombs of dynamite and fertilizer to blast coral reefs apart. Some of the fish in such blasts will float to the surface, providing a short-term harvest. Such practices are terribly damaging. Here, a coral reef damaged by dynamite fishing has not recovered in twenty years. Philippines.

ABOVE: This dead coral reef, located near the mouth of a river on Babeldaob Island in Palau, was choked by sediments flowing from a once-clear river. The river is now laden with sediments produced in a massive road-building project. Palau.

RIGHT: The crown-of-thorns star is a voracious predator on coral. Population explosions of these animals have occurred on numerous coral reefs. This explosion of crown-of-thorns in Palau might be explained by its occurrence near a sewage outfall. Science has yet to determine if these population explosions are part of a natural cycle, or if they are caused by manmade factors. Palau.

figures, to watch a Texas shrimper toss silver shovelsful of dying fish overboard is to ponder our view of the sanctity of life. Longliners troll the oceans with twenty-five-mile lines bristling with thousands of hooks, catching what they want, and what they don't—swordfish, sharks, dolphins, sea birds, and sea turtles spinning slow, lifeless pirouettes. The world's aquatic species are going extinct five times faster than land animals. And once rare, many creatures (including keystone species that play an especially significant role in their ecosystem) are functionally extinct because the services they would provide are absent.

Human population growth is a primary contributing factor. Each day the global population grows by 219,000 people. By 2000, more than 3 billion people occupied the world's coastal regions. That figure is expected to double by 2050.

Humans, more and more of us, are placing our hands on the oceans, devouring more and

ABOVE: Coral reefs grow in narrow temperature ranges; extremely high or low temperatures can kill entire reefs. Coral around the world have experienced a phenomenon known as bleaching—as a result of elevated temperatures, the coral expels all of its symbiotic algae, which normally produce energy needed for coral growth and maintenance. In 1998, an El Niño warming event damaged or destroyed many of Palau's reefs. This reef shows some signs of regrowth, but others may never recover. Palau.

BOTTOM, LEFT: Most shrimp are caught by trawling, a wasteful process in which huge nets scrape the sea bottom, collecting nearly all sea life there. For every pound of shrimp caught, up to twelve pounds of other marine life are killed unnecessarily. Here, a trawler has caught crabs, squid, fish, and numerous other animals besides shrimp. All except for the shrimp will be discarded. Gulf of Mexico.

BOTTOM, RIGHT: Longlines are simply long fishing lines bristling with thousands of hooks. They hook countless unwanted animals—here, a loggerhead turtle. Baja Mexico.

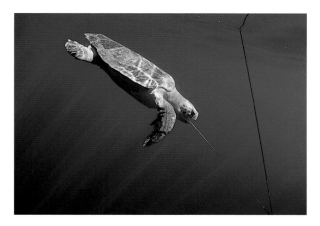

WHALE TALE OR SWAN SONG: THE DECLINING ORCAS

Sadly, man's impact on the seas reaches far afield, touching creatures small and great. Researchers have recently noticed alarming declines in some orca populations in the Pacific Northwest. Researchers believe the primary culprit may be an insidious, and in the lay world nearly unpronounceable, set of chemicals, ranging from polychlorinated biphenyls (PCBs) to dichlorodiphenyltrichloroethane (better known as DDT).

What's happening is easier to understand than to pronounce. PCBs—which researchers believe are the primary culprit—are oily, colorless liquids, once used as lubricants and insulators for transformers and electric motors. These chemicals are doggedly long-lasting. Though outlawed in the United States since the 1970s, they lie in the bottom sediments in places like Puget Sound, where they have leached from inadequate disposal sites. The PCBs are consumed by invertebrates that are fed upon by bottom-feeding fish like halibut and rockfish. These, in turn, are consumed by salmon, the primary food source for many orcas. The concentration of PCBs increases up the food chain, a phenomenon that scientists call "bioaccumulation." For the orcas,

at the top of the food chain, this translates as a heavy chemical dose. Scientists have found that as a result certain pods of orcas are among the most contaminated marine mammals in the world.

More important than the label, orcas are dying. Salmon have been sorely over fished. The orcas store PCBs in their blubber. With their primary prey (salmon) now overfished and in short supply, the orcas must burn their blubber for energy, and this releases the toxins into their bloodstream. Some scientists also believe that with salmon in short supply, the orcas have turned to eating the toxic bottom fish.

Whatever the food source, orca calves and adults are dying. The PCBs don't kill the majestic mammals directly. They work more insidiously. PCBs mimic some hormones in females, disrupting the estrous cycle and making it difficult to conceive. Females who can give birth offload a portion of their PCBs to their offspring both in the womb and in their milk. In males, the chemicals can reduce fertility. PCBs also reduce the potency of immune cells in the orcas' blood. With their reduced immunity, a stress they might normally slough off, can now kill them.

Canada has already listed certain orca populations as endangered. In the waters off British Columbia, the populations of orcas are already small (in the low hundreds). Researchers are working toward solutions, but the obstacles are great. For one thing, the PCBs can travel great distances—through the air, the water, and the food chain. Airborne PCBs have been traced halfway around the planet.

Awareness of the problem is the critical first step toward correcting it.

more, dumping more and more, leaving less and less. It isn't a leap to imagine mankind facing the same fate as the bacteria in the Gulf of Mexico.

"We are ruining the natural economy on which the market economy depends," states E.O. Wilson, biodiversity guru and scholar of evolution at Harvard University. "And, as an unintended consequence, we may extinguish half the species of plants and animals by the end of the 21st century. . . . If these considerations don't make us change our ways, I'm afraid nothing will."

It's easy to ignore problems that seem so monumental and overwhelming. The statistics numb. The warning cries of endless experts blend to a bleating. Our minds fog, wander, then give up. Ignorance is easy and comfortable. But in the face of headline-grabbing ills, some success stories exist. People and nations are making a difference.

Tubbataha Reef National Marine Park sits in the very heart of reef destruction. Established in 1988, the park spans two atolls in the Philippines and covers 128 square miles. Off-limits to fishing, it is home to some 450 thriving fish species. (But even Tubbataha isn't immune. In February 2002, Chinese and Filipino fishermen were caught fishing in the National Park. Park rangers confiscated fishes (including sharks), giant clam and sea turtles, along with dynamite and cyanide.) Similar "marine zoning"—protecting chunks of ocean to varying degrees, from permissive multi-use areas to completely hands-off marine parks—is on the upswing. In 2000 the United States announced a plan to put 20 percent of its coral reefs into designated ecological reserves by 2010. Optimists will note that more than a quarter of the world's reefs are under the ownership of the world's wealthiest nations— the United States, United Kingdom, Australia, and France. But protection without enforcement is not enough; ironically, the more remote a reserve, the more vulnerable it is to poaching.

Reacting to the indiscriminate killing of sea turtles, in 1989 the United States required that offshore shrimpers fit their trawling nets with

turtle excluder devices (TEDs) A TED is a small net or metal grid inside the shrimping net, designed to let the shrimp pass into the main net while ejecting turtles back into the wild. By late 1994, all U.S. shrimpers were required to install the devices. Before that, as many as 55,000 sea turtles—mostly loggerheads and Kemp's Ridley turtles—died from drowning in shrimp nets each year. Thousands of turtles have been saved.

ABOVE: Coral reefs rival tropical rainforests in diversity. Hanauma Bay, a reserve in Oahu, provides refuge for marine life and a great spot for snorkeling. Hawaii.

RIGHT: Turtle exclusion devices (TEDs) are a success story. Required on all U.S. shrimping vessels since 1994, these devices have saved thousands of sea turtles. Here, a loggerhead turtle in a NMFS research project demonstrates the efficacy of a TED, a metal grate that allows turtles to escape a shrimp trawl. Florida.

LEFT: This sea lion was caught in a gill net while hunting at night. It escaped drowning by biting off the net. Unfortunately, the remaining net cord will slowly strangle the animal unless humans are able to catch the sea lion and remove the net. California.

Boycotts of tuna, and subsequent U.S. "dolphin safe" policies, led to a tremendous reduction in dolphins killed by tuna boats of many countries. (But read on to discover the unintended consequences.) Island nations and territories across the South Pacific have begun creating a patchwork of whale sanctuaries to protect the mammals from whale hunters. Australia has closed its ports to boats scooping up tons of undersize Chilean seabass, a new, booming fishery that often takes illegal licenses in the distant and difficult-to-police waters of the Southern Ocean where the seabass are found.

Australia has also adopted a model bluefin tuna fishery, in which individual fishermen are property owners of their own portion of wild tuna. Rather than kill all the bluefin they can before the other fishermen do (the mode of operation in most countries), each fisherman owns what is called an individual transferable quota (ITQ), the right, which they pay for, to catch a specific percentage of the yearly haul and no more. Only

so many ITQs are available. When a fisherman retires, he sells his ITQ, like a farmer would sell his land, to someone else. With the number of permits limited, each individual is assured a bigger share of the catch, and each fisherman recognizes that he has a stake in the future of the fishery.

Thanks to groups like the National Audubon Society (which provide lists and website information), diners who wouldn't know a TED from a tea service can come to the table knowing which entrees are ecologically wise choices (wild Alaskan salmon and halibut, striped bass, mackerel, mahi-mahi), and which aren't (Atlantic swordfish, the illegally fished Chilean seabass, the slow-to-mature orange roughy).

The problem is, like it or not, our world—politically, socially, culturally—is a complex and often imperfect place. Powerful lobbyists push scientists into questionable recommendations, and politicians into questionable action or inaction. Power and money are strong motivators, whether they are swaying votes or feeding a family. It's easy for a sport-diver who has witnessed the shocking fallout of a fish bomb—fish spinning aimlessly in convulsions, or drifting gape-mouthed and belly up, their peacock colors fading to sorrowful gray—to rail against fish bombing on reefs; less so for the Indonesian fisherman who is paid $8.35 for a blast-killed haul of parrotfish, triggerfish, and bream, more than five times the average daily wage in his country. It's not always easy to take the long-term view when your family waits hungry at the dock.

Ours is not a world of amicable cooperation or Boy Scout morals. Countries pilfer fish from inside each other's two hundred-mile territorial waters. They ignore international mandates, or make good use of convoluted rules. In 1986 the International Whaling Commission (IWC) issued a worldwide moratorium on commercial whaling. Under a provision of IWC rules, the Japanese are allowed to take minke whales for scientific purposes, most years killing more than four

A vendor in Tokyo's Tsukiji Market prepares whale meat, ostensibly from minke whales taken for scientific purposes. However, scientists who have obtained samples of whale meat sold in Japan have found that the meat includes the flesh of endangered species as well: humpbacks, blue whales, and fin whales, for instance. Japan.

Tuna are swimming machines, their bodies designed to maximize speed in the water. These once-wild bluefin tuna are caught and raised in captivity for eventual export to foreign fish markets, where they command huge sums of money. South Australia.

Minke whales are hunted by the Japanese for "scientific purposes." In most years Japanese whalers kill up to five hundred minkes. However, what is not used for genetic studies and other experiments ends up satisfying the Japanese consumer's appetite for whalemeat delicacies.

A manta ray is caught in a gill net in Baja Mexico. These animals, so friendly and popular with divers, have been fished relentlessly for their meat in the Sea of Cortez. Large manta rays were once a diving attraction off the seamounts of La Paz, but now divers travel three hundred miles south, to the Revillagigedo Islands, to see the giant manta rays that once called the Sea of Cortez home. Baja Mexico.

in wholesale mass. And, adding economic insult to environmental injury, the free trade provisions written into the new global economic treaties disallow interfering with such slaughter.

Public outcry led to "dolphin-safe tuna," major U.S. canneries refusing to buy tuna from fishermen who also encircled dolphins in their nets (in the open seas, tuna often follow dolphins). Thousands of dolphins were saved, but recently a twist has surfaced. Trying to avoid dolphins and net tuna, fishermen often encircle logs or artificial fish-attracting devices (fish, including tuna, often drift with floating objects). In doing so they net, and kill, tons of fish they can't use, including juvenile yellowfin tuna. Dr. Martin Hall of the Inter-American Tropical Tuna Commission calculates that fishing around these floating objects to avoid dolphins saves one dolphin at the expense of killing and discarding roughly 16,000 unmarketable small tunas, 380 mahi-mahi, 190 wahoo, 20 sharks and rays, 1,200 triggerfish and other small fishes, one marlin, and, now and again, a sea turtle.

hundred minkes in the high seas around Antarctica and one hundred in the North Pacific. The carcasses, the Japanese claim, are needed to carry out genetic studies and gauge rates of growth and reproduction. But plenty of minkes show up in Japanese restaurants and fish markets (thanks to a scientific whaling provision requiring full use of the by-product) as slabs of raw flesh, smoked wafers, salted bacon, and packets of crunchy cartilage.

And on we plunge, often in wanton excess. To see a shark finned, then dropped overboard to spiral downward to slow death, is to assume an unshakable memory and sorrow, and to see what apex killers, fueled by greed, can truly become.

Even well-meaning solutions don't always produce storybook endings. Turtle excluder devices have been a success, but thousands of turtles still die. Adult turtles, caught again and again, are eventually killed. Young turtles can slip through the gaps in the TED bars and into the main net. Other countries, refusing to use TEDs, still drown turtles

MAN BITES SHARK: RETHINKING THE CONSUMMATE PREDATOR

Schlocky Hollywood movies and persistent myth have portrayed the shark as a wanton and ruthless killer. But to understand true ruthlessness is to stand on the deck of a fishing boat while the fins of a shark are summarily hacked off and the still-living creature is shoved overboard, drunkenly navigating in a bloodstained sea.

This is neither hyperbole nor an isolated incident. Shark finning, driven by the outrageous profits the fins bring, is the primary culprit in a mass carnage that has increased exponentially. In 1980, reported Hawaiian shark landings barely exceeded one thousand pounds. Twenty years later, Hawaiian landings exceeded six million pounds. This is the reported catch, in an industry not noted for objective recording. And Hawaiian waters are not the only place where sharks are fished. Statistics numb, so take just this one with you. Roughly 100 million sharks die at man's hand each year, killed by sportfishermen, or for soup, meat, teeth, even their cartilage—the latter advertised as a cancer deterrent though science has deemed this yet another shark myth.

Man's greed and soulless conscience are compounded by another problem. Myth holds the shark invincible, Lord of the Seas for over 400 million years. It's true that the shark is an evolutionary marvel, and most shark species are consummate predators. But it's also true that sharks mature slowly, and breed slowly too. This is not an animal that spews thousands of eggs on a nightly basis. Dusky sharks may not mature sexually for twenty years. Blacktip sharks, a commercially desirable species, produce four to six offspring every other year. With birth rates like these, shark populations can't survive our current intense fishing pressures.

The shark is at our mercy.

BOTTOM, LEFT: Shark fins dry in the sun at a fishing camp in Baja Mexico. Sharks are slaughtered by the millions to satisfy a relatively recent Asian demand for shark fin soup. Baja Mexico.

BOTTOM, RIGHT: A blue shark is hooked on a longline. It is likely that all but the fin of this shark will be wastefully discarded. Baja Mexico.

This small drift-net boat laid out several miles of net over one night, all by hand. The fishermen caught only four small skipjack tuna for their many hours of labor. Factory-driven drift-net operations can lay out hundreds of miles of net each night in the open ocean, ensnaring all varieties of marine life. It is estimated that enough drift net is laid each night to circle the equator. Philippines.

meteoric surge in aquaculture. Aquaculture has caused excitement. Salmon, catfish, trout, and shrimp raised in ponds, tanks, and pens take fishing pressure off their wild counterparts. But aquaculture has also raised plenty of concerns. High-density salmon farms pollute the waters with excess feed and feces, and the cooped-up fish are more susceptible to sea lice and diseases like infectious salmon anemia, which can spread to wild salmon. Salmon farms in Chile were accused of dosing fish with large amounts of antibiotics; more than two hundred tons of Chinese shrimp were found to be laced with chloramphenicol, a potent antibiotic that can disrupt blood cell production in humans. The twists continue. Though intended to protect wild fish, scientists say fish farming is beginning to put a dent in wild schools of herring, sardines, mackerel, and other fish used to make fish feed—two to four pounds of this meal is needed to grow a one-pound fish. Concerns spiral like sci fi. Farmed salmon escape regularly, some of them genetically modified for

Conservationists are now rethinking tuna fishing methods, including going back to circling tuna and dolphins with nets.

The world's growing appetite for seafood and the depletion of fisheries has produced a

These shrimp ponds will be used to raise shrimp, but farming shrimp is, unfortunately, not an answer to the environmental problems of shrimp trawling. Mangroves and other coastal habitats are being destroyed to build shrimp farms; critical habitat loss and pollution are associated problems. Thailand.

fast growth. What might be the impact of these mutant fatties if they begin to breed in the wild?

It is also difficult to pinpoint fault. Shrimp farmers in Thailand, Vietnam, and Myanmar destroy miles of precious mangroves and poison local waters with waste runoff, but diners across America, Europe, and Japan gobble up the pond-raised shrimp and demand more. At the edge of a muddy Georgia marsh, a lifelong shrimper, his livelihood battered by farmed imports, rubs his chin.

"Hell, I can't blame folks for eating pond-raised shrimp," drawls Hunter Forsythe. "To somebody who's never been to the coast, imported pond-raised shrimp taste just fine. The only way they'd know the difference is if I were to come to Kansas with five pounds of wild shrimp. And as long as they're eating it, the shrimp farmers will keep supplying it." Simple answers, and solutions, are rare.

A large part of the problem is that we have become ruthlessly efficient at ferrying nature's dwindling bounty into our stomachs. Enormous freezer trawlers can catch and process a ton or more fish an hour. Spotter planes help tuna boats off New England find bluefin tuna. Speared and netted, the majestic giants, almost as pricey as gold, are on planes to Japan the next day. Bluefin tuna—speared off New England, chased on the high seas, netted

off Sardinia, Italy, in the melee ritual killing of the Mattanza—are sorely assaulted. Debate rages over how greatly wild stocks have been impacted. But every day, in the wee morning hours at the Tokyo Central Wholesale Market, row upon row of bluefin tuna lie beheaded, definned, frozen, and awaiting auction in a smoky mist, cocoons from which life will never spring. A 444-pound bluefin might sell for $175,000. And bluefin isn't the only sea life passing through the Tokyo market. Eel from Taiwan, sea urchin from Oregon, octopus from Athens, crab from Cartagena, salmon from

ABOVE, LEFT AND RIGHT: Mangrove forests and seagrass beds act as sediment traps and nurseries for a variety of marine life. Filling in mangrove swamps to create land for development destroys marine ecosystems. Palau.

Thousands of giant tuna are auctioned off in the Tokyo's Tsukiji Market each morning. Fishing is a huge global industry, with Japanese buyers surfacing in all corners of the globe. Japan.

Trawling has been likened to "clear-cutting the sea." Huge nets are weighed down at the front with chains and rollers. The nets are then dragged on the sea bottom, flattening everything in their path, and destroying the bottom community that is a food source and nursery for many species. Florida.

Santiago, shrimp from Thailand—the seafood moves through the market so quickly the place is oddly hung with little odor. Against such efficiency, what chance do the fish have?

We are destroying our environment at an ever-accelerating rate. In this century, mega dams (in 1950 there were 5,000 large dams worldwide, by 2000 there were 45,000) have helped see to the end of nearly 50 percent of our freshwater and salt-water wetlands. Coral colonies grow slowly, rarely more than half an inch a year. Some atolls, after 50 million years, are almost a mile thick. In only a few decades, a tenth of the Earth's coral reefs have been destroyed and a third have been seriously degraded. Nature's patience has found its match.

In the past fifty years we have quadrupled our catch of seafood. In the late 1980s, walleye pollock flooded Washington's Puget Sound. Roughly ten years later, trawl surveys found these pollock stocks greatly depressed. Steller sea lions and their young feed on pollock. Without pollock, sea lions, young and old, die. This is a web both fascinating and

TOP, RIGHT: In a tradition that has lasted for centuries, giant bluefin tuna are captured and slaughtered in Sardinia, Italy. Fishermen in this fishery lay huge nets for several weeks to trap tuna when they gather in the Mediterranean Sea to spawn. There were once over forty-eight of these fisheries, or tonnara, *in Sardinia; now there are enough fish to sustain only two. Scientists have proved that these bluefin tuna are the same ones seen on the east coast of North America. Many fish, including the bluefin, cross international boundaries, so efforts to conserve fish stocks locally have largely been unsuccessful. Sardinia, Italy*

RIGHT: Giant bluefin tuna are whipped into a frenzy as a net draws them together during the traditional mattanza. *Sardinia, Italy*

Steller sea lion populations have plummeted from hundreds of thousands to just thirty thousand in the past three decades. Their population decline may be in response to a variety of pressures: climate change, shooting by fishermen, predation by orcas and sharks, incidental take in fishing gear, and the fishing pressures on their food source—pollock, which is used to make imitation crab meat. Alaska.

unnerving, emblematic of consequences throughout the food chain that we can't always see.

If we continue on the path we are on, one day need and greed may come together with a resounding crash. And if greed wins, need will be obsolete.

Yet hope still provides reason why we should resist from going numb. Life in the oceans is resilient. Left alone, sea life in many marine reserves has performed a remarkable comeback. Giving up is foolish. Ample reason for optimism still exists.

FAR, LEFT: Human-generated pollution has numerous ill effects on marine life. The coral reefs of the Florida Keys seem to be dying of it. Here, a diseased sea fan has been stricken by a virus or bacteria, probably linked to sewage. Florida.

LEFT: In some countries collectors for the aquarium fish trade use cyanide to stun fish, killing corals and other animals in the process. Fish caught in this way often die within a few days of being put in a home aquarium in North America, where most of these fish end up. Home aquarists should be sure that the fish they buy have been captive-bred, or that they have been caught in an ecologically sensitive manner. Organizations like the International Marinelife Alliance work to ensure that fish caught for the aquarium market have been caught using methods that are environmentally sound. Philippines.

TODAY'S CATCH: KNOW THE MENU, SAVE A SPECIES

The politics of fishing seem to have become impossibly complex. But fishing—bureaucracy and vested interests aside—has always boiled down to a simple basic. We catch fish to eat them. And if you want to promote wise fishing practices, the best way to do so is to think about what is going into your mouth.

Governments, fishermen, and global organizations all react to what you eat at the table. Consumer demand for "dolphin safe" tuna reduced direct dolphin deaths in tuna nets by 99 percent. A boycott of Atlantic swordfish by cruise lines, leading chefs, and informed consumers led to improvements in the fishery—improvements that will help preserve this magnificent fish.

Awareness makes all the difference. Before ordering from a menu or plucking a package at the supermarket, know the answers to a few simple questions. Are the populations of this fish healthy or are they being sorely overfished? Does the fishing method harm habitat, or kill incidental bycatch? Does the fish reproduce slowly or rapidly?

No, you don't need a degree in ichthyology from the Scripps Institution of Oceanography. Information, straightforward and decipherable, is right at hand. The National Audubon Society's Living Oceans Program (www.audubon.org/campaign/lo), for instance, has its own guide to seafood in the form of a downloadable seafood wallet card (what to eat, what to boycott) and a book, *Seafood Lover's Almanac,* complete with recipes and information. Other organizations— the Monterey Bay Aquarium, seafoodchoices.com, The California Academy of Sciences, and ecofish.com—offer information on wise choices.

Wild Alaskan salmon or Chilean sea bass? Our educated decisions can make the difference in whether a species survives—or not.

The Atlantic swordfish is a magnificent animal, but not an ecologically wise seafood choice. This fish is in danger of crashing to critically low population levels. An effective campaign was recently mounted to convince chefs to take this fish off their menus, but once the campaign ended, Atlantic swordfish crept back onto the dinner plate. Sardinia, Italy.

ACKNOWLEDGMENTS

It would be impossible to thank everyone who has contributed to the making of this book. To those who have so graciously lent their time, energy, and facilities to the making of the photographs and experiences in this book, thanks from the bottom of my heart.

Thanks go to my family—Deanna, my parents, Bing, Alanna, and Lance—for their love, support, and patience. The Day clan in Atlanta has been a second family, and Andy Day has been the brother that I wish I never had. Alberta, I miss you very much.

Thanks go to Peter Brueggeman for his tireless and unending enthusiasm for all my projects. He has lent a sympathetic ear and intelligent advice on every project I have undertaken, and is the one person most responsible for the success of my larger projects.

Many of these photographs were made possible by a fellowship from the Pew Fellows Program in Marine Conservation, an initiative of The Pew Charitable Trusts in partnership with the New England Aquarium. For their help with my fellowship, thanks to Cynthia Robinson, Angel Alcala, Pam Baker, Michael Bean, Heidi Dewar, Steve Drogin, Paul Engelmeyer, Chuck Farwell, Ornella Girosi, Gary Graham, Bob Johannes, Jane Lubchenco, Jay Maclean, Debie Meck, John Mitchell, Jeff Noel, Gerry Reyes, Enrique Soto, Satoshi Tada, and Ian Workman; of Baja on the Fly, the Environmental Defense Fund, International Marine Life Alliance, Isla Diving Center, and National Marine Fisheries Service, Mississippi Laboratories.

ANTARCTICA

In Antarctica, I received logistical support for my expeditions by the United States Antarctic Program, National Science Foundation. I thank NSF's Office of Polar Programs for their support of my time in Antarctica, particularly Guy Guthridge, Erick Chiang, Dwight Fisher, and Polly Penhale.

The members of my teams to Antarctica were instrumental to the success of my time there: Beez Bohner, Peter Brueggeman, Dug Coons, Andy Day, Christian McDonald, Doug Quin, and Dale Stokes. A special thanks to Kristin Larson, Jim Mastro, Robbie Score, and Rob Robbins, who helped me navigate treacherous waters. Robin Abbott, Trent Myers, Rhonda Rhodriguez, Brett Wilson, and the staff of Raytheon Polar Services Company supported my work there with good cheer.

The pilots and staff of Petroleum Helicopters Inc. and Kenn Borek Air Ltd. endured my many requirements for flights and open doors with good cheer.

OPPOSITE: Daybreak at Roca Partida in the Revillagigedo Islands of Mexico reveals huge schools of jacks surrounding this undersea pinnacle. Tiny Roca Partida, miles from any other land, takes but fifteen minutes to swim around at the surface, but countless dives to see everything that calls it home underwater.

BELOW: The soulful eyes of the Weddell seal are also very useful hunting tools; these animals have sharp enough vision to allow them to hunt for prey by sight rather than sound. Antarctica.

Organizations which deserve applause for their work in Antarctica include the U.S. Air Force, Air Mobility Command (AMC); 109th Tactical Airlift Wing, New York Air National Guard; and the U.S. Coast Guard, including Aviation Polar Operations, Detachments 146 and 149.

Scientists and their crew showed me their work, allowed me to use their camps and fish huts, and welcomed my intrusion during their short work season. Thanks to Bill Baker, Sam Bowser, Randy Davis, Paul Dayton, Art Devries, Kevin Hoefling, Jim McClintock, Teri McLain, Paul Ponganis, and Terrie Williams.

THE SOUTH PACIFIC

In Australia, thanks to Jim Thiselton of Kangaroo Island Diving Services, and John Rumney and crew on the *Undersea Explorer*.

My trip to French Polynesia was made possible by Paul Sloan of Tahiti Tourism, the Moorea Beachcomber Parkroyal Hotel, Top Dive Resort, Hotel Raira Lagon, The Six Passengers Diving Center, Bathy's Club. Thanks to Nanou Chapuisat, Juan-Pedro Duran Lopez, Ugo Mazzavillani, and Olivier Petitjean.

In Papua New Guinea: thanks to Dik Knight and Michael Burden at Loloata Diving Resort, Alan Raabe on the *Febrina*, and Max Benjamin of Walindi Plantation Resort.

In the Solomon Islands, thanks to Air Pacific, Solomon Airlines; Adventure Sports (Gizo), Bilikiki Cruises, the *Solomon Sea*, and Solomon Sea Divers (Munda). Thanks to Rick Belmare, Dave Cooke, Fred Douglas, Meredith Eder, Dannie and Kerrie Kennedy, and Rob Pforzheimer.

My photographs from Palau are the result of several visits over the span of six years. Thanks to Continental Airlines, Fish N Fins, the *Ocean Hunter*, *Palau Aggressor*, Sam's Tours, and the *Sundancer*. Thanks to Tova and Navot Bornovski, Tony Campbell, Ethan Daniels, Noah Idechong, and Dermot Keane.

In Indonesia, thanks to the staff of Kungkungan Bay Resort, Greg Gapp, and Mark Ecenbarger.

In Borneo, thanks to Ron Holland, Graham and Donna Taylor, and the staff of Borneo Divers.

THE NORTH PACIFIC

In Japan, thanks to Miyuki and Koji Nakamura and Tadahiko Matsui of Japan Underwater Films; and Niki Papakonstantinou.

In California, I had the luck to fall in with a remarkably talented and generous group of friends, whose time together I will always treasure: Dan Auber, Brandon Cole, Ed Cooper, Bob and Cathy Cranston, Steve Drogin, Howard and Michele Hall, Kevin McDonnell, Marty Snyderman, and Dan Walsh. My office staff, past and present, has held down the fort and put up with my impossible managerial style. Thanks to Kris Ingram, Phil Sharkey, Andrew Fornasier, Camilla Mann, Kathryn Beliunas, Katy Barber, and Mike Ready. Further thanks go to Ernest Brooks, Andy Case, Ralph Clevenger, John McCosker, Richard Rosenblatt, Gil van Dykhuizen, and HJ Walker for sharing their work and expertise with me.

In Mexico, Mike McGettigan and Sherry Schaefer aboard the *Ambar III* showed me the wonders of the Revillagigedos and the Sea of Cortez.

In Hawaii, thanks to Marsha Green, Jeff Pantukhoff, Jim Watt, and Ann Zoidis, for showing me so much of their world and research. Jim Watt showed me oceanic whitetip sharks on a day I will never forget.

A nudibranch, or sea slug, breathes through gills on its back. Solomon Islands.

ACKNOWLEDGMENTS

In Costa Rica, Avi Klapfer and the crew of the *Undersea Hunter* showed me Cocos Island, as did the crew of the *Okeanos Aggressor*.

In the Galapagos Islands, I was hosted by the *Galapagos Aggressor* and the *M/Y Eric*. Thanks to Mathias Espinosa, Herbert Frie, Doris Welsh, and Peter Witmer.

THE NORTH ATLANTIC

In Florida, I was helped by Hal and Shirley Brown, Superintendent Billy Causey of the Florida Keys National Marine Sanctuary, Don Demaria, and Craig and Deevon Quirolo of Reef Relief.

In my travels throughout the Caribbean I thank Anthony's Key Resort and the Institute for Marine Sciences in Roatan, Honduras; the *Dream Too*, the *Shearwater*, Stuart Cove's, and Walker's Cay in the Bahamas; American Airlines, Buddy Dive Resort, Carib Inn, and Toucan Divers in Bonaire; and the *Caribbean Explorer* in Saba. Thanks to Jim and Anna Abernethy, Gary Adkison, Bruce Bowker, Stuart and Michele Cove, Julio and Sam Gallendo, Robin Sabino, Scott Smith, Inez Wagner and Mike Walker.

THE INDIAN OCEAN

In the Red Sea, thanks to Bob Goddess, Egypt Air, Sea Divers, and Rolf Schmidt and the staff of Sinai Divers.

In the Seychelles Islands, thanks to Air Seychelles, the Seychelles Ministry of Tourism, and Seychelles Underwater Center.

In Thailand, thanks to Ocean Rover Diving Cruises, South East Asia Yacht Charters, and Thai Airways International; Maarten Brusselers, Jeroen Deknatel, and Mark Strickland.

Many companies have been particularly helpful in my work through the years. Ikelite Underwater Systems, Lowepro USA, Oceanic Products, and Pelican Products have been unstinting in their continual support of my work. I could not do what I've done without them. Thanks to Ike Brigham, Jim Graham,

A sea lion and a diver swim above beds of giant plumose anemones. Monterey, California.

Bob Hollis, Nicole Mummenhoff, Nestor Palmero, and Barry Warner at these companies.

Green's Camera World and Bay Photo in Monterey, California; and Repro Images in Vienna, Virginia, have ushered my precious film with care. Backscatter Photo and Video, Camera Tech, and Sub-Aquatic Repair keep my underwater camera gear running. Thanks to Dan Blodgett, Geoff Semorile, and Berkley White. Ty Sawyer and Daryl Carson at *Skin Diver* and *Sport Diver* have been instrumental in helping me get to places, as have Cindi Laraia of Dive Discovery and Ken Knezick of Island Dreams Travel.

The following companies provided support for my expeditions and equipment needs: A&I Color, Aggressor Fleet, Diving Unlimited International (DUI), Fuji Film, Kodak Professional, Light & Motion, Nikon, Really Right Stuff, Scubapro, Sea and Sea Underwater Photography, Sherwood Scuba, and URPRO Filters. Thanks to Sergio Angelini, David Alexander, Matthew Armand, Bryan Geyer, Jill Haines, Barrett Haywood, Kirk Kreutzig, Dick Long, Susan Long-Holland, Jim Lyon, Bill Pekala, and Eric Squires at these companies.

Ken McAlpine, the world's most patient writer, contributed a wonderful text; Jeanne-Marie Perry Hudson handled all the details involved with this book; Lori Malkin put together a wonderful design of the photographs and text. Finally, thanks to Hugh Levin, the world's most understanding and supportive publisher.

PAGE 380: A lionfish patiently waits to ambush an individual in a school of baitfish. Richelieu Rock, Thailand.

INDEX

Page numbers in *italics* refer to photographs.

A spine-cheek anemonefish ventures out from the stinging tentacles of its host anemone. Papua New Guinea.